"For the most part, public theology so far has been an endeavor of religious 'experts' who belong to a single tradition exploring how their faith should serve the common good. David Moe argues that in a religiously pluralistic world we need ordinary practitioners of diverse religions coming together and, each drawing on their own tradition, pursue together the common good. In a divided world, this is a very needed book."

—**Miroslav Volf**, professor of systematic theology, Yale Divinity School

"This is the most imaginative, absorbing, and remarkable book I have ever read!"

—**Pum Za Mang**, associate professor of world Christianity, Myanmar Institute of Theology

"In journalism, we stress the importance of not just writing about abstract ideas, but going out on the street to see how everyday people live it out. David Moe does this in *Beyond the Academy* by moving beyond the ideas of Asia's public theologians and examining what Christian faith looks like for real grassroots Christians in Myanmar. This is an important book for anyone interested in Christianity in Southeast Asia."

—**Angela Lu Fulton**, Southeast Asia editor, *Christianity Today*

"Public theology too often involves dialogue between scholars, but without hearing from the grassroots voices. David Moe confronts this criticism directly as he offers an Asian public theology emerging from everyday people during the coup in Myanmar. *Beyond the Academy* is public theology at its finest. I enthusiastically recommend it."

—**Gregg A. Okesson**, professor of leadership and development, Asbury Theological Seminary

"Noting the ways in which Christian theology is primarily an ecclesial activity, David Moe argues for a closer integration of academic work with the life of the church. From the context of a minority church within the Buddhist culture of Myanmar, he points to ways in which theological reflection can contribute more effectively to Christian social engagement. His volume offers us a valuable resource for public theology today."

—**David Fergusson**, regius professor of divinity, University of Cambridge

"*Beyond the Academy* explores the implications of Christian theology in the setting of an oppressive and deeply divided Asian society, namely Myanmar. Throughout, David Moe centrally emphasizes lived experience, as he allows us to see through the eyes of grassroots Christians. The book is thoughtful, innovative, and it is truly moving to hear the voices of those ordinary believers as they live their faith. Thoroughly recommended."

—**Philip Jenkins**, distinguished professor of history, Institute for Studies of Religion, Baylor University

"If two thousand years ago, diaspora Jews gathered from every nation under heaven on the streets of Jerusalem heard in their own languages about the wondrous works of God, today, ethnic Burmese Christians from across the small towns and rural villages of Myanmar's countryside are declaring via their own accents not only about God's saving deeds but also about Christian faith and discipleship in their pluralistic public square. Readers of the Third Evangelist's sequel volume can now also listen in on the grassroots witness of the Southeast Asian church as scholar-practitioner David Moe's second book resounds such to the ends of the earth."

—**Amos Yong**, professor of theology and mission, Fuller Seminary

"David Moe's probe into grassroots Christian theology is deeply rooted in his home environment of Myanmar where his faith was formed and where he practiced his faith amid systemic violence. Moe makes a distinction, not only between grassroots and academic theology, but also between grassroots and public theology that tends to be top-down. He insists that the grassroots reality of actual Christians practicing actual faith is the most elemental articulation of faith. Moe's vigorous attestation of practical faith is sure to be instructive for Christians who live and practice faith elsewhere, most especially in the West where our faith is much too often accommodating to cultural expectation. This book is an invitation to step outside our conventional assumptions in order to face the stark reality of Gospel mandates."

—**WALTER BRUEGGEMANN**, professor emeritus of Old Testament, Columbia Theological Seminary

"David Moe writes in response to the ongoing violence of the military coup in Myanmar. There is an urgency in his work. His context is far removed from the 'unhappy gap' that exists between the academy and lives of ordinary believers. What unfolds is unlike public theology in the West. In a manner that is both prophetic and irenic, Moe crafts a lived Asian public theology that listens to the grassroots that inspires and which it serves in return."

—**CLIVE PEARSON**, former editor-in-chief, *International Journal of Public Theology*

"I was much enlightened and heartened when I read David Moe's book, not least because he has pushed the boundaries of doing contextual theology even beyond what I had done in my *Grassroots Asian Theology*. This is what theological works should be."

—**SIMON CHAN**, editor, *Asia Journal of Theology*

"David Moe opens up new Asian perspectives to public theology by inviting to the dialogue table not only theologians and leaders from academia but also grassroots Christians. From his own background of ethnic and religious conflict in Myanmar, he explores how Christians from marginalized communities experience and express their faith, and by highlighting their significant contribution, he widens the dialogue. I highly recommend it."

—ANNA MAY SAY PA, professor emerita of Hebrew Bible, Myanmar Institute of Theology

"David Moe is a leader of a new generation of S.E. Asian theologians seeking to move beyond their N.E. Asian and S. Asian predecessors who offered helpful local correctives to long-dominant Western presumptions. Focusing on his native Myanmar, Moe employs a 'synthetic methodology' that values previous contributions while expanding the field to include the hitherto neglected voices of grassroots Christian communities. This book is uniquely situated at the interface of world Christianity and public theology."

—THOMAS JOHN HASTINGS, former executive director, Overseas Ministries Study Center at Princeton Theological Seminary; former editor, *International Bulletin of Mission Research*

Beyond the Academy

Princeton Theological Monograph Series

K. C. Hanson, Charles M. Collier, D. Christopher Spinks,
and Robin A. Parry, Series Editors

Recent volumes in the series:

Robert A. Hand
Theological Epistemology in Immanuel Kant's Transcendental Idealism and Karl Barth's Theology

Scott P. Rice
Trinity and History: The God-World Relation in the Theology of Dorner, Barth, Pannenberg, and Jenson

Hakbong Kim
Person, Personhood, and the Humanity of Christ: Christocentric Anthropology and Ethics in Thomas F. Torrance

Lisanne Winslow
A Trinitarian Theology of Nature

Matthew T. Prior
Confronting Technology: The Theology of Jacques Ellul

Edmund Fong
Obedience from First to Last: The Obedience of Jesus Christ in Karl Barth's Doctrine of Reconciliation

Chad Michael Rimmer
Greening the Children of God: Thomas Traherne and Nature's Role in the Ecological Formation of Children

Steven Schafer
Marriage, Sex, and Procreation: Contemporary Revisions to Augustine's Theology of Marriage

Beyond the Academy
Lived Asian Public Theology of Religions

DAVID THANG MOE

Foreword by Simon Chan

☙PICKWICK *Publications* · Eugene, Oregon

BEYOND THE ACADEMY
Lived Asian Public Theology of Religions

Princeton Theological Monographs Series

Copyright © 2024 David Thang Moe. All rights reserved. Except for brief quotations in critical publications or reviews, no part of this book may be reproduced in any manner without prior written permission from the publisher. Write: Permissions, Wipf and Stock Publishers, 199 W. 8th Ave., Suite 3, Eugene, OR 97401.

Pickwick Publications
An Imprint of Wipf and Stock Publishers
199 W. 8th Ave., Suite 3
Eugene, OR 97401

www.wipfandstock.com

PAPERBACK ISBN: 979-8-3852-1808-0
HARDCOVER ISBN: 979-8-3852-1809-7
EBOOK ISBN: 979-8-3852-1810-3

Cataloguing-in-Publication data:

Names: Moe, David Thang [author]. | Chan, Simon [foreword writer].
Title: Beyond the academy : lived Asian public theology of religions / David Thang Moe.
Description: Eugene, OR: Pickwick Publications, 2024 | Series: Princeton Theological Monographs Series | Includes bibliographical references and index.
Identifiers: ISBN 979-8-3852-1808-0 (paperback) | ISBN 979-8-3852-1809-7 (hardcover) | ISBN 979-8-3852-1810-3 (ebook)
Subjects: LCSH: Theology of religions (Christian theology). | Christianity and other religions. | Public theology. | Theology, Doctrinal—Asia. | Burma—Religious aspects—Christianity.
Classification: BT83.85 M64 2024 (paperback) | BT83.85 (ebook)

VERSION NUMBER 10/09/24

Dedication to

The Presbyterian Church of Myanmar
in my native village of Khin Phong

and

My wife Prissila Moe, who accompanies me
from the remote Village to the Ivy League—Yale University

Contents

Foreword by Simon Chan | ix

Preface | xiii

Acknowledgments | xvii

1   Paradigm Shifts in Lived Asian Public Theology of Religions | 1
2   Motivations and Methods for Engaging Lived Community | 33
3   Engaging Grassroots Christian Witnesses of Lived Faith | 57
4   Revisiting Asian Public Theology of Religions and Liberation | 84
5   Synthesizing Academic-Grassroots Voices for Lived Public Theology of Religions | 113

Conclusion | 150

Appendix: Interview questions with the Grassroots Ethnic Christians | 153

Bibliography | 157

Index of Subjects and Names | 175

Foreword

I AM MUCH ENLIGHTENED and heartened when I read David Moe's book, not least because he has pushed the boundaries of doing contextual theology even beyond what I had done in my *Grassroots Asian Theology*. This is what theological works should be. As the title of the book suggests, Moe seeks to go beyond the academy to develop a public theology of religions that takes account of the "first theology" (*theologia prima*) of grassroots Christians. For good reason, Moe uses Myanmar as his case study. He spent a greater part of his life in that conflicted country ministering to Christians from a harassed minority ethnic group. His theology is forged in the crucible of inter-racial and inter-religious violence.

From such a context, Moe introduces us to a modified version of the "triple dialogue" of Federation of Asian Bishops' Conference. Moe's is a "new triple dialogue" between the academy and the grassroots within the church (intra-Christian dialogue), Christians and Buddhists at the level of both their "big" and "little" traditions (inter-religious dialogue), and the Asian and non-Asian theologians (glocal dialogue). This new approach reflects an increasing awareness especially among Protestant theologians that good theology is not merely the result of the theologian's reflection but also of his/her deep engagement with the lived theologies of ordinary Christians—what Catholics call the *sensus fidelium*.

I can see at least four ways in which this work contributes to a more holistic Asian public theology of religions. First, neglected aspects of the Asian contexts are fleshed out that previously were not even on the elite theologian's radar screen. For example, we begin to see both the beautiful and the ugly sides of a religion. Moe does not romanticize or fudge: "Buddhism in Myanmar and Sri Lanka has two opposing forms—the ugly side of nationalism and the beautiful side of compassion." Using a grassroots approach, we encounter a postcolonial Buddhism which is not quite like the timeless and idealized "metacosmic" religion that Aloysius Pieris pictures, but one that is very much rooted in history and politics, concerned with protecting its vested interests. As Moe puts it, "Post-colonial Buddhist nationalists maintain the colonial legacy of internal colonialism against ethnic minorities." But Moe does not merely critique Buddhism; by highlighting its ugly and beautiful sides, he also shows the potential of a lived theology of religions to transcend ethnic and religious barriers and, consequently, find common ground for resisting an oppressive military regime. I find this part of his constructive theology very illuminating (chapter 5).

Second, the nature of public theology is redefined. The public theology arising directly from engaging with grassroots Christians is somewhat different from the kind found in academic theology. What Moe offers is a richly contoured theology that defies the usual definitions. It is "first the lived reality of the worshiping community; only then is it a critical engagement." Moe recognizes that direct public engagement may be relevant in the West where the church as a public institution is still acknowledged (if somewhat grudgingly by its cultured despisers) but not in Asia. The public theology that Moe proposes is perhaps closer to Hauerwas' than Moltmann's. It has more to do with "reflection on the church's public and private witness of its lived faith in the world where God rules with love, truth, and justice" than with public protests and pronouncements.

Closely related to the second, is the ecclesiological starting point of his theology. In this respect Moe faults the Asian pioneers of public theology, M. M. Thomas and Shoki Coe, for failing to "incorporate the ecclesial voices of the grassroots Christians."

A fourth feature is that grassroots public theology needs the input of the social sciences especially ethnography. But in the Myanmar situation, the work of professional ethnographers is incredibly difficult. Thus, Moe takes upon himself to do his own ethnographic research. The task is challenging and much remains to be done. But what emerges are some overlooked "first theologies" of ordinary Myanmar Christians. For example, the Christus victor theme and the priestly work of Christ feature prominently in their soteriology. There are many other fascinating insights from the book, especially the final chapter, but it's best that I leave them to the readers.

Simon Chan
Editor, *Asia Journal of Theology*

Preface

MY THESIS IS SIMPLE and suggestive. We need to move beyond the academy. There are two reasons for moving beyond the academy. First, an overtly academic public theology is in crisis today. Although public theology may be flourishing among the academic thinkers within the academy, its external relevance for real life is limited. Call this the "external crisis of public theology." Second, there is the "ecclesial flourishing" among grassroots Christian communities across Asia who witness their lived faith. There are far more Christians in the village churches of Asia than in the academy. I have decided that since grassroots Christians are the largest segment of Christian population in Asia, we must utilize their lived voices as sources for developing a relevant sort of lived Asian public theology. Thus, I argue the methodological case for reimagining the paradigm shifts in lived Asian public theology in the context of world Christianity.

I am not claiming that we should uncritically romanticize and praise grassroots voices and experiences. Grassroots Christians have limitations. I am rather saying that we should start a lived Asian public theology by engaging with grassroots Christian communities who practice their lived faith. It is my conviction that we need a fresh methodology that bridges the gap between the academic and grassroots voices. There has long been the gap between the academy and the church. The question is: who will bridge this gap? Both academics and church people can play a role in bridging the gap. Yet it is more sensible for the academics to take the initiative by engaging with grassroots communities. It is because of this that I chose the title for this book to be *Beyond the Academy*.

PREFACE

It will be clear that this book has been the fruit of my conversation with grassroots Christians and academic Christians. My intention in this study is to explore a conversation between the description of the grassroots Christian practices and lived public theology that emerges from their practices. Since my inquiry relates to the description of lived practices on the ground and their relation to the formation of public theology, this book is placed at the intersection between grassroots Christian communities and the lecture and research studies of the academy. Having been born in a rural village and participating in a grassroots church as a Sunday school teacher and as a youth leader for some years, I see myself both as a grassroots insider (experienced person) and as an academician Christian (researcher). My methodology is rooted in a conviction that seeks to synthesize the grassroots voices and the academic voices for the contextual formulation of a lived Asian public theology of religions.

I have presented some themes of this book at some formal scholarly occasions in the academy over the past few years. I have presented the first chapter at the World Christianity Conference, Princeton Theological Seminary (March 2019). I have presented the Parable of the Good Samaritan and its implication for ethnic reconciliation, healing, and hospitality at the AAR/SBL meeting, Denver, CO (November 2018), Myanmar Institute of Theology (November 2021) and at Tahan Theological College (December 2021). I also have preached a sermon on the Good Samaritan at the Yale Divinity School's Marquand Chapel (March 2023). I have given a talk on Romans 13:1–7 as a Hidden Transcript of Public Theology at the Chinese University of Hong Kong (March 2023). I have presented the Lukan banquet of hospitality and its contextual implication for the public theology of reaching out and receiving in at the meeting of the American Society of Missiology at the University of Norte Dame (June 2019). All these presentations are discussed in chapter five. I thank the academic audiences for their helpful comments.

The book has five chapters. In chapter one, I have discussed some research problems and the need of moving beyond the academy. I have examined the state of Asian public theology and called for reimagining the paradigm shifts in a lived Asian public theology in the context of world Christianity. I have invited us to engage with the grassroots community as conversation partners in the performance of a lived Asian public theology of religions. In chapter two, I have discerned and described some motivations and methodologies for engaging with the grassroots Christian community.

Particular attention has been paid to why and how one should engage with the grassroots church. In chapter three, I have shown how I have engaged with the grassroots Christian community. I have carefully studied how they express their lived faith and witness the gospel in public life.

In chapter four, I have revisited the origins and foundations of the Asian public theology of religions and liberation. I have described some distinctive contributions of some select Asian theologians to Asian public theology of religions and liberation. I have also analyzed their strengths and limitations. In chapter five, which is the final chapter of the book, I have put together both the academic and grassroots voices. Using a synthetic methodology as a hermeneutical tool, I have attempted to find the gaps and fill the bridges between the academic and grassroots Christian views on faith, theology, and public life. In doing this, I have positioned myself as a theologian of the bridge—bridging some gaps between the academic and grassroots Christian voices.

Acknowledgments

I WAS BORN IN a village that no longer exists. Our village has moved to two different locations from the place where I was born. The village comprised about seventy households: 100 percent of the villagers are Christians. Born and raised in the peasant village, I spent most of my life in the village church—The Presbyterian Church of Myanmar—as a Sunday school student, a Sunday school teacher, and a youth leader. My lived experiences and works with these peasant Christians are the seeds for this book.

At its core are many debts—my teachers, colleagues, and friends. The gifts they have offered are so immense that I can never fully pay them back. I can only do so with a word of deep thanks.

First, I would like to express my heartfelt thanks to my parents and my village church for their spiritual support of prayer throughout my long academic journey from the remote village to the Ivy League—Yale University. This book is dedicated to them.

Second, I must express my deep thanks to the committee of "Equipping the Saints for Burma" at the Presbyterian Church of the Way in Shoreview, MN, USA, for their financial support. In particular, I thank Dick Stone and Judy Stone, Russ Cummings and Anita Cummings, Christ Martin and Sheila Martin, Joe Killpatrick and Carol Killpatrick. I also extend my thanks to Dr. Timothy Geoffrion, his wife Dr. Jill Geoffrion, and their Faith, Hope, and Love Global Ministries (Minnesota), Grace Foundation (California), and CMF International (Indianapolis) for their financial support that made my study in the U.S. possible.

ACKNOWLEDGMENTS

Third, my thanks go to Dr. Gregg Okesson, Dr. Stephen Offutt, and Dr. Lalsangkima Pachuau, for their helpful comments on the earlier drafts of the book. They have provided a combination of skills and expertise that have contributed to the integrated nature of this work: they have done so as a public theologian, a sociologist, and missiologist. I must also thank my friend and colleague at the editorial team of the *International Journal of Public Theology*, Dr. Clive Pearson, for reading my manuscript with the competent eyes of a public theologian and a language editor. I am forever grateful for his helpful comments.

Fourth, I thank the anonymous interviewees who agreed to share with me their inspiring stories and lived faith. Some of them are grassroots pastors, church elders, music leaders, Sunday school teachers: others are charity workers, social activists in Myanmar's villages. Their voices have never been heard in the academy. In the academy, we are trained to engage with famous scholars and influential thinkers and make them even more famous. While this kind of academic engagement remains crucial, I am fully convinced that it is necessary to engage with the grassroots people and unknown practitioners and to make their voices heard by engaging with academic voices. I believe that one of the most important things to do in life is to tell the untold stories of others.

Fifth, I owe special debts to Professor James C. Scott (aka Shwe Yoe in Burmese), Dr. Brandon Milliate, former librarian of Southeast Asian Studies at Yale University, Dr. Thomas Hastings, former Executive Director of OMSC and his wife Carol Hastings, for their warm hospitality during my research at Yale in 2019. Scott was my mentor and colleague at Yale's Council on Southeast Asia Studies. I am most grateful for his mentorship and inspiration, especially with regards to the methodology of learning from peasant Christians. I sincerely thank another mentor and colleague Professor Erik Harms, Chair of Yale's Council on Southeast Asia Studies, for his kind support and mentorship. I also thank Ei Ei Khin, Senior Manager, Brent Bianchi, librarian of South and Southeast Asian Studies, and the entire community of the Council on Southeast Asia Studies for their friendship. Prof. Steve Wilkinson, Director of MacMillan Center and Mrs. Heidi McAnnally-Linz, former Deputy Director of MacMillan, have been wonderful supporters of my work at Yale. Richard Lesage, librarian of South and Southeast Asian Studies at Harvard University, also deserves my thanks for his help during my research there in 2019.

ACKNOWLEDGMENTS

I am grateful to friends and colleagues at Wipf and Stock, especially my editor Dr. Robin Parry, acquisitions editor Michael Thomson, Matthew Wimer, and George Callihan, for publishing this book in the Princeton Theological Monograph Series.

Finally, I am most thankful to my longsuffering and beloved wife, Prissila Moe ("the prudent wife from the LORD," Proverbs 19:14), for her constant encouragement, sacrificial care, and spiritual patience throughout my research. Without her companionship, I would not have been able to complete this book. I am dedicating this book to her with love and gratitude. The triune God has been faithful throughout my life and research. Without him, I would not have been able to complete this book, and apart from him, I would have nothing to say here! May this humble work be blessed to the glory of the triune God!

DAVID MOE
New Haven, CT
March 24, 2024, Palm Sunday

ONE

Paradigm Shifts in Lived Asian Public Theology of Religions

Introduction: The Unhappy Gaps

THIS YEAR, 2024, BEARS witness to fifty years of the official rise of public theology in the academy. The term "public theology" was introduced by American Lutheran historian Martin E. Marty in an article in which he depicted the writings of Reinhold Niebuhr as a paradigm for public theology in America.[1] Since then scholarly discussions on public theology have become more popular in academic circles and gained wide support from scholars around the world.[2] This expansion of interest is evident in the wide range of publications now available on the subject. The establishment of the Global Network for Public Theology (GNPT) in 2007 at the Center of Theological Inquiry in Princeton and its several centers in different institutions in both hemispheres, North and South, reflect and contribute to this growing interest. The GNPT itself brings together research centers in more than thirty academic institutions around the world.[3] The GNPT uses the *International Journal of Public Theology* as a vehicle for sharing insights into the global flow of public issues, often from explicitly global perspectives.[4]

1. Marty, "Reinhold Niebuhr," 332–59.
2. Kim, "Public Theology," 40–66.
3. See "Mission," https://gnpublictheology.net/about/#mision&history [accessed on April 4, 2022].
4. See Kim, "Editorial," 285–89; Kim, "Public Theology," 40–66.

Since its inception in 2007, the journal has published some themes arising out of the triennial conferences of the GNPT held in Chester, Stellenbosch, Bamberg, and Curitiba. There have been country-bound, for instance, public theology in China, South Africa, Brazil, Ukraine, and Myanmar. Others have been theme-based—for example, climate change, urban spaces, NGOs, development, peacemaking, and animals.[5] While the growing trend in academic public theology is impressive, many observers note that public theology tends to be done more as an *academic* enterprise. The complaint sometimes made is that there can often be a lack of an empirical foundation and engagement. Scholars write academic public theology by dialoguing with their fellow scholars. They write public theology for academics as audiences within the narrow academy. They appear to write about public theology without sufficiently incorporating the voices of the grassroots Christians into their theological reflections.

Two Asian scholars may be cited as examples. The first is the Sri Lankan liberation theologian Aloysius Pieris. Pieris is widely cited in Western theological texts as an example of an Asian liberation theologian. His book *An Asian Theology of Liberation*[6] is widely used and engaged as a landmark source for an Asian public theology of Christian–Buddhist dialogue and liberation.[7] But, his theology of liberation does not sufficiently incorporate the voices of the grassroots poor. Moreover, his theology hardly addresses the politics of Sinhalese Buddhist nationalism and ethnic conflict in his home country of Sri Lanka. My second example is an Indian public theologian, Felix Wilfred. Wilfred is a theologian who develops an explicit term "Asian public theology." Yet in his *Asian Public Theology*, he hardly incorporates the lived voices of some grassroots Asian Christians. Overemphasizing political powers, his public theology also fails to address the issues of spiritual powers.[8]

These two Asian theologians and others of similar academic approaches fail to sufficiently engage with the lived voices of the grassroots Christians and religious activists. Scholarly writings on public theology do not sufficiently reach the hearing of the grassroots church and their place in public life. In general, the grassroots church is less interested in the fine points of abstract and somewhat detached arguments. They pay a much keener

5. https://gnpublictheology.net/about/#IJPT [accessed April 6, 2024].
6. Pieris, *An Asian Theology of Liberation*.
7. Fleming, *Asian Christian Theologians*.
8. Wilfred, *Asian Public Theology*.

attention to popular preachers and their inspiring messages of the prosperity gospel.⁹ The Yale public theologian Miroslav Volf rightly notes that:

> A sense that academic theology has lost its voice is widespread today. Many observers note, as Jeffery Stout did in *Ethics After Babel*, that theology is unable "to command attention as a distinctive contributor to public discourse in our culture."¹⁰ Equally, if not more, disturbing is the loss of interest in academic theology on the part of the church; as scholars write for scholars and students, the ear of church folk is tuned in elsewhere. Helped by the mass media, popular preachers and a diverse chorus of social critics are dominating the discourse in church and in wider culture. Theologians are on the sidelines. Like the street corner preachers of yesterday, they find themselves talking to a crowd too hurried to honor them with more than a fleeting glance.¹¹

Volf's statement reveals the gaps that exist between the academy and the church. If public theology is truly for the sake of all people, not just for scholars, I argue that we need to reimagine the paradigm shifts and move beyond the academy. Moving beyond the academy means engaging with the grassroots community and utilizing their lived experiences and voices as the sources for creating a lived Asian public theology.

My argument is built on the claim of a Singaporean theologian, Simon Chan: "Theology is first a lived experience of the church before it is a set of ideas formulated by church theologians."¹² Some Asian theologians, such as Simon Chan and Hwa Yung, among others, have proposed the need for a grassroots Asian theology. They have considered how an Asian theology should be done in a way that is relevant for ordinary Christian communities. To that end, they have suggested that we should utilize the lived experiences and voices of the grassroots communities as the primary source. In a related sort of way, the British theologian Mark Cartledge developed a methodology using collated data as a source for the doing of a more practical expression of a public theology.¹³ In an edited anthology on *Lived Theology*, some American theologians—Charles Marsh, Peter Slade,

---

9. I presented a paper on bridging the unhappy gaps between the academy and the church at the World Christianity Conference, Princeton Theological Seminary, Princeton, NJ, March 15–18, 2019.

10. Stout, *Ethics after Babel*.

11. Volf, "Theology, Meaning & Power," 45–66, at 45.

12. Chan, *Grassroots Asian Theology*, 15.

13. Cartledge, "Public Theology and Empirical Research," 145–66.

Sarah Azaransky, and others—have also placed attention on new perspectives of method, style, and the pedagogy of the lived experience of faith.[14] It is arguably the case that the ensuing Western manifestation of a lived public theology focuses on Christian witness against political powers: it fails to address spiritual powers. By way of comparison a lived Asian public theology of religions must address *both* political powers *and* spiritual powers.

My immediate context for this project is my homeland of Myanmar. The contemporary revolutionary movement that has risen in the face of the most recent in a series of the military coups demands a lived Asian public theology of religions grounded in real life. This particular context will not specifically address matters to do with the unfolding of that revolutionary movement that arose in response to the 2021 Myanmar coup. I have written that elsewhere. The focus of this work is on how some ordinary Christians, religious practitioners, pastors, and activists witness to their faith in such a particular context. The model of witnessing to faith or the performance of a lived Asian public theology in a Myanmar's dictatorial context is different from other contemporary Asian contexts, such as Indonesia, Malaysia, Singapore, the Philippines, South Korea, Taiwan, India, and others. The aim of this book is to engage with the lived voice of these particular grassroots Christians and place them in dialogue and a process of reconciliation with the Asian (and in some instances from the North Atlantic) academy. The book is built on three areas of the research inquiry.

First, this book examines critically the origins and foundations of an academic Asian public theology of religions and liberation. Second, it studies how grassroots Christians express their lived faith and witness the gospel in the context of social injustices, suffering, and conflict. Third, it suggests how grassroots and academic Christians should witness the holistic gospel of reconciliation in the context of Buddhist nationalism and ethnic conflict. It is in this third area of inquiry that I seek to reconcile the grassroots voices with the academic voices. The aim of this book is to show how the grassroots and academic theologians should enrich each other by bridging the gaps.

In synthesizing two voices, I see myself as a public theologian of the bridge. I bring my interpretative voice as an ethnic minority person who has the firsthand experience of Buddhist nationalism (insider) at the grassroots levels, and as a researcher (outsider). In the circumstances it is only appropriate that I provide a brief ethnographic background of my identity

---

14. Marsh et al., *Lived Theology*.

as a minority Christian with nurture in a grassroots faith and subsequent vocation as a researcher. I was born and raised in the rural village of Khin Phong in Mindat, Chin State of Myanmar (to which I dedicate this book). I was actively involved in the village Presbyterian Church as a Sunday school student, as a teacher, and as a youth leader for several years. I have spent most of my life with those grassroots village Christians who embodied their faith in many ways as preachers, missionaries, evangelists, persons of prayer, singers, social activists, and charity workers. I have preached, taught, and sung the embodied theology of the church along with those humble Christians. With my current role as a postdoctoral scholar and lecturer at Yale University, I have never lost touch with my village people. It is always important to remember where we are from. I have been in contact with them consistently for the sake of a public vision of democracy, education, and mission.

Having been born and raised in a Buddhist-dominant nation, I, along with those some ethnic minority Christians, have experienced the public and political issues of Buddhist nationalism and ethnic discrimination. That experience informs my inquiry and raises the following questions: what does it mean to be a faithful Christian in the context of political oppression and ethnic persecution? What does it mean to witness the gospel of salvation as reconciliation and liberation in such a context? How should we, a lived community of faith and prayer, respond to the public issues of political oppression and ethnic conflict? My aim is to study some grassroots Christians' local expressions of their lived faith and their witnesses of the gospel in private and public life. I will do this in chapter three. In chapter five, I will use my interpretative lenses to reconcile some grassroots Christians' voices with the academic voices and synthesize their voices and expressions for developing a lived Asian public theology of religions.

Moving beyond the Academy: The Invitation

After describing the unhappy gaps between the academy and the church, we will now turn to the invitation for moving beyond the academy. Seeking to do so, it would be helpful to briefly revisit the purpose and shape of Asian theology. Scholars agree that the 1960s and 1970s were a time when Asian contextual theologies were emerging as "resistance against a Western theology that posed as universal, normal, and axiomatic."[15] In order

15. Sugirtharajah, *Jesus in Asia*, 200. For an overview of the emergence of third world

to resist Western theology, the theologians needed the academic training and ability. While celebrating the contextual formation of Asian theology over sixty years, we need to rethink Asian theology and its relevance for the Asian context. The Sri Lankan Catholic theologian Aloysius Pieris makes the often-cited point that a serious theological inquiry in Asia should deal with its two twofold reality: "religious diversity and mass poverty." The first reality calls for interreligious dialogue and the second reality calls for liberation.[16] An academic contextual theology in much of Asia is grounded in Pieris's paradigm of interreligious dialogue and liberation.

First, an Asian theology of religions and liberation is the main product of an interreligious dialogue. Academic theologians here employ an interreligious dialogue as a controlling tool for doing an Asian public theology of religions.[17] They focus extensively on *inter*religious dialogue rather than on *intra*religious dialogue or academic–grassroots dialogue within a Christian community. Theologians tend to engage with people of other religions as their key dialogue partners for the doing of an Asian theology. In Myanmar, academic theologians promote the academic form of interreligious dialogue (Christian–Buddhist dialogue), but often neglect the need of academic–grassroots Christian intrareligious dialogue.[18] While the former form of interreligious dialogue is crucially important, we cannot neglect the latter.

Second, an Asian theology of religions and liberation is the product of an interacademic dialogue. Theologians do Asian theology by engaging with their fellow academicians. The local expressions of the grassroots Christians are often absent from their reflections on Asian theology. Consider an Asian liberation theology, which is one of the unified themes for doing an Asian public theology.[19] Take *Minjung* theology, which Jürgen Moltmann calls "the first liberation theology to come from Asia,"[20] as an example. *Minjung* theology was developed in the 1970s in South Korea as

---

contextual theologies, see Fabella and Sugirtharajah eds, *Dictionary of Third World Theologies*.

16. Pieris, "Two Encounters in My Theological Journey," 141–46, at 141; Pieris, *An Asian Theology of Liberation*, 36–50.

17. Swamy, *The Problem with Interreligious Dialogue*, 145–62.

18. See Ling, *Ecumenical Resources for Dialogue*.

19. Battung, "Commonalities," 95–99.

20. Moltmann, *Experiences in Theology*, 250.

a contextual political theology in response to the regime.²¹ While it gains a wide acceptance from global theologians, it has been criticized by some Korean Pentecostal theologians as a "theology from above," represented by a group of elites.²² Korean Pentecostal theologian Koo Dong Yun argues that some of the Korean Christian *minjung* who had been marginalized by the ruling class in the 1970s later became an upper-middle class or members of the ruling political party in the 1990s. "These people who used to be the oppressed *minjung* were being accused by others of being oppressors as they became organized and acquired socio-political power."²³

Third, an Asian public theology of religions and liberation has been developed on behalf of some grassroots Christians. It has been developed *for* the grassroots Christians rather than *with* them. Some Asian theologians may engage with some grassroots Christians, but they do not incorporate the grassroots voices and lived practices into their reflections on Asian theology. M. M Thomas of India represents this approach. As we will see in chapter four, Thomas is a lay theologian with highly intellectual thinking. He seemed to engage with the grassroots Christians, but he did not bring their grassroots voices and practices of public preaching, prayers, and social charity into his writings. By engaging with some academicians who see a theology of the church's direct engagement in politics as the only relevant public theology in Asia, Thomas appeared to write an Asian public theology of religions and revolution *for* the grassroots Christian communities rather than *with* them.²⁴

Simon Chan observes that Thomas's writing is not about grassroots Asian theology because he failed to incorporate some grassroots Christians' lived practices.²⁵ It is my conviction that writing about Asian public issues of oppression and suffering on behalf of some grassroots people does not sufficiently meet the needs of the grassroots Christians. Theologians may theologize about the grassroots Christians' experiences of social injustices and political liberation for them, but grassroots Christians, as I will show in

21. See, for instance, Kim, *Minjung Theology*.

22. While I was working at two different Korean Presbyterian Churches in the U.S (at Korean Central Presbyterian Church in Virginia as children pastor and at Lexington Korean Presbyterian Church in Kentucky as youth pastor), I asked some lay Korean Christians about *minjung* theology. The vast majority of lay Korean Christians did not know about *minjung* theology at all.

23. Yun, "Pentecostalism from Below," 89–114, at 97.

24. Thomas, *The Christian Response to the Asian Revolution*.

25. Chan, *Grassroots Asian Theology*, 23–37.

chapter three, are interested in a different kind of liberation from spiritual powers. In order to do a more relevant grassroots Asian public theology, we must start theology from the ground up by engaging their voices and by incorporating their practices into theological reflections. My understanding of a lived Asian public theology is thus methodologically grounded in using the ecclesial practices, experiences, and interests as primary sources. In other words, grassroots Asian public theology methodologically emerges *from below*.

Some theologians argue that an Asian public theology of religions and liberation tends to be the result of "top-down approach" rather than "bottom-up approach."[26] The problem with a top-down approach, according to a Sri Lankan theologian Vinoth Ramachandra and American New Testament scholar Craig Keener, is that it becomes another opportunity for the academicians to speak in the name of the grassroots Christians, and sometimes profit in their academic status by so speaking, without relinquishing personal privilege.[27] American Catholic theologian Robert Schreiter also observes that theologians can be academic oppressors if they do not incorporate the congregational voices. He explains:

> To allow the professional theologian to dominate the development of a local theology seems to introduce a new hegemony into often already oppressed communities. In the development of local theology, the professional theologian serves as an important resource, helping the communities to clarify its own experiences and to relate to the experience of other communities past and present. Thus, the professional theologian has an indispensable but limited role.[28]

In his book *Spirit Hermeneutics*, Craig Keener also observes on the danger of the inter-academic dialogue without engaging with some grassroots Christian voices:

> In many cases academicians listen only to fellow academicians, and often to those of the same basic theological persuasions, whatever their cultures. It is not yet a problem, but is a warning for the future. Indeed, in some scholars' hands, postcolonialism

26. Chan, "Asian Christian Spirituality in Primal Religious Context," 32–52, 42–43.

27. Ramachandra, *Subverting Global Myths*, 240–42. Keener, *Spirit Hermeneutics*, 294. Brian Stanley also observes that majority world theologians "do theology from above," which is not much relevant to their local grassroots communities, see Stanley, "Inculturation," 21–27, at 26.

28. Schreiter, *Constructing Local Theologies*, 18.

has become another opportunity for an educated elite to speak in the name of an underclass, and sometimes profit in their academic status by so speaking, without relinquishing personal privilege or helping the oppressed.[29]

We may then ask: is an Asian liberation theology emerging from the academic dialogue relevant for the grassroots Christians and for the public life? In his *The Genesis of Asian Theology of Liberation*,[30] Aloysius Pieris defends that an Asian theology of liberation remains relevant. He said:

> Some think—and would want others to think—that liberation theology is out of fashion if not out of date altogether for the simple reason that it is not mentioned today as frequently as it used to be a few decades ago. This inference is flawed. That liberation theology has lost its novelty does not imply that it has lost its relevance. It is far from being extinct. For its framework can be detected even in certain tracts published by the Federation of Asian Bishops' Conferences (FABC). Some evangelicals in our country are also showing overt interest in it.[31]

There is no denying the fact that an Asian theology of liberation is relevant for the political liberation of the oppressed, but its public relevance for real life is insufficient. The example is made here. While liberation theology opts for liberation from political powers, grassroots Christians opt for liberation from spiritual powers. Academic liberation theologians focus on structural sin, whereas the grassroots Christians focus on personal sin. The liberationist understanding of salvation emphasizes a horizontal dimension, whereas grassroots Christians focus on a vertical dimension. There is a gap between grassroots voices and academic voices. In order to fill the gaps, I will use a synthetic methodology of social science interviews with some grassroots Christians and literature. A synthetic methodology of doing a lived Asian public theology is based on a new triple dialogue. I will now suggest why and how a new triple dialogue is needed in the context of world Christianity.

---

29. Keener, *Spirit Hermeneutics*, 294–95.
30. Pieris, *The Genesis of Asian Theology of Liberation*.
31. Pieris, *The Genesis of Asian Theology of Liberation*, 1.

Beyond the Academy

A New Triple Dialogue in the Context of World Christianity

In 1972, the Federation of Asian Bishops' Conferences (FABC) proposed a famous triple dialogue among Asian Catholic Christians—"the dialogue with Asian cultures (inculturation), the dialogue with Asian religions (religious meeting), and the dialogue with the poor (human liberation)"—as a way for doing Asian theology.[32] Peter Phan and other Asian theologians adopted a triple dialogue as a tool for doing ecumenical Asian theology.[33] The task of the first dialogue with cultures is to achieve inculturation or the adaptation of Christian teachings and practices to Asian cultures. While "inculturation" is more widely used among the Catholics associated with the FABC, "contextualization" is more widely used among mainline Protestant Christians who are associated with the World Council of Churches (WCC). In either way of inculturation and contextualization, the aim is to build Christianity *on* Asian cultures, not to build *against* Asian cultures. Doing theology with Asian cultures has been popular among ecumenical theologians.[34]

The task of the second dialogue with Asian religions is to perceive people of non-Christian religions (especially Buddhism, Confucianism, Hinduism) as pilgrimage neighbors for the common witness of transforming society. Theologians utilize religious ethics as sources for the common witness of transforming society. Since religions and cultures are inseparable in Asia, it is difficult to distinguish between the two. When holding dialogue with Asian cultures, religions are naturally involved, too. Interreligious dialogue has become a common model for the mission of the Asian church among Catholic and mainline Protestant Christians. Theologians suggest that mission is perceived in terms of interreligious dialogue.[35] Third, but related to the second, the task of the third dialogue is to call the church to be in solidarity with the poor for their liberation from poverty.[36]

---

32. See Eilers, *For All Peoples of Asia*, 3–4.

33. See Phan, *Christianities in Asia*, 256–61; Chia, "Receptive Ecumenism through Asia's Triple Dialogue Theology," 126–36.

34. See Bosch, *Transforming Mission*, 430–42; 458–68; Yeow, *Doing Theology with Asian Resources*, 1–94.

35. Bosch, *Transforming Mission*, 468–78.

36. Eilers, *For All Peoples of Asia*, 3–4.

While this old triple dialogue remains crucial for doing an Asian theology, I wish to propose a fresh triple dialogue in a slightly different manner. My aim is not to compete with the old triple dialogue, but rather to complete it. It is my hope that a fresh triple dialogue serves as a helpful tool for doing and performing a lived Asian public theology of religions in the context of World Christianity. I use a new triple dialogue to refer to—the academic–grassroots intrareligious dialogue (academy–grassroots church dialogue), the Christian–non-Christian interreligious dialogue (Christian–Buddhist interreligious dialogue in this study), and the Asian–non-Asian public theologian dialogue (glocal dialogue). Each of these dialogues needs clarification.

The first form of dialogue, that is, the academic–grassroots intrareligious dialogue has been neglected in the development of Asian theology. If public theology is to be done from the ground up, this dialogue is necessary for creating a relevant lived Asian public theology. It creates a space for Christian theologians of the academy and ordinary Christians of the grassroots church to exchange their lived experiences and theological insights. If theology is about God-talk in terms of how God works among each believer in the villages and the cities, theology should not be seen as the dominant business of the academicians within the academy, but should transcend the narrow academic boundary and be open for the collaborative work between Christian theologians and ordinary people of the lived church as the body of Christ (1 Cor 12:27).

The second form of dialogue is the Christian–non-Christian interreligious dialogue. As noted earlier, this form of dialogue is nothing new in Asia. It calls for the church's dialogical engagement with people of other faiths. What I emphasize is a kind of interreligious dialogue that engages not only with academics and clergies of other faiths, but also with ordinary practitioners and activists. In a post-colonial period, the church is no longer the colonial missionary that sees people of other faiths as the mere objects for conversion: it should see them as God-image bearing neighbors (Gen 1:27) for witnessing to the common good of eco-justice and social justice without losing the church's mandate of the last commission (Matt 28:19–20).

The third form of dialogue is the glocal dialogue between Asian Christians and non-Asian Christian theologians. Thus, my use of the subtitle "lived Asian public theology of religions" is not a parochial form of theology for Asia. It engages not only with Asian theologians, but also with non-Asian public theologians as dialogue partners or as global body of Christ. As the global body of Christ, Asian Christians and non-Asian Christians are called to share similar and different gifts for the glory of God. Scholars of World Christianity emphasize that this form of dialogue is demanded in the context of World Christianity. This dialogue invites theologians from diverse global contexts to exchange their similar and different cultural issues and insights for doing a public theology. Doing theology in the context of World Christianity proves itself to be a cross-cultural and glocal team game and no one is the dominant referee. Only the Holy Spirit is the referee, and everyone is the collaborative player with different and similar gifts for the exchanges of theological insights.[37] A Malaysian American New Testament scholar K. K Yeo rightly said:

> Global Christologies seek creative dialogues toward: (1) a catholic faith based on biblical Christologies that honor multiple and interacting worldviews; (2) a global theology that respects cross-cultural and shifting contexts in which faithful communities embody real-life issues; (3) a translatability of the Scripture that upholds various dynamic vernaculars and hermeneutics; and (4) a roundtable symposium of proclaiming and worshipping a biblical Christ portrayed in varied Christologies.[38]

In response to the creative dialogues among global theologians, K. K. Yeo, Gene Green, and Stephen Pardue took the lead in editing the Majority World Theology Series.[39] This comprehensive series serves as a good example for doing public theology through the third form of dialogue. While decentralizing Western theology remains necessary, the third form of dialogue creates a cross-cultural space for exchanging and enriching the public and global issues of public theology among global theologians. Andrew Walls's celebrated typology of "indigenizing principle and pilgrim principle"[40] sums it up well.

The twin principles are not in opposition, but they are in tension for expressing the local and global body of Christ. While the indigenizing principle tends to focus on localizing public theology by interacting with local Christians, the pilgrim principle tends to focus on universalizing public

---

37. See Tennent, *Theology in the Context of World Christianity*.
38. Yeo, "Biblical Christologies of the Global Church," 162–79, at 168.
39. Green at al., *Majority World Theology*.
40. Walls, *The Missionary Movement in Christian History*, 53–54.

theology by interacting with global Christians.[41] Doing a lived Asian public theology of religions through a triple dialogue enables us to see theology not as a single endeavor of academicians. A lived Asian public theology of religions does not see individuals as the colonial agents of imposing their ideas on the other. A lived Asian public theology of religions invites different agents as dialogues partners for the exchanges of their lived experiences and theological insights for the common good. This triple dialogue will be evident throughout this book.

A Threefold Reality of Asian Context: Beyond Pieris's Twofold Typology

Sri Lankan liberation theologian Aloysius Pieris sums up the context of Asia in a twofold reality: "multifaceted religiosity" (in which Christianity is a minority) and "mass poverty" (both Christians and other faiths suffer together).[42] I believe Pieris neglects the third reality of Asia, that is, majority–minority ethnic conflict. Pieris's home country of Sri Lanka is known for the conflict between the Sinhalese Buddhist majority and Tamil Hindu and Christian minority.[43] There is also a conflict between the Bamar Buddhist majority and ethnic Christian minority in Myanmar, and other parts of Asia.[44] We cannot neglect the third reality of an identity-based ethnic conflict in Asia. Lived Asian public theology of religions must address a threefold reality of multifaceted religiosity, poverty, and conflict and advocate for the interreligious dialogue, liberation from poverty, and ethnic reconciliation. I wish to elaborate on the third reality of ethnic conflict in Southeast Asia.

---

41. Walls, *The Missionary Movement in Christian History*, 54.

42. Pieris, *An Asian Theology of Liberation*, 69–86.

43. See Deegalle, *Buddhism, Conflict, Violence in Modern Sri Lanka*; Chelvadura, *Ethnic Conflict and Reconciliation in Sri Lanka*.

44. According to the third edition of *World Christian Encyclopedia*, Christians compose 6.2 percent of the population, and the majority of Christians are found among the ethnic minority groups of the Chin, Kachin, and Karen, while 87.9 percent of Theravada Buddhists are found among the Bamar. See Johnson and Zurlo eds., *World Christian Encyclopedia*, 555–59.

Beyond the Academy

Ethnic Conflict and Religious Nationalism

Theologians tend to solve the problem, but some political scientists and anthropologists tend to understand the root causes of the problem. Political scientists observe that there are some root causes of ethnic conflict. Ethnic conflict does not rise in a cultural vacuum. Ethnic conflict is the result of the religious nationalism and political domination. The identity politics of majority–minority ethnic conflict and religious nationalism are interwoven.[45] Where there is political domination, there is the minority groups' resistance in the name of conflict.[46] In their book *Ethnic Conflict*, Karl Cordell and Stefan Wolff show how such nationalism and ethnic conflict are related to each other.[47] Ethnic conflict is based on "demands for respect, recognition, minority rights, power, and self-autonomy."[48]

In his celebrated book *The Clash of Civilizations and the Remaking of World Order*, Samuel Huntington claimed that in the post-Cold War world, "the most pervasive, important, and dangerous conflicts will not be between social classes, rich and poor, or other economically defined groups, but between people belonging to different cultural entities."[49] While Huntington's thesis is debatable in the present context of Russia's invasion of Ukraine, what is generally acceptable about his argument is that the conflicts in the post-colonial world are not between different countries, but what he calls "local conflicts" between different religions and ethnicities.[50] This is true to the Buddhist and Islamic Southeast Asian contexts where the local conflicts between the ethnic minority Christians and majority Buddhist and Muslim nationalists are rampant in public society.[51]

In *Nationalism*, Anthony Smith and John Hutchinson observe that "nationalism is one of the most powerful forces in the modern world, yet

---

45. See Soper and Fetzer, *Religion and Nationalism in Global Perspective*, 1–31; Kingston, *The Politics of Religion, Nationalism, and Identity in Asia*; Fukuyama, *Identity*, 67–73; Smith, *Nationalism*.

46. See Anderson, *The Spectre of Comparisons*, 318–32; Cheesman and Farrelly, *Conflict in Myanmar*; Thawnghmung, *The "Other" Karen in Myanmar*.

47. Cordell and Wolff, *Ethnic Conflict*, 25.

48. See Glazer and Moynihan, "Introduction," 1–28, at 5; Fukuyama, *Identity*, 67–73.

49. Huntington, *The Clash of Civilizations*, 28. Huntington first published his article in 1993. See Huntington, "The Clash of Civilizations?" 22–49.

50. Huntington, *The Clash of Civilizations*, 29.

51. See Esman, "Communal Conflict in Southeast Asia," 391–419; Phan and Tan, "Interreligious Majority-Minority Dynamics," 218–40.

its study has until recently been relatively neglected."⁵² Southeast Asianist Benedict Anderson's theory of nationalism in terms of "imagined communities"⁵³ is helpful for our understanding of nationalism and ethnic conflict. In his celebrated book *Imagined Communities,* Anderson defines nationalism as "imagined communities" where the dominant ethnic groups imagine the nationhood in Southeast Asia.⁵⁴ Religion and nationalism are equally imagined communities that can unite or divide people across South and Southeast Asia. While the majority Sinhalese Buddhists in Sri Lanka imagine the Sri Lankan community by discriminating against the Tamil minority Christians and Hindus. The majority Muslims in Malaysia and Indonesia imagine the nation by dominating and discriminating against non-Muslim ethnic minorities. In Myanmar and Thailand, the majority Buddhists imagine the nations by dominating and discriminating against the non-Buddhist ethnic minorities.⁵⁵

The Western people's perception of Buddhism is the Dalai Lama's promotion of peace and compassion. Yet Buddhism in Myanmar and Sri Lanka has two opposing forms—the ugly side of nationalism and the beautiful side of compassion. Buddhist nationalism in Sri Lanka and Myanmar took its roots in a colonial period as an anti-colonial movement.⁵⁶ The anti-colonial nationalist movement in Myanmar, for instance, was first led by some Buddhist monks who stimulated the *Sangha* to call for "home rule."⁵⁷ The anti-colonial movement was later joined by some Bamar Buddhist university students, such as Aung San (the hero of national independence), U Nu and Dr. Ba Maw in the 1930s.⁵⁸ They founded *Dobama Azi-ayone. Dobama* means, "We Burmans" and *Azi-ayone* means "association."

---

52. Hutchinson and Smith, eds., *Nationalism,* 4.

53. Anderson, *Imagined Communities,* xi–xv. Anderson, "Western Nationalism and Eastern Nationalist," 31–41.

54. Anderson, *Imagined Communities,* 6; Mehden, *Religion and Nationalism in Southeast Asia,* 115–69; Liow, *Religion and Nationalism in Southeast Asia.* 1–61; Gravers, *Nationalism as Political Paranoia in Burma,"* 41–121.

55. Cady and Simon, *Religion and Conflict in South and Southeast Asia.*

56. Gier, *The Origins of Religious Violence,* 45–98. Smith, *Religion and Politics in Burma.* Myanmar's nationalist movement of Young Men's Buddhist Association (YMBA) was inspired by the Sri Lankan nationalist movement of the YMBA founded in 1889.

57. Mendelson and Ferguson, *Sangha and State in Burma,* 199–205. Smith, *Religion and Politics in Burma,* 106–7.

58. Butwell, *Burma,* 11; Myint-U, *The Hidden History of Burma,* 29; Suu Kyi, *Freedom from Fear,* 8–12.

Beyond the Academy

Dobama Azi-ayone's slogan runs along the lines of race, language, and religion: Burman is our race, Burmese is our language, and Buddhism is our religion.[59]

During the strikes against the British, Buddhist nationalist students shouted, "love our race, cherish our language, and uphold our religion."[60] Their protest song, the basis of today's national anthem, includes the refrain *da-do-mye, da-do-pyi*: "this is our land, this is our country."[61] *Dobama Asi-ayone* gave birth to the Burma Independence Army in 1941. If there is one positive impact of the Buddhist anti-colonial nationalist movement, it could be as a way to gaining national independence from the British in 1948.[62] But how does Burmese Buddhist nationalism play a role in the politics of post-colonial nation-building?

Post-colonial Buddhist nationalists maintain the colonial legacy of internal colonialism against ethnic minorities.[63] When the regime took power in 1962 as a colonial analogy of British, Buddhist nationalism turned into the anti-ethnic minority movement characterized by political domination, ethnic discrimination, and cultural assimilation of ethnic minorities.[64] Aung San's vision of national integration in 1947 and U Nu's nationalization of Buddhism in 1961 caused minority assimilation into the Bamar culture.[65] U Nu's vision of ethnic assimilation was driven by a slogan: *amyo* (only the Bamar race), *batha* (only the Burmese language), and *thathana* (only the Buddhist religion). U Nu defined national identity through a lens of race and religion: "to be a Burman is to be a Buddhist."[66] This slogan has become a basis for Burmanization and Buddhistization that shapes a post-colonial imagination of faith (religious identity) and flag (political identity).

---

59. Myint-U, *The Hidden History of Burma*, 29.

60. Yi, *Dobama Movement in Burma (1930–938)*, 5, 63.

61. Myint-U, *The Hidden History of Burma*, 29.

62. See Hutchinson and Smith, *Nationalism*, 4; Smith, *Religion and Politics in Burma*, 81.

63. Schober, *Modern Buddhist Conjunctures in Myanmar*, 57. Furnivall, *Colonial Policy and Practice*.

64. Smith, *Religion and Politics in Burma*, 320–22; Anderson, *Imagined Communities*, 5–7.

65. Sakhong, *In Search of Chin Identity*, 206–16; Silverstein, *The Political Legacy of Aung San*, 51–58. Mang, "Burman, Burmanization, and Betrayal," 169–88.

66. Smith, *Religion and Politics in Burma*, 83.

It was during this period in 1966 that nationalist state expelled Western missionaries from the nation.[67] Ethnic minority Christians became vulnerable on the ground of their embrace of Christianity as a foreign religion that shapes their religious and ethnic identity. The irony of such a nationalist stance is how it ignores the fact that Buddhism is itself a foreign religion, coming from India in the eleventh century. Buddhist nationalism has a stronger sentiment of an anti-Westernism rather than an anti-foreignization. The regime is open to friendly relationships with China and Russia, but not with the U.S or some Western countries. All this leads to the ethnic minority Christians being perceived as pro-Western, and therefore facing religious discrimination and ethnic marginalization.

The minority Christian experiences of discrimination are both personal and communal. The ethnic minorities are treated as aliens in their ancestral lands.[68] For instance, a Chin ethnic minority politician and activist Lian Hmung Sakhong said:

> In the name of Hill Regions Buddhist Mission, the junta brought in an army of Buddhist monks who were then dispatched to various towns and villages across Chin State. Protected by the soldiers, these Buddhist monks have considerable powers over the Chin population. In many cases, local people have pointed out that the monks are military intelligence operatives who are more powerful than local army commanders.[69]

Buddhist nationalist practice of political domination, ethnic discrimination, and religious persecution is evident not only in Chin regions, but also in the Kachin and Karen regions. David Steinberg, an expert in the history of Myanmar, also observed:

> The Burmans are prejudiced against the minorities and consider them to be less civilized. The state military have unfairly been dominated by the Burmans. The coercive power of the state is in the hands of the Burman leadership. The traditional autonomy of the minorities has been eliminated, even though the traditional leadership of some of the ethnic minorities was retained during colonial rule. The autonomy promised the minorities under the first constitution of the Panglong Treaty has never been fulfilled. Although minority areas are rich in natural resources, especially

---

67. Sowards and Cartee, *The Last American Baptist Missionaries to Burma 1946–1966*.
68. Kung, "Love Your Enemies," 81–99.
69. Sakhong, *In Defence of Identity*, 53.

> Kachin, the profits from their exploitation have not been shared with the minorities, and the minorities have been denied adequate economic development. Minority religions have been placed in jeopardy by the state. The minorities have been denied the right of education in their native language.[70]

Political domination and ethnic discrimination consist of ethnic marginalization, religious persecution, restricting on freedom of worship, arresting pastors, and demolishing the Christian crosses, and replacing them with the Buddhist pagodas.[71] Political domination and ethnic discrimination cause what I call "the clash of imaginations." When the ethnic majority Bamar Buddhists imagine nationalism by claiming the exclusive ownership of the nation, ethnic minority Christians imagine a sort of ethno-tribalism by claiming the sovereignty of their ethnic regions. Two sides of their identity imaginations are clashing against each other. The Sri Lankan scholar Vinoth Ramachandra rightly discerns how:

> National minorities do not feel secure, no matter how strongly their individual civil and political rights may be protected, unless the state desists from engaging in these sorts of nation-building projects. When a majority community defines itself as a nation and claims the cultural ownership of the state, it provokes its minorities to define themselves too as nations. Minority ethnic nationalism is often a defensive reaction against a majority nationalism. This is the bloody postcolonial history of countries, such as Sri Lanka, Indonesia, India, and Burma.[72]

The ethnic minority reaction to Buddhist nationalism is to build upon trends and practices established prior to national independence from Britain. Prior to those period, the independent ethnic minority communities chose their own tribal leaders or village chiefs to rule the ethnic regions and to imagine their identity. John Hutchinson and Anthony Smith provide six features of shared ethnic identity: "(1) a common name; (2) a myth of common ancestry; (3) memories of a common past; (4) elements of a common culture; (5) a link with a homeland; and (6) a sense of solidarity."[73] These features are helpful for understanding the identity formation of ethnic

70. Steinberg, *Burma*, 191.

71. Sakhong, *In Defence of Identity*, 49–59. See also Ling, and Mang, *Religious Persecution: A Campaign of Genocide Against Chin Christians in Burma*.

72. Ramachandra, *Subverting Global Myths*, 142.

73. Hutchinson and Smith, *Ethnicity*, 6–7.

minorities. The politics of the conflict between the ethnic minorities and majorities and their conflictual imaginations of identities call for the moral vision of ethnic reconciliation and political liberation.

Doing Public Theology for Four Communities: Church, Academy, Society, and State

If Martin Marty coined the term "public theology," in the 1970s, David Tracy developed it further during the 1980s. Tracy is arguably the "most influential Catholic public theologian writing in English of the past fifty years, both internationally and beyond confessional borders."[74] He suggests that there are three kinds of publicness in public theology, and the task of public theology is to engage three communities—church, academy, and society.[75] I will briefly reflect on each of these communities and suggest that a lived Asian public theology needs to move beyond the three communities and engage with the fourth community (the state). In his celebrated book *The Analogical Imagination*, Tracy explains about those three this way:

> If one is concerned to show the public status of all theology, it becomes imperative first to study the reference groups, the publics of all the theologian. The fact is that theologians do not only recognize a plurality of publics to whom they intend to speak, but also more and more the theologians are internalizing this plurality in their own discourse. The results are often internal confusion and external chaos. Just whom does the theologian attempt to address in theological discourse?[76]

While I appreciate Tracy's creative proposal for the need of theology's public engagement with three communities, I would specify that the church is a grassroots community. The church in the U.S. where Tracy locates might be a balanced community of lay people and intellectuals. The church in Asia, especially in the rural villages, as we will describe later in chapter two, is a community of grassroots believers. Most of the church people in Asia are economically poor, politically oppressed, uneducated, religiously persecuted, and ethnically discriminated against. Unlike the grassroots church, the academy is a community of scholars with critical thinking and

74. Palfrey and Telser, *Beyond the Analogical Imagination*.

75. Tracy, *The Analogical Imagination*; Tracy, "Three Kinds of Publicness in Public Theology," 330–34.

76. Tracy, *The Analogical Imagination*, 3–5.

creative imagination, and society is a public and pluralistic community of interreligious people. The question of how we should engage these three communities for doing lived public theology of religions will require careful consideration.

Public Theology with Confession—Grassroots Church

The first nature of public theology is *confessional*. If we define theology as the study of God, we tend to think that there is theology only in the academy. But if we redefine theology as a confessional meditation on God with the expression of lived faith, there is an embodied theology in the church.[77] The father of liberation theology, Gustavo Gutiérrez, proposes "meditation and practice" as the first act and "theological reflection" on that meditation and practice as the second act.[78] Gutiérrez's theological method arose as a critique of the traditional way of doing theology. In the traditional form of doing theology, theologians first think theologically and then apply it. For Gutiérrez, the grassroots church's meditation on God comes first and theology as a reflection that follows meditation is the second act.

Therefore, theology is not just to be learned, thought, and taught in the academy, but it is also to be lived, experienced, and meditated first in the church. Grassroots Christians do not articulate the doctrine of God in abstract ways, but they do embody God through their meditative and doxological engagement.[79] Their embodiment of theology begins with the grateful heart. Although they do not critically articulate the doctrine of God with their head, they express how much they love God with their heart. If mission begins with the heart of God (John 3:16), theology should also begin with the heart, which expresses a joyful relationship with God and a joyful public witness of God's love and salvation.

We stress that a lived public theology is first and foremost to be performed in the church with the heart of worship. Pentecostal theologian Amos Yong seeks to correct stereotypes of Pentecostalism, both political and theological, and argues that worship should not be understood in isolation from the public witness of God. For Yong, political or public praxis is not merely about the church's public engagement but also about the church's

---

77. Tracy, *The Analogical Imagination*, 203–18; Moltmann, *Experiences in Theology*, 4–5.

78. Gutiérrez, *On Job*, xviiii; Gutiérrez, *A Theology of Liberation*, 4–18.

79. A grassroots pastor, interviewed by the author, July 21, 2020.

liturgical performance of worship, prayer, and preaching.[80] Yong's thesis is helpful for a transformative understanding of Pentecostal Christians' role in political witness to the Spirit beyond a Pentecostal dancing with the Spirit in the church. A lived public theology is first to be performed in the church. Its goal is to renew our minds (Rom 12:2) in order for us to be moral agents for socio-political transformation in public society. The task of Christians is not just to advocate for social transformation, but also to prepare for internal transformation of the mind.[81]

Scholars like Walter Brueggemann, Stanley Hauerwas, others also emphasize the relationship between worship and its implications for public witness. We must stress that such public theology does not begin in public life, but in the worshiping life of the church.[82] Hauerwas is known for suggesting that "theological politics" starts in the worshiping life of the church as a "community of character" shaped by the apostolic tradition of Jesus's teaching.[83] He states the relation between social engagement and the practice of worship:

> Liturgy is social action. Through liturgy we are shaped to live rightly the story of God, to become part of that story, and are thus able to recognize and to respond to the saints in our midst. Once we recognize that the church is a social ethic then we can appreciate how every activity of the church is a means and an opportunity for faithful service to and for the world.[84]

In a similar way, Brueggemann makes a connection between liturgy and public witness by providing two disciplines of resistance. One is liturgical and the other ethical in ancient Israel's attempt to live as a distinctive community in a world dominated by empires.[85] For the liturgical resistance, Brueggemann expounds Exodus 1–15 as the reenactment of Israel's foundational story. This liturgy begins with the Israel's public voicing of pain to God. Liturgical life then shapes Israel's prophetic resistance against hegemony.[86] Liturgy is a spiritual moment to transform one's mind in order to

---

80. Yong, *In the Days of Caesar*, 155.
81. Yong, *In the Days of Caesar*, 155–56.
82. Brueggemann, *Texts That Linger, Words That Explode*, 75–78; Hauerwas, *A Community of Character*, 36–52.
83. Hauerwas, *A Community of Character*, 36–52; 57–71.
84. Quoted in Scharen, *Public Worship and Public Work: Character*, 19.
85. Brueggemann, *Texts That Linger, Words That Explode*, 75–78.
86. Brueggemann, *Texts That Linger, Words That Explode*, 76–78.

be a light and salt to the world (Matt 5:13–16). While the light symbolizes a Christian's shining life through which others could see Jesus's true life, the salt symbolizes preserving the integrity of faith in the world.

Brueggemann enables us to see worship as a doxological moment of character transformation for becoming ethical and political agents. Since liturgical practices shape the moral, political, and apostolic agents for social transformation, we may see "worship as an alternative political praxis."[87] It is fair to conclude that grassroots Christians' lived contribution to public theology begins in the church's liturgical space where Christians celebrate salvation as a joyful witness of Jesus's victory over evils and of reconciliation.

Public Theology with Critical Reflection—Academy

The second nature of public theology is *critical*. The academy is where public theology is to be critically reflected beyond the church. The nature of public theology in the second community is a reflective and analogical imagination. It is widely suggested that public theology is to be critically reflected.[88] As an academic discipline, public theology is critically reflected in conversation with other academic disciplines, especially Christian ethics.[89] Although Tracy does not incorporate the grassroots voices of the church as the primary sources for reflecting public theology, he does emphasize the need of relationship between the academy and church. He said, "as a discipline, theology belongs, therefore, to the churches and its seminaries and possibly to church-related institutions of learning."[90]

It is my concern that the academy exists for reflecting public theology in conversation not only with other academicians, but also with church people. Since grassroots Christians already embody an implicit theology without thinking about it academically, they just need academics to think about it critically together. Moltmann rightly points out that "There is implicit theology of modern times—a theology always already existent, but not critically thought through—and that this demands an explicit theology."[91] There is theology in the congregation. An explicit nature of public theology can be done through the synthetic voices of the academic and grassroots

---

87. Yong, *In the Days of Caesar*, 55.
88. Tracy, *Fragments*, 241–68. See also Kim, *Theology in the Public Sphere*, 3.
89. Tracy, "Three Kinds of Publicness in Public Theology," 333.
90. Tracy, *The Analogical Imagination*, 16.
91. Moltmann, *God for a Secular Society*. 1.

Christians. This will be taken up later when integrating some grassroots and academic Christian voices in chapter five.

Public Theology with Conversation—Public Society

The third nature of public theology is *conversational* or *dialogical*. Unlike the first community of faith, the third community represents a more pluralistic space where Christians and people of other faiths are encountering in public sphere as neighbors and colleagues. This encounter requires a dialogical engagement. One of the best ways of understanding Tracy's public theology is through his focus on dialogue or conversation.[92] Public theology can be seen as a theology of conversation. As a theology of conversation, Christians and ordinary people of other faiths bring their different faiths and exchange their diverse gifts and wisdom for enriching each identity and for witnessing the common good of public life. Christians should not see people of other faiths as the mere objects for conversion, but as neighbors to whom the hospitality of giving and receiving insights must be both extended and received.[93] While holding the distinctive nature of faith, Christians must learn to see people of other faiths as partners in sharing the gifts for performing a lived Asian public theology of religions.

In his book, *A Public Faith*, Miroslav Volf rightly said that "as witnesses, Christians are not mere teachers who instruct. A teacher can learn something that remains very much external to her own life and then pass it on as useful information to others."[94] A good witness, according to Volf, must be humble in actions. Christians should witness to Jesus not only by speaking to the other as the message receivers about him in words, but also by imitating Jesus in their actions. The point is to respect the other as a neighbor who has gifts to give us too. Volf wrote:

> Good givers will respect the integrity of receivers. There are limits to what other may be willing or able to receive, and givers should honor these limits. Christian should share wisdom in the way that the first letter of Peter instructs them to give an account of their hope—"with gentleness and reverence" (1 Pet 3:15–16).[95]

---

92. Tracy, *Fragments*, 145–86; 146–53; Tracy, *Dialogue with the Other*; Okey, *A Theology of Conversation*.

93. See Yong, *Hospitality & The Other*, 99–128; Shepherd, *The Gift of the Other*.

94. Volf, *A Public Faith*, 108.

95. Volf, *A Public Faith*, 109.

Volf emphasizes the right and respectful relationship between Christian faith and people of other faiths. Our public engagement is the result of following Christ who is at work in public society beyond the academy and the church. A German public theologian Jürgen Moltmann is right when he depicted the society-oriented public theology as the kingdom theology. He said:

> As kingdom-of-God theology, it is of necessity missionary theology, linking the church with society, and the people of God with the peoples of the earth. It becomes a public theology, which participates in "the sufferings of this present time," and formulates its hope for God at the places where contemporaries are and exist. Kingdom-of-God theology intervenes critically and prophetically in the public affairs of a given society, and draws public attention, not to church's interests but to God's kingdom, God's commandment, and His righteousness.[96]

Since the nature of God's kingdom encompasses all dimensions of private and public life, public theology must be dialogically performed in all dimensions of life from the *church* through the *academy* to the *society*. Despite an academic discipline, public theology should be done in an accessible way for ordinary people to join in.

Public Theology with Courage—Political State

The fourth and final nature of public theology must be *prophetic*. Most public theologians suggest that public theology must be "prophetic in action."[97] In order for Christians to prophetically engage with the state, the church needs the moral courage. A prophetic engagement with the state should be built on interreligious cooperation (Christian–non-Christian interreligious engagement). The task of a Western political theology is to examine how the church and the state should relate to each other. Such an approach to a Western political theology can be seen in Yale political theologian Nicholas Wolterstorff's book *The Mighty and the Almighty: An Essay in Political Theology*.[98] The church's direct engagement with the state may be relevant

---

96. Moltmann, *Experiences in Theology*, xx.

97. Tracy, *The Analogical Imagination*, 203–18; Tracy, "Three Kinds of Publicness in Public Theology," 331–34. See also Moltmann, *God for a Secular Society*, 1; Volf, *A Public Faith*, 104; Kim, *Theology in the Public Sphere*, 5.

98. Wolterstorff, *The Mighty and the Almighty*, 1–10.

to the West where the church remains powerful, but such an approach is not quite relevant for Asia where Christianity is only a minority religion, with the exceptions for the Philippines and Timor-Leste in Southeast Asia.

Rather than engaging first with the state, as a Western political theology tends to, I would suggest that a lived Asian public theology of religions should first seek to engage with the non-state people of other religions in society and to interreligiously confront the unjust state. This makes more sense in Asia where Christianity is a minority prophetic religion and its interreligious dimensions of courageous collaboration with people of other faiths is necessary for their stronger prophetic resistance to the state. This approach will be evident throughout the book.

Lived Asian Public Theology of Religions

What is public theology? What is lived Asian public theology of religions? In his *Faith Speaking Understanding*, Kevin Vanhoozer helpfully defines the first question:

> Public theology is the church's demonstration of life in Christ—to the glory of God and for the sake of the world. There is a public dimension to the gospel. The relatively new discipline of public theology studies ways in which Christian faith should impact public life. The assumption is that the gospel has a significant bearing on all people, not Christians only. Much of what the church says and does takes the form of public witness.[99]

There is no authoritative definition of public theology.[100] I define public theology as a reflection on the church's public and private witness of its lived faith in the world where God rules with love, truth, and justice. I depict the kingdom of God as the foundation and Jesus Christ as the model for defining a public theology.[101] The public dimension of God's reign or kingdom demands the church's identity and its vocation for the public and personal witness of the triune God in all dimensions of life. According to Jürgen Moltmann, "There is no Christian identity without public relevance,

---

99. Vanhoozer, *Faith Speaking Understanding*, 7.

100. For a definition of public theology, see Harold. "Defining Public Theology," 3–20.

101. See Moltmann, *God for a Secular Society*, 1–5; Moltmann, *The Trinity and Kingdom*.

and no public relevance without theology's Christian identity, since for Christ's sake theology is kingdom-of-God theology."[102]

Now we ask the next question. What is a lived Asian public theology of religions? I define a lived Asian public theology of religions as a renewal theology that critically examines an academic Asian public theology of religions and reconsiders the lived experiences of the church and other faiths seriously. Lived Asian public theology is built around the personal confession and public commitment of the church that the renewal of Asian public theology of religions must fill the gaps between the church, the academy, and society. In *Lived Theology*, Charles Marsh suggests that "lived theology examines practices, objects, and beliefs in order to understand God's presence in human experience."[103] Lived theology is not about doctrine in abstraction, but about engaging real life. He said, "by creating space in language, and by organizing spaces of conversation and exchange in and outside the academy, lived theology welcomes to the table both friend and stranger."[104] Marsh does not emphasize the interreligious role in lived theology. However, I go a step further and take the interreligious ethics of Christian and other faiths (Buddhism and spirit religion in this case) as sources for developing lived Asian public theology of religions.

A public theology of religions and comparative theology of religions share some relationships under the umbrella of interreligious engagement, yet they hold their distinctions based on their orientations. "Faith seeking understanding" is the slogan of comparative theology, while "faith speaking action" is the slogan of public theology. The aim of comparative theology of religions is to compare some religious doctrines across religious traditions for the vision of seeking the mystery of God deeper,[105] while public theology of religions emphasizes reflections on the ethical role of interreligious engagement for the moral vision of seeking the welfare of the city (Jer 29:7).[106] While comparative theology of religions tends to engage with academic thinkers as its main dialogue partners, a lived public theology of religions expands the horizons of its dialogue partners by engaging with both the academics and ordinary practitioners. Comparative theology of

102. Moltmann, *God for a Secular Society*, 1.
103. Marsh, "Introduction," 1–22, at p. 7.
104. Marsh, "Introduction," 17.
105. See Clooney and Stosch, *How to Do Comparative Theology*; Clooney, *Comparative Theology*.
106. See, for instance, Volf, *A Public Faith*, 35–74; Winter, *Seek the Welfare of the City*.

religions chooses good religious insights, while public theology of religions approach religions paradoxically: "religions are alive today—for good and for ill."[107] A public theology of religions criticizes the amoral sides of religio-political practices and utilizes the moral sides of religions as alternative sources for healing and the common good.

In filling the gaps between the church, the academy, and society, I discern a relevant approach to a lived Asian public theology of religions. There are two ways of approaching an Asian public theology. The first approach is to see the world as God's public reign and to start public theology there in society and then bring it to the church. Among Asian public theologians, Felix Wilfred, as we will see in chapter four, represents this approach. In his book, *Asian Public Theology*,[108] Wilfred argues that public theology must start first in the world and before moving to the church. He states that the "addresses of Asian public theology are not church in the first place, but the public."[109] For him, the ecclesial movement to the society is motivated by a "theology for public life, rather than a public theology."[110] He classifies "theology for public life" as a Western version of theology, and "public theology" as an Asian version of doing theology."[111] Taking the majority status of other religions in Asia, he suggests that Asian public theology be initiated by other religious thinkers and political activists, such as Mahatma Gandhi and other political activists.[112]

While Wilfred's method can be applauded, it has some weaknesses. It weakens the identity of the church. If public theology is about the society's moving to the church, we have lost the meaning of mission. Mission (*missio* in Latin or *apostellein* in Greek) means sending the church into the world in imitation of God's sending Jesus into the world (John 20:21–22; Acts 1:8).[113] Mission means sending the church to spread the good news to the world. This practice does not mean that mission is merely about sending the church to the world without staying for doxology. Mission means both

---

107. Volf, *Flourishing*, 59.
108. Wilfred, *Asian Public Theology*.
109. Wilfred, *Asian Public Theology*, xix.
110. Wilfred, ed., *Theology to Go Public*, xiv.
111. Wilfred, *Asian Public Theology*, xv–xix.
112. Wilfred, *Asian Public Theology*, xix.
113. See Kostenberger, *The Missions of Jesus and the Disciples according to the Fourth Gospel*, 27–37; Bosch, "Reflections on Biblical Models of Mission," 175–92, at 176. Bosch observes that the idea of mission as being sent to spread the good news of Jesus's life and message is mentioned in the New Testament 2,016 times.

being sent out and staying.[114] In reaching out to the world, the church must not see people of other religions as mere objects for conversion. This is Wilfred's concern, and thus he suggests that public theology must start in pluralistic society.[115] The church must rather see adherents of other faiths as co-doers of public theology of religions. This kind of engagement echoes my previous suggestion of the second form of dialogue, that is, Christian–non-Christian interreligious dialogue.

The second approach is to start in the church. This approach asks the ontological and functional questions of the church. It asks the identity question of what it means to be the church for the triune God and the vocation question of how the church should play its function in engaging public society to bear witness to the Trinity's work of justice, peace, and reconciliation. Like the first, this approach sees the world as the public realm of God's reign and asks how the church should engage with it. According to Miroslav Volf, Karl Barth is the most significant advocate for the role of the church for the world.[116] Volf observes, "Barth got it right when he insisted that the first task of the church is to be the church. But the church is truly itself when it isn't about itself but about God and God's mission in the world."[117] Barth has a high view of the role of the church for the world or, as Volf terms it, "church theology." Barth interprets the church Christologically and Christ politically in terms of their prophetic witness for the society where God reigns.[118] Barth's public theology was deeply grounded in what we may call "first theology."[119]

First theology is rooted in a threefold relation of the Trinity-Bible-Church.[120] In terms of its ontological relationship with God, first theology is seen as "Liturgical Theology."[121] First theology proceeds to "second theology," which is rooted in a threefold relation of the Trinity-church-world. The church plays a hermeneutical role in first theology by interpreting

---

114. Moe, "The Word to the World," 68–85.
115. Wilfred, *Asian Public Theology*, xviii–xix.
116. Volf, "Faith, Pluralism and Public Engagement," 813–34, at 823.
117. Volf, "Faith, Pluralism and Public Engagement," 823.
118. For a study of Barth's concept of the church and its role in public theology, see Barth, *Community, State and Church*.
119. Vanhoozer, *First Theology.* 28–31.
120. Vanhoozer, *First Theology,* 28–31.
121. Chan, *Liturgical Theology,* 21–40.

the identity of faith and its public relevance.[122] The church plays a role in second theology by asking how the church should dialogically engage with the world. In terms of bridging first theology of the Trinity-Bible-Church and second theology of the Trinity-Church-World, a lived public theology starts in the church and is implied for the world. This approach is rooted in the economic and immanent Trinity. Emphasizing the economic Trinity, we often ignore the significance of the immanent Trinity. If we start lived public theology in the church, we rediscover the significance of the immanent Trinity for the church's inner communion, whereas the church's public engagement with the world embodies the economic Trinity's relation to the world.[123]

A lived trinitarian public theology takes the church as its ground for the love of the Trinity through a spiritual engagement with God and for the love of neighbors in society through a social engagement (Mark 12:30–31).[124] It asks the identity question of what it means to be the church for the Trinity on the one hand, and provides some methodological questions for how the church as the image of the Trinity should engage with the world as God's public reign, on the other. A lived Asian public theology is not just about engaging lived voices, but also about recognizing their voices as the primary means of social and spiritual witnesses.[125] This bottom-up approach assumes that lived "theology arises as much from how being the church is practiced as how it is understood."[126] Adopting this bottom-approach opens up a fresh understanding of how the church's internal dimensions of lived practices of praise, prayer, preaching, and social charity could make a distinctive contribution to a lived Asian public theology.

In his *In the Days of Caesar: Pentecostalism and Political Theology*,[127] Amos Yong also takes the liturgy of the church as a starting point for doing public theology. He suggests that the liturgy should not be seen in isolation from the church's public praxis.[128] While the internal life of the church is

---

122. Moltmann, *The Trinity and Kingdom*, 1.

123. This first appeared in *Asia Journal of Theology*, Moe, "The Church as the Image of the Trinity," 22–49.

124. Volf, "Faith, Pluralism and Public Engagement," 823.

125. See Chan, *Grassroots Asian Theology*; Chan, "Grassroots Asian Ecclesiologies," 595–614; Chan, *Spiritual Theology*.

126. Chan, "Grassroots Asian Ecclesiologies," 295.

127. Yong, *In the Days of Caesar*, 155–65.

128. Yong, *In the Days of Caesar*, 155–65.

crucial for the church's relationship with God, its external life is crucial for the church's public engagement. The internal movement and the external movement of the church are equally crucial for a lived Asian public theology. The thick identity of the church is rooted in this twofold movement.[129] The reciprocal idea of the internal and external movements of the church takes its root in the people of Israel's imagination of their identity as the relationship with God and with the world. In his landmark book, *Theology of the Old Testament*, Walter Brueggemann explains:

> The testimony of Israel concerning Yahweh is always of two kinds, one to reorder the internal life of the community in ways faithful to Yahweh, the other to invite the world out beyond this community to reorder its life with reference to Yahweh. Both enterprises are preoccupied with the recognition that the acknowledgement of Yahweh at the center of life (the life of Israel or the life of the world) requires a reordering of everything else.[130]

The internal witness and the external witness of the church are in tension. In terms of the church's *intra*religious witness within the church, we get a public theology of religion (in the singular). We emphasize the role of Christian faith in theology. In terms of the church's *inter*religious witnesses to the world, we get a public theology of religions (in the plural). As the church turns its witness to the world, its task is to engage with people of other faiths as partners in resistance to the unjust state. It is in this sense that we emphasize the role of Christian faith and people of other faiths in lived Asian public theology of religions.

We must also acknowledge that there is the challenge of performing the publicness of lived Asian public theology in some dictatorial contexts. In Western liberal democracy contexts, a public witness of prophetic faith against the state is safe. Yet such a public and open witnesses are risky in some dictatorial contexts, like Myanmar, North Korea, and others. In this respect I must argue that public theology is not just about the church's public witnesses of lived faith in public life, but it is also about the church's hidden and symbolic forms of witnesses. As I will develop in chapter five, James Scott's theory of "hidden transcripts" is helpful in holding the tensions between the hidden and public witnesses of faith. Scott was described

---

129. Clifford Geertz popularized thick description, but he got the term from Gilbert Ryle. Geertz, *The Interpretation of Cultures*, 3–32. Volf uses thin and thick faith as a way for the church's public engagement, see Volf, *A Public Faith*, 39–41.

130. Brueggemann, *Theology of the Old Testament*, 747.

by Jennifer Schuessler in *The New York Times* as a "Professor Who Learns from Peasants."[131] Schuessler was well aware of how Scott is a big thinker and how his work relates to the real world by engaging with lived practitioners in Southeast Asia.[132]

In his two sibling books, *Weapons of the Weak*,[133] the result of his fieldwork among peasants in Malay village in the 1978–1980 years, and *Domination and the Arts of Resistance*,[134] Scott took great interest in understanding the power relations of the dominant groups and subordinate groups and the latter's various ways of resistance to the former.[135] In these, Scott explores the ways peasants and grassroots practitioners used evasion and subterfuge, rather than open confrontation, to thwart efforts at the state.[136] Scott's theory of "hidden transcripts" and everyday forms of ordinary people's resistance to the politics of domination is relevant for developing and performing lived Asian public theology of the hidden and public witnesses of faith within and outside the Christian community.[137]

Conclusion

This opening chapter has described the unhappy gaps between the academy and the church and has proposed some needed paradigm shifts for a lived Asian public theology of religions. We have examined the state of Asian public theology and invited readers to move beyond the academy. We have provided some reasons for moving beyond the academy. One of the key reasons for doing so is that public theology has lost its voice and meaning in both the church and public society. Its voice has been loud only within a

---

131. Schuessler, "James C. Scott," https://www.nytimes.com/2012/12/05/books/james-c-scott-farmer-and-scholar-of-anarchism.html, [accessed January 2, 2021].

132. James Scott is touted by Benedict Anderson as "a true Southeast Asianist stature." See the back cover of Scott, *The Moral Economy of the Peasant*.

133. Scott, *Weapons of the Weak*.

134. Scott, *Domination and the Arts of Resistance*.

135. Scott, *Domination and the Arts of Resistance*, 1–15.

136. Scott, *Weapons of the Weak*, 37–47; Scott, *Domination and the Arts of Resistance*, 4–16. Scott adopts Irving Goffman's concept of offstage resistance; Goffman, *The Presentation of Self in Everyday Life*.

137. I have shared four panel discussions with James Scott at Yale University, Columbia University, Yonsei University, and The Chinese University of Hong Kong on the subaltern politics of Buddhist nationalism and everyday forms of subalterns' resistance to political powers of the coup and I am indebted to him for his insights.

narrow academic community. Seeking to readdress the relevance of theology for real life, we have proposed a rethink in order to develop a lived Asian public theology of religions. Lived Asian public theology of religions ought to be done through a fresh methodology of a new triple dialogue—(i) the academy–grassroots Christian intradialogue; (ii) Christian–non-Christian interreligious dialogue, and (iii) Asian–non-Asian public theologians. We concluded the chapter by constructing a framework of a lived Asian public theology of religions.

Two

Motivations and Methods for Engaging Lived Community

Introduction

IT IS NOW CLEAR that a new triple dialogue serves as a driving force for developing a lived Asian public theology. It is time to focus on an often-neglected dialogue (the academy–church intrareligious dialogue). Asian public theologians tend to choose the second of the three prospective dialogues (the interreligious) as a dominant methodology for developing an Asian public theology of religions and liberation. With their overemphasis on the interreligious dialogue, Asian public theologians often neglect the academic–church *intra*religious dialogue. We need to reconsider seriously the academic–grassroots church intrareligious dialogue as a fresh methodology for developing and performing lived Asian public theology of religions. Lived public theology is not just to be thought conceptually, but also to be performed practically.

It is impossible to do a lived Asian public theology without engaging with the grassroots community who bear witness to their lived faith. I would suggest that our willingness to engage with grassroots Christian communities must be rooted in a transformative understanding of two things. One is a transformative understanding of the crisis of an overtly academic public theology. Although it may be flourishing among academics within the academy, academic public theology in many parts of the world is in crisis in terms of its external relevance for real life. It should be designated an "external crisis." What we have discussed about public theology in the academy is not sufficiently relevant for real life beyond the academy. We cannot bring public theology as a solution for real life without engaging with practitioners. A theology that comes from the interaction with practitioners must necessarily address real life.

The other one is a transformative understanding of the flourishing of Christian faith among the grassroots and marginalized communities in Asia. While an academic public theology is in crisis in terms of its insufficient relevance for real life, there is the ecclesial flourishing among some grassroots Christians, especially in the Asian villages. There is much evidence to support the contention that a grassroots Christian faith is flourishing wonderfully among ordinary and marginalized communities. Some political hardships do not stop their grassroots faith from witnessing to Jesus. Their grassroots understanding of lived faith is less about a system of beliefs and a set of doctrinal articulations in abstract: it is more about a joyful way of life.

This twofold reality—the crisis of an academic public theology and the flourishing of grassroots faith—has become the motivation for engaging the lived community of faith. Such an approach is consistent with the work of Miroslav Volf and Matthew Croasmun in their *For the Life of the World*, where they express their dissatisfactions with an academic theology that fails to engage with real life for human flourishing. It allows for public theology which they name as "an everyday theology." They rightly note:

> Theology that has lost its way is above all professional academic theology, which is only subset of Christian theology as a whole. In an important sense, all Christian are theologians. As Christians, we seek to think and speak plausibly our journeys with Christ into our own and the world's fullness to make the practice of faith coherent. Call this "everyday theology."[1]

This sort of approach to public theology emerges from how people are understanding and performing their lived faith in everyday lives rather than how academics might impose their ideas and systems on grassroots practitioners. To develop a lived Asian public theology as an everyday theology, it is indispensable to engage with the grassroots community of lived faith. There might be several motivations for engaging the grassroots Christian community. I wish to propose some main motivations for engaging the grassroots community of lived faith. I will suggest how we should engage

1. Volf and Croasmun, *For the Life of the World*, 13.

with them and show the methodology for how I have engaged with them for the purpose of this book.

Motivations for Engaging the Grassroots Christian Community

We begin by asking some questions concerning both teleological and methodological issues. What are some motivations for engaging with the grassroots Christian community? What is a new perspective on the grassroots Christianity that demands such a response? How might a new perspective on the grassroots Christianity then shape some methodological and theological studies in the life of the church? What becomes of the role of the trained theologian—how should he/she engage with the lived experience of the grassroots Christian persons and communities? How might different storied accounts of the church's experiential encounter with God shape a contextual reimagination of a lived Asian public theology of religions?

A New Perspective on the Grassroots Christianity

First, in order to reimagine a lived Asian public theology, we need a new perspective on the grassroot Christian community. As an academic discipline, public theology has often ignored the lived experiences of the grassroots Christian communities. Public theology has long been and still is the main business of academic theologians. If public theology is for the sake of all people, not just for a small community of academics, we need to expand a wider horizon of the dialogue partners with a new perspective on theology and lived community. I will suggest that a new perspective should seriously rethink the five features of Asian Christianity for developing a lived Asian public theology. They are listed as follows: grassroots Christianity as a lived religion; lived Christianity as a grassroots religion; Christianity as a majority religion of the minorities; Christianity as a discriminated against and persecuted religion; grassroots Christians as storytellers. Each of these features is closely related.

Beyond the Academy

Grassroots Christianity as a Lived Religion

Our new perspective on grassroots Christian community is based on a transformative understanding of Christianity as "lived religion."[2] As a lived religion, the members of the grassroots Christian community embody their faith in everyday life. Their embodiment of their faith is multiple in actions between the church and public society. Some grassroots Christians embody their faith as pastors and preachers, while others embody their faith as social workers and activists. Lived experiences and different practices are individually and communally inherent in their everyday lives and actions. They individually and communally practice Christianity as a way of life rather than as a mere system of doctrines. Grassroots Christians tend to understand Christianity not merely as a religion of systems and articulations, but as a way of life and as a relationship with God through practices.

It is in this regard that grassroots Christianity can also be understood as a way of life. In his book *Christianity as a Way of Life*, Kevin Hector helpfully explores how academic theologians and ordinary Christians should reconsider "Christianity as a way of life."[3] Hector argues that Christians are called to witness to God not only through words and teaching, but especially through spiritual practices that train persons to conduct themselves well daily lives.[4] To make sense of Christianity as a way of life, Hector argues that we understand Christianity not merely as a set of religious beliefs, but rather as a set of practices designed to transform one's way of perceiving God, the self, and others in the world. As a way of life, Christianity is understood as a lived religion that orients us to God, our transformative way of being in the world, and reshape our way of being with others.[5] Hector defines this claim by looking at three broad sets of Christian practices:

> So, then, three sets of practices: practices of being oriented, of being in the world, and of being with others. Taken together, the aim of these practices is to transform not only one's way of perceiving and acting but one's very self. This is what I have in mind, in sum, when I claim that Christianity is a way of life.[6]

---

2. See, for instance, Hall. *Lived Religion in America;* McGuire, *Lived Religion*, 3–18.
3. Hector, *Christianity as a Way of Life*.
4. Hector, *Christianity as a Way of Life*, x.
5. Hector, *Christianity as a Way of Life*, 2.
6. Hector, *Christianity as a Way of Life*, 3.

To make sense of these sets of practices, Hector emphasizes "wonder, lament, love, and prayer" as four essential aspects of Christian faith. First, wonder trains Christians to appreciate the goodness of God as a gift. Wonder plays a key role in the grassroots Christians' joyful way of life. Despite poverty their lives are full of joy. Second, lament enables Christians to feel sympathetic to the other in suffering. Lament also enables Christians to recognize the vulnerability of human beings. Third, love plays a key role in a transformative way of compassionate relationship with others. One way of cultivating love is through acts of beneficence for others. In this sense, we imitate Jesus. Finally, prayer shapes Christianity as a way of spiritual life in its relationship with God.

Grassroots Christians' understanding of Christianity is not based on the academic articulations about God and the church. They practice their faith as a way of life even if they do not express it theologically. Thus, our engagement with them comes from the conviction that there is embodied theology in the church. Christian theology does not start in the academy. It starts in the church. Theology is already existent in the life of the church through its acts of worship, wonder, lament, joy, praise, prayer, and preaching.[7]

In his book *Experiences in Theology*, Jürgen Moltmann regards theology in the church as a "shared theology."[8] He described how "In sermons, hymns and prayers, in teaching, and when I talked to people in their homes, I experienced theology as a *shared theology* of believers and doubters, the oppressed and the consoled."[9] For Moltmann, theology is not just the product of academicians. Theology is a shared product of the collaboration between the grassroots and academic Christians.[10] This line of understanding is consistent with our previous discussion on the second form of dialogue (academic–grassroots Christian intrareligious dialogue). Simon Chan and Hwa Yung paid serious attention to the necessity of doing lived Asian theology by engaging with the grassroots communities as respectful dialogue partners.

---

7. See Hastings, *Worshiping, Witnessing, and Wondering*.

8. Moltmann, *Experiences in Theology*, 5.

9. Moltmann, *Experiences in Theology*, 5. He reflected on this when he was a pastor for five years in the Reformed Congregation of Bremen-Wasserhorst, a little country congregation of about four hundred people.

10. Moltmann, *Experiences in Theology*, 4–5. Some theologians regard theology in the church as "primary theology." Schmemann, *Church, World, and Mission*, 135. Chan, "Asian Christian Spirituality in Primal Religious Context," 42.

In his book *Mangoes or Bananas,*[11] Yung has made the case for doing Asian theology that is relevant for the grassroots Asian Christian communities. He has urged:

> A serious effort must be made to bring theology down to the grassroots level of the church. One non-Christian academic, in private conversation, has observed that most of the Asian theologians today are writing for the academic. A change of orientation is needed. This involves consciously writing much of the material discussed above with the needs of the laity in mind.[12]

While Yung has proposed to do what he calls "Asian theology for and from the grassroots," he has not sufficiently developed it. It is only Chan who has comprehensively developed the methodological idea of why and how grassroots Asian theology ought to be done. Chan argued that Asian theology should emerge from the ground up rather than from the top-down. Chan confesses in his book *Grassroots Asian Theology: Thinking the Faith from the Ground Up* that, although he is a systematic theologian, grassroots Asian theology does not represent a systematic theology, but a contextual theology. He said:

> This is not a systematic theology. My main focus is on how theology ought to be done. This book as much concerned with the process as the contents of theology. Only the content that has a particular bearing on the Asian context is highlighted in each theological focus. My aim is to force a rethink on the way Asian theology is currently undertaken and in so doing show the distinctive contributions of Asian grassroots Christianity to the wider church's theological endeavors.[13]

Chan suggests that a more pertinent methodological question we need to ask in order to develop a relevant theology in Asia is: "what spiritual and intellectual resources of the Christian faith can we bring to bear on the Asian context."[14] Chan invites us to reconsider grassroots ecclesial experiences and lived practices as the primary sources for doing grassroots Asian theology. Amos Yong praises Chan's "methodology as exemplary."[15] While Chan's methodology shapes my own way of thinking, he tends to discredit

11. Yung, *Mangoes or Bananas?*
12. Yung, *Mangoes or Bananas?*, 15.
13. Chan, *Grassroots Asian Theology*, 8.
14. Chan, *Grassroots Asian Theology*, 10.
15. See Yong's endorsement on the back cover of the book.

too quickly academic theologians in favor of grassroots voices.[16] I do agree with Chan's exemplary methodology, which calls for doing Asian theology from the ground up, but I have a concern that his conclusion seems to highly praise grassroots voices at the expense of the academic. I will show in chapter five that one should neither discredit academic voices nor romanticize grassroots voices. In this regard, we should critically and creatively synthesize their different voices by analyzing their strengths and limitations.

Lived Christianity as a Grassroots Religion

The second motivation for engaging with the grassroots Christian communities comes from our transformative understanding of lived Christianity as a grassroots religion. To be sure, Christianity in Asia is not an elite religion. It is a grassroots religion, the vast majority of whose practitioners are ordinary, and poor, people from ethnic minority backgrounds.

In recent years, some scholars and historians of World Christianity have paid serious attention to a transformative understanding of the center shift of Christianity to the Global South from the Global North. They have observed that the center of Christianity has shifted to the Global South from the Global North since the early twentieth century. No one had ever expected that the center of Christianity would be shifted to the Global South from the Global North.[17] It is an unexpected change in the eyes of humans. Yet it is the miraculous work of the Holy Spirit. A historian of Asian Christianity, Scott Sunquist, appropriately called the twentieth century "the unexpected Christian century" because of this surprise shift to the Global South.[18] In her book, *Global Christianity*, Gina Zurlo, an expert scholar in the demographic study of Global Christianity likewise acknowledged that "Christianity is no longer a Western-majority faith, as most Christians

---

16. Chan, *Grassroots Asian Theology*, 18–27. Chan criticizes C. S. Song, M. M. Thomas, and some pioneer *Minjung* theologians and argues that their "theologies are hardly qualified as Asians."

17. See Walls, *The Missionary Movement in Christian History*; Walls, *The Cross-Cultural Process in Christian History*; Sanneh, *Disciples of All Nations*; Sanneh, *Whose Religion Is Christianity?*; Jenkins, *The Next Christendom*; Kim and Kim, *Christianity as a World Religion*; Robert, *Christian Mission*, 10–20.

18. Sunquist, *The Unexpected Christian Century*, xv–xxi.

today live in Asia, Africa, and Africa. Many adherents in the United States are unaware of this shift in Christianity's center of gravity."[19]

Scholars of World Christianity regard Christianity as a world religion.[20] While many scholars of World Christianity are right in celebrating the macro-global shift of Christianity to the Global South from the Global North, they do not pay sufficient attention to the micro-reality of the flourishing of Christianity among the grassroots people. It is understandable that they do not pay sufficient attention to the flourishing of Christianity among grassroots people, because most of the recognized scholars of a World Christianity do not come from grassroots backgrounds. They come from the educated middle classes. It should be reemphasized that Christianity is not just shifting to the Global South demographically, but it is flourishing among the poor, persecuted, and grassroots people. Christianity is not just a world religion, but in the non-Western world it is a religion of the poor.

The vast majority of the receiving people are grassroots people. Philip Jenkins, in his seminal book *The Next Christendom*, admits that "global Christianity is flourishing wonderfully among the poor, persecuted, while it atrophies among the rich and secure."[21] Although Jenkins's category of the "next Christendom" could be contestable as to how some marginal Christians could represent the powerful nature of the next Christendom, his observation on the flourishing of Christianity among the grassroots communities is correct. Zurlo also observes that "much of Christian flourishing has been among poor and marginalized people."[22] In the following we will explore why and how Christianity is flourishing among such people.

Christianity as a Majority Religion of the Minorities

There is the paradox of Christianity in Southeast Asia. The paradox is that the majority of those living out Christianity are to be found among the minorities. It is a majority religion of the minorities. Christianity is represented by most of the minority groups. Christianity in Southeast Asia, for instance, is found especially among what I would call the "double minorities." By the double minorities, I mean the minority status in terms of both the ethnic and religious minority identities. Christianity in Southeast

---

19. Zurlo, *Global Christianity*, xv; Sanneh, *Whose Religion Is Christianity?* 13–93.
20. Kim and Kim, *Christianity as a World Religion*.
21. Jenkins, *The Next Christendom*, 275.
22. Zurlo, "A Demographic Profile of Christianity in East and Southeast Asia," 4.

Asia, except the Philippines and Timor-Leste, is found among the double minorities.[23] Two of the most common features of Asian Christianity, according to Peter Phan, are their existence among the ethnic minorities and amidst overwhelming economic poverty.[24] While Christianity in five economic Asian Tigers—South Korea, Japan, Hong Kong, Taiwan, and Singapore—do not represent the economic poverty of Christian faith, Christians in most of the Asian nations face an economic poverty.

Take, Malaysia, for instance. Malaysia, an Islamic-majority nation, is the first country in Southeast Asia to have received the earliest Catholic missionaries from Portugal in 1511. Portuguese Catholic missionaries conquered port of Malacca and set up residence and ruled there. They built an incomplete church building called the Church of Saint Paul.[25] Christianity in Malaysia has grown since its reception in 1511 to register 2.39 million adherents (9.2 percentage of the population) in 2010. While 61.3 percentage of Muslims is found among the Malay majority groups, most of Christians are found among some ethnic minorities, such as Kandazan-Dusun from Sabah, Iban from Sarawak, Chinese, and Tamils across the nation. Islam is a religion of the Malay majorities and Christianity has become a religion of the ethnic minorities.[26] Also in Thailand, a Buddhist-majority nation, most of the Christians, who form less than 2 percent of the population, are not of Thai descent or Siamese, but are Chinese, Vietnamese, and from tribal minority groups. Since the arrival of foreign missionaries, "Christians have always been a tiny minority in Thailand."[27]

Myanmar is another important country to consider for the status of Christianity among the ethnic minorities. While Buddhism is widely practiced by the Bamar ethnic majority groups, Christianity is found among the ethnic minority groups, such as the Chin, Kachin, Karen, and other ethnic minorities who make up of 6 or 8 percent of the population. The flourishing of Christianity is found among the ethnic minorities in the villages. Today the stronger significance of Christianity in Southeast Asia is found among the ethnic minorities from the peasant villages rather than from the industrial cities. In the village of the author, 100 percent of villagers are Christians

23. See Kwa and Law, eds, *Missions in Southeast Asia*.

24. Phan, "Introducing Christianity in Asia," xxxiv–xxxv.

25. The author of this book had a chance to visit this historic church building in Malacca in 2010.

26. Tan Sooi Ling, "History of Christianity in Malaysia," 47–60.

27. Dahfred, "History of Christianity in Thailand," 136.

and peasants. Being a Christian and being a peasant are inseparable in most of the Southeast Asian villages. In Chinland, a state in Northwest Myanmar, most of the Christians are found among the village people who are economically poor, academically low, politically oppressed, ethically marginalized, and religiously persecuted. Their peasant Christian identities echo the context in which Jesus did his ministry in the first century.[28]

As a religion found mostly in the rural villages, grassroots Christians also face the challenge of spiritual powers in the Southeast Asian spirit world. Grassroots people in the Southeast Asian villages share a spirit world where people and spirits live together. Spirits are encountered in their everyday activities.[29] As a consequence, their common understanding of salvation is the healing and liberation from the spirit-possessed sicknesses and from the power of sin. The most distinctive contribution from the village Christianity is the understanding of salvation as healing the spirit-possessed sick and as delivering from sin and of Jesus as a healer and as a mediator. Their understanding of the mediatorial role of the village priest shapes the contextual understanding of Jesus as a healing mediator between God and sinners (1 Tim 2:5).[30]

Minority Christianity as a Discriminated-Against Religion

To understand Christianity as a discriminated against and persecuted religion, we need to understand the grassroots Christians encounters of two different powers: spiritual powers and political powers. We have noted earlier how they encounter spiritual powers. To understand Christianity as a persecuted and discriminated against religion, we will focus on political powers here.

Political powers are the burdens and threats for the existence of ethnic minority Christians. If Islam in Malaysia and Indonesia and Buddhism in Myanmar and Thailand are misused by people in power as oppressing religions for the ethnic minorities, Christianity in those non-Christian countries is an oppressed religion. Ethnic minority Christians in Myanmar and Sri Lanka face Buddhist domination, religious persecution, and ethnic discrimination. Likewise, ethnic minority Christians in Malaysia

28. See Bailey, *Poet and Peasant and Through Peasant Eyes*. For a comprehensive study of the peasantry cultures in Southeast Asia, see also Scott, *The Moral Economy of the Peasant*.

29. Endres and Lauser, eds., *Engaging Spirit World*, 1–18.

30. Ki, *From Darkness to Glorious Light*.

and Indonesia face Islamic domination and religious nationalism. Ethnic minorities face the politics of religio-ethnic discrimination based on their different identities in their respective countries. How do the ethnic minorities maintain, then, the integrity of their minority faith? What can the academic theologians learn from the grassroots minority Christians and their struggles for identities and their faithfulness as minority communities in the context of political domination?[31]

Academic theologians must learn from minority Christians' faithful witnesses of Jesus. Minority Christians in a military nation like Myanmar do not *seek* persecution and suffering, but their experiences of religious persecution and political suffering come as the consequences of their faithful witnesses to Jesus. Although the ethnic minorities face the politics of religious persecution and ethnic discrimination, they remain spiritually strong and vocationally faithful. They not only represent the quantitative majority of the Christian population, but they also represent the qualitative life of faithfulness. They remain faithful to following Christ amidst political suffering, economic poverty, ethnic discrimination, and religious persecution. The significant presence of Christianity among ordinary people is truly admirable. This state of affairs calls for the urgent need of "rethinking Asian theology from the ground up."[32] Their firsthand experiences of persecution and faithfulness even echo the social-cultural situations of the first-century minority and grassroots Christians and their experiences of persecution and faithfulness.[33] In their book *The New Testament in Its World*, two New Testament scholars, N. T. Wright and Michael Bird carefully observed:

> Many early Christians were functionally illiterate, at least, at the time of their conversion. Part of the glory of the gospel, however, is that it is for everyone, that there should not be an elite who get it while everybody else is simply going with the flow. So, the leaders and teachers in the early church taught people to read, so that they could become thinking, reflective, and contributing actors in the drama.[34]

Wright and Bird show the need of recognizing the role of ordinary Christians in the drama of witnessing to the gospel. My conviction is that

---

31. Ramachandra, *Christian Integrity in a Multicultural World*, 11.

32. See Chan, *Grassroots Asian Theology*.

33. For the stories of the first-century Christian communities, see Wright and Bird, *The New Testament in Its World*, 849.

34. Wright and Bird, *The New Testament in Its World*, 849.

ordinary Christians in the first century share some similarities of their faithful witnesses of Christ with some grassroots Asian Christians in the twenty-first century. Like the first-century Christians, twenty-first-century grassroots Christians in Southeast Asia remain faithful to witnessing to Jesus Christ amid political oppression, ethnic discrimination, and religious persecution. Take, some ethnic minority Christian witnesses in Myanmar, as an example. Myanmar is what David Steinberg, an expert in the politics and history of Myanmar, calls a country that practices the "longest-ruling military elite in Modern Asia, and perhaps in the contemporary world."[35] Although grassroots Christians have been living under the regime and Buddhist nationalism for over six decades with concrete experiences of religious persecution, ethnic discrimination, and political domination, they practice their lived faith as the faithful followers of Jesus by the healing power of the Spirit.

Their lived experiences and their everyday witnesses that tell the stories about their faithful and spiritual relationship with God are essential sources for developing a lived Asian public theology as a story theology. We are trained to engage with the existing written literatures, but we often neglect the oral witnesses of people's stories.[36]

As we reimagine the paradigm shifts in a lived Asian public theology of religions, we must reconsider the function of the stories of ordinary people in doing theology. A pioneer Asian theologian from Taiwan C. S. Song strongly emphasized the role of stories in doing Asian theology. Song is best known for his long emphasis on the central role of people stories in developing Asian theology.[37] His contextual approach to story theology is deeply rooted in the thesis that sees Jesus as the storyteller and the public witness of the reign of God in action.[38] Song eloquently said:

> Strictly speaking, Jesus did not bring God's reign into the world, for it is already there. What he did was to engage people in the manifestation of it, to enable them to know it is there, to open their minds' eyes to see it. The reign of God is among them because it is

---

35. Steinberg. *The Military in Burma/Myanmar*, 1.

36. I am deeply indebted to James C. Scott for inspiring me to think seriously about the role of the oral stories of peasant people in writing research on Southeast Asia. Scott often told the author that "I decided that since peasants were the largest segment of the world's population, it would be honored and worthy career to devote my life to the study of peasants and agriculture."

37. See Song, *Tell Us Our Names*; Song, *The Believing Heart*.

38. Song, *Jesus and the Reign of God*, 161–67.

a matter of human experience. It does not come in such a way that it can be found by looking at the march armies or the movement of heavenly bodies; it is not to be seen in the coming of messianic pretenders. Rather, it is to be found wherever God is active decisively within the experience of an individual and people have faith to recognize this for what it is. Jesus is the witness pointing to the reign of God in the very midst of the people excluded from the official religious community.[39]

According to Song, the way Jesus lived and went about his public ministry is powerful witness to God's reign. Jesus witnessed to God's reign through the stories of ordinary people. Jesus associated with ordinary people by eating and drinking with them. The Jesus who was with ordinary people in the first century must also be present among the grassroots Christians and non-Christians as the public witness of God's reign. The lived stories of Jesus's active and public presence among ordinary people become some crucial motivations for our contextual reimagination of doing lived Asian public theology. I will suggest ways as to why and how theologians should learn from and listen to the unheard yet inspiring stories of some grassroots Christians. Their stories of ethnic discrimination, political suffering, religious persecution, and their lived experience of faithful witnesses should be utilized as rich sources for developing storied Asian theology.

Grassroots Christians as the Storytellers

In his latest book *In the Beginning Were Stories, Not Texts*, C. S. Song made the claim that the Bible is fundamentally a story. "Life begins with story. Creation begins with God's story."[40] People in the Bible live their faith by telling their stories. Jesus himself is a storyteller; he spoke of God's reign through stories and parables. Stories are, thus, the most basic mode of communicating a lived theology. At the heart of Christian faith are stories, not theories or ideas. Stories come first, and theories and ideas come later.[41] Song said:

> Doing Christian theology through stories has become a major trend in Christian theology today. This is the way it should be. After all, the Bible is a storybook. Take away stories, and is the

39. Song, *Jesus and the Reign of God*, 162.
40. Song, *In the Beginning Were Stories, Not Texts*, 5.
41. Song, *In The Beginning Were Stories, Not Texts*, 153–70.

Christian Bible still the Bible? Writers are story tellers. Painters are story tellers. The strange thing is that Christian theology, while trying to serve the storybook called the Bible, has often been largely a theology of ideas and concepts. This non-biblical trend has to be reversed.[42]

Song suggests five approaches to lived story theology. I personally found each of these approaches helpful for the motivations for engaging grassroots Christian communities whose pre-Christian and Christian stories are very much based on the oral witnesses.

First, we must not see story in isolation from theology. We must see story as a lived theology because stories consist of some symbolic theological meanings. According to Song, "A story is not simply a story; it is already a story theology, though not in an overt or conspicuous way."[43] In a similar vein, Moltmann rightly said, "a theology is always already existent but not critically thought through—and that this demands an explicit public theology."[44] Seeing story as lived theology enables us to believe that "theology is used neither in the restricted sense of teachings and doctrines authorized by the church nor in the sense of conceptually developed systems of beliefs, premises, assertions more by theologians."[45] It is noted that theology in "story as story theology" takes upon itself the task of explaining what it has perceived God to be and what God is doing in the lives of ordinary people through their sorrowful and joyful stories they live and tell.[46]

Second, a lived theology is telling stories in practice. Song argues that "you do story theology not only to listening to stories; you are practicing it when you tell stories—stories of others, stories of the past, and above all you own stories."[47] While the first approach employs researchers as story-listeners, the second approach treats grassroots Christian communities as storytellers. Listening and telling stories are the reciprocal ways of doing lived public theology. For example, the stories of the victims of the Nazi atrocity were told by a young Jew Elie Wiesel, who survived the Holocaust.[48]

42. Song, *In The Beginning Were Stories, Not Texts*, vii.
43. Song, *In The Beginning Were Stories, Not Texts*, 153.
44. Moltmann, *God for a Secular Society*, 1.
45. Song, *In The Beginning Were Stories, Not Texts*, 153.
46. Song, *In The Beginning Were Stories, Not Texts*, 155.
47. Song, *In The Beginning Were Stories, Not Texts*, 156
48. Wiesel, *Night*.

Doing political theology in Germany, for example, is the product of listening and telling the stories of the victims.[49]

Third, Song depicts "story theology as empathetic response to stories."[50] Lived stories are not only to be told and listened to, but also to be responded to with compassionate actions. Song argues that Asian theology is not just to be learned, but to be experienced. He urged "Asian theologians to be engaged in theology with a heart."[51] Doing public theology with the heart is sensitive to recognizing the stories of the grassroots Christian community and human community. Song uses a beautiful analogy of fish and water to express how a lived Asian public theology in action and human stories should be related to each other. He said, "humanity to theology is something like water to fish. Fish die when taken out of water. Theology dies when divorces from human life and history."[52]

Fourth, there is the need for doing a lived story theology within a larger community of neighbors. The ethic of storytelling and story-listening is not just a dialogue between storytellers and story-listeners, but it invites us to become one community. Your stories are your stories, and yet not your stories only. Your stories are stories of the community of faith and of the community of one human race from the perspective of neighborliness.[53]

Fifth, and finally, Song suggests that there are four essential elements involved in the formation of a lived Asian story theology: "curiosity, association, empathy, and imagination."[54] In order to understand truths hidden in the lives and stories of grassroots Christian communities, it is important for theologians and/or researchers to ask them with curiosity. As I will show later, I did ask some grassroots Christians with the curious mind. The second thing is *association*. God is not in isolation from human lives. God is actively associated with humanity from personal lives through political stories.[55] The third thing is *empathy*. Empathy is more than sympathy. Empathy takes an action for the associated other in need.[56] The fourth thing is *imagination*. According to Song, "imagination is different from fantasy

---

49. Song, *In The Beginning Were Stories, Not Texts*, 157.
50. Song, *In The Beginning Were Stories, Not Texts*, 159.
51. Song, *Tell Us Our Names*, 39.
52. Song, *Tell Us Our Names*, 10.
53. Song, *In The Beginning Were Stories, Not Texts*, 161.
54. Song, *In The Beginning Were Stories, Not Texts*, 166–70.
55. See, for instance, Song, *Tears of Lady Meng*.
56. Song, *In The Beginning Were Stories, Not Texts*, 167.

and daydream—it is the ability to create new things or ideas or to combine old ones in new forms."[57] It is for this goal of creating a fresh vision of a lived Asian public theology that we engaged grassroots Christian voices in dialogue with academic voices.

This research deals with the empirical inquiry into how some grassroots Christians understand their ecclesial and ethnic identity, express their faith and witness Christ. I am trying to figure out how I should approach this subject. I am more familiar with the literatures. These analyses are politically strong, but ecclesiologically weak.[58] They do not sufficiently address how grassroots Christians witness their faith. This requires for the ethnographic interaction with Christians and for recognizing their witnesses of their faith. Gregg Okesson's book *A Public Missiology: How Local Churches Witness to a Complex World*, for instance, invites us to listen to the voices of the congregations and to recognize their lived practices as the primary means of public witness to the complex world.[59]

While recognizing the church's political witness against the regime in the context of the political oppression, I wish to suggest a more nuanced approach that goes beyond a mere political dimension of social engagement and recognizes the grassroots Christian community's multiple witnesses of preaching, prayer, charity, evangelism, healing, and hospitality, and others. This way of nuanced approach enables us to reimagine a more relevant Asian public theology. It further enables us to reconsider the ecclesial experiences and lived practices of preaching, prayer, social charity, evangelism, healing, and hospitality as the primary means of public witness in and for the world. It does not consider the church's direct and open engagement with politics as the only type of public theology.

Public theology is not just about the church's engagement in politics, but it is also about the church's engagement in public realms as the prophetic pastors, priestly persons of prayers, apostolic gospel preachers, activists, and advocates for holistic mission. American public theologian Max Stackhouse is right in seeing "pastor as public theologian."[60] We are trained to see scholars who write about public theology as the only public

57. Song, *In The Beginning Were Stories, Not Texts*, 168–69.

58. See Smith, *Religion and Politics in Burma*; Schober, *Modern Buddhist Conjunctures in Myanmar*; Myint-U, *The Hidden History of Burma*; Sakhong, *In Search of Chin Identity*.

59. Okesson, *A Public Missiology*, 245–56.

60. Stackhouse, "Pastor as Public Theologian," 106–29; Stackhouse, *Public Theology and Political Economy*.

theologians. Some pastors are actually public theologians because they witness their faith in congregations and society. For too long, pastoral witness has not been heard in the reflections on public theology. Their voices have been lost in the academy. In *The Pastor as Public Theologian*, Kevin Vanhoozer and Owen Strachan have reclaimed the lost vision of the pastoral witness and shown how pastoral witness has played the key role in the history of Christianity. Drawing on the Bible, key figures from the history of Christianity and theology, they offered a clarion call for pastors to serve as public theologians in their local congregations and public society as public preachers and social charity workers.[61]

It is fair to say that academicians are not the primary agents of doing public theology. Doing public theology requires a collaborative work between the academic and lay theologians. Martin Luther, one of the greatest theologians in the history of Christianity, declared that "We all are theologians—every Christian. Theology means God's Word; theologian means one who speaks God's words. Each and every Christian should be such a person."[62] Miroslav Volf admits, "public intellectuals are too detached from life as it is lived on the ground; what they say or write may be correct in theory but is of no use in practice."[63] I agree with Volf that the time has come for the academicians and non-academic practitioners to exchange their voices and their insights for creating a lived Asian public theology of religions. I will explore how the members of local congregations should be reconsidered not merely as the practitioners, but also as the hermeneutics of public theology in dialogue with academics.

How to Engage the Grassroots Christians

There is a need for bridging ecclesiology and ethnography. Although ethnography takes its roots in the nineteenth-century anthropology, its renewed relationship with ecclesiology has been a recent development among scholars of ethnography.[64] The British missionary theologian Lesslie Newbigin's idea of "congregation as hermeneutic of the gospel" profoundly inspired the development of the relationship between the ethnographic

---

61. See Vanhoozer and Strachan, *The Pastor as Public Theologian*.
62. Luther, "Sermon Psalm 5," 9–11.
63. Volf, "On Being a Christian Public Intellectual," 3–20, at 8.
64. Ward, "Introduction," 6.

study of congregations and their role in interpreting the gospel.[65] Although Newbigin did not say anything about ethnography, his concept of "congregation as hermeneutic of the gospel" shapes the relationship between ecclesiology and ethnography in a sense that the ethnographer must recognize the authoritative role of local congregation in interpreting theology.

Some significant books on the relationship between ecclesiology and ethnography have come from some anthropologists, sociologists, and ecclesiologists. They include Helen Cameron's *Studying Local Churches*,[66] Nancy Ammerman's *Studying Congregations*,[67] Pete Ward's *Perspectives on Ecclesiology and Ethnography*,[68] and Christian Scharen's *Explorations in Ecclesiology and Ethnography*.[69] Pete Ward wrote of how the relationship of "ecclesiology and ethnography demand[s] our attention because it has the potential to make significant and urgently needed contribution to the contemporary discussion of the church."[70] Since 2014, *Ecclesial Practices: Journal of Ecclesiology and Ethnography* has been published as a premier forum for the intersection of ecclesiology and ethnography. Public theologians and ecclesiologists consider the congregations to be central for interpreting a public theology. They emphasize the lived experiences, doxological practices, and witnesses of local churches as the resources for doing lived public theology. They prioritize the role of the local churches in doing a lived public theology.[71]

Ethnography is understood as a common methodology for doing theology in the context of World Christianity. "Currents, Perspectives, and Ethnographic Methodologies" was taken up by Princeton Theological Seminary as the theme for the second World Christianity conference held on March 15–18, 2019. I attended this conference and presented a paper on "Ethnic Identity and World Christianity: Grassroots Ethnic Theology of Salvation and Sin in Myanmar." In my presentation, I asked three questions: (1) do we scholars listen to the voices of the grassroots Christians? (2) Do

---

65. Newbigin, *The Gospel in a Pluralist Society*, 222.
66. Cameron et al., *Studying Local Churches*.
67. Ammerman et al., *Studying Congregations*.
68. Ward, *Perspectives on Ecclesiology and Ethnography*.
69. Scharen, *Explorations in Ecclesiology and Ethnography*.
70. Ward, "Introduction," 1–12, at 4.
71. See Ward, "Introduction," 4–5; Okesson, *A Public Missiology*, 95–116; Hunsberger, "The Missional Voice and Posture of Public Theologizing," 15–28; Guder, *Called to Witness*.

grassroots Christians listen to our scholarly discourses? How can we fill the gap between the intellectual and grassroots voices for doing lived theology in the age of World Christianity? This conference was a way of affirmation for ethnography as a method for doing a lived Asian public theology.

Methodology: How Did I Engage the Grassroots Community?

Our research methodology is based on interviews with fifteen grassroots Christians and participatory observation.[72] The interviews were mainly conducted in July and August of 2020. Since it was a crucial time of preparation for the nation's election on November 8, common people, including the interviewees, were excited about sharing the role of their faith in political and public life. The second part of interviews were conducted in March and December of 2021 and January of 2022 after the rise of the coup on February 1, 2021. I incorporated the interviews, but I depended mainly on my interviews before the 2021 coup.

As we will see later, the way they understand the role of faith in political and public life is different from one to another. Such diverse voices arose from their varying roles in different locations. Some participants work at the churches in some towns or cities as pastors, church elders, and Sunday school teachers, while others work among Bamar Buddhists in the plain area as missionaries and evangelists. Some of them work at the refugee camps in the rural villages as the practitioners and philanthropists for the victims of war. What they have in common is that all participants identify themselves as devout Christians. In my interview with them, I also experienced a challenge. That challenge had to do with theological meaning related to my conversations with them. In our conversations with our fellow academicians, we do not much experience that particular challenge because we are all generally familiar with theological terminologies, concepts, and ideas.

Yet our conversations with grassroots Christians are different. Since they did not readily understand some technical terms, I adjusted my conversations with them in accessible ways. For example, I used some analogies

---

72. There are seven characteristics of the relationship between ethnography and qualitative interviews: (1) participation; (2) immersions; (3) reflections/reflexivity; (4) representation; (5) thick description; (6) empowerment; and (7) understanding. See Jones and Watt, eds, *Ethnography in Social Science Practice*, 6. See also Ward, "Introduction," 6.

that relate to the everyday lives of grassroots people. One of the main tasks and goals of doing a lived public theology is to express the concepts in accessible ways for both academic and ordinary audiences. Conversations with the ordinary Christians in accessible ways are important for gaining relevant data. I would call this "a symbolic practice of incarnational conversations." It is rooted in Jesus's incarnational practices of what Andrew Walls calls "translating divinity into humanity"[73] for all humanity to understand in their own cultures. Jesus uses parables as the mediums for his accessible conversation with his audiences. As Kenneth Bailey, who has rich personal experience of life in Middle Eastern cultures, rightly said:

> Jesus was a metaphorical theologian. That is, His primary method of creating meaning was through metaphor, simile, parable, and dramatic action rather than through logic and reasoning. He created meaning like a dramatist and a poet rather than like a philosopher. In the Western tradition serious theology has almost always been constructed from ideas held together by logic. In such a world the more intelligent the theologian, the more abstract he or she usually becomes, and the more difficult it is for the average person to understand what is being said.[74]

Like Jesus did, I used some metaphors and stories as the mediums for conversations with the grassroots Christians. In his celebrated book *Water Buffalo Theology*,[75] the Japanese missionary theologian Kosuke Koyama has done countryside Asian theology of Christian–Buddhist engagement by using water buffalo as a metaphor for the Thai Buddhist farmers who used water buffaloes at their daily works. Using stories, metaphors, and symbols was helpful for a conversation with the grassroots Christians who tell their stories. Doing theology in this way is meaningful for Christians and non-Christian alike because we use the metaphors as the helpful mediums for communicating theology in everyday life. If a lived Asian public theology is not just for academics, then it is essential to speak about public theology in accessible ways for ordinary Christians to join us.

We need to make a hospitable room for them to join in our conversation. One of the best ways to do this is by sharing our own similar and different stories of lived faith. Given the fact that a lived public theology is a theology of conversation between storytellers and storylisteners, I do not

---

73. Walls, *The Missionary Movement in Christian History*, 47–51.
74. Bailey, *Jesus through Middle Eastern Eyes*, 279–80.
75. Koyama, *Water Buffalo Theology*.

see my faith exclusively as an internal and private conversation with God: it is an inclusive and a public conversation between God, others, and myself. My conversation with some grassroots Christian communities proceeded in three steps.

Step One: Selecting Congregations and Sampling Interviewees

In order to collect data, I have selected three ecclesial traditions—Presbyterians, Baptists, and Pentecostals—the Chin, Kachin, and Karen backgrounds. I have selected fifteen interviewees based on their different roles as pastors, elders, Sunday school teachers, and charity workers. After the coup, I have interviewed seven activists and advocates.

In relation to sampling, I have employed snowball sampling. The term "snowball sampling reflects an analogy to a snowball increasing in size as its rolls downhill."[76] Snowball sampling is a method that uses a small pool of initial informants to nominate through their social networks. I have found snowball sampling helpful because connecting with one another as a small group of Christians is the strength for identifying research problems and collecting the data.[77] Using snowball sampling, I have made initial contacts with a small group of some Christians who are relevant to my research. I have asked them to put me in contact with other Christians who would be willing to be interviewed and to discuss their faith in the context of Buddhist nationalism with me.[78] In deciding who to interview and who to not interview, my interview has been conducted with a small group of some grassroots Christian leaders.

By the grassroots Christian leaders, I do not generally mean those who are totally illiterate. It is difficult to identify and define the exact concept of grassroots Christians. By grassroots Christians, I basically mean those who have basic knowledge of Christian doctrines, but have not done any advanced degrees. To be more specific, by the grassroots Christians, I do not mean those have basic knowledge of theology and teach at the seminaries. By the grassroots Christian community, I primarily mean those who are ordinary people and the main body of the local churches. They are working at the churches in the small towns and rural villages as senior and/or youth

---

76. Morgan, *The SAGE Encyclopedia of Qualitative Research Methods*, 816.

77. Bryman, *Social Research Method*, 100.

78. Bryman, *Social Research Method*, 100–101. An example of snowball sampling method can be seen in Becker, *Outsiders*, 45–46.

pastors, church elders, women leaders, Sunday school teachers, missionaries, church planters, social activists, and charity workers for the poor and wounded victims of civil war.

I used Burmese as the key medium for communicating with the grassroots Christians. I asked them some open-ended questions. I assembled open-ended questions in three main areas: (1) church; (2) salvation; and (3) the salvation–public life relation. Raising open-ended questions allowed them to express their own voices in whatever they found most helpful. These open-ended questions included: (1) how do the grassroots Christians understand the church? (2) What is the gospel of salvation? (3) What role can the church play (or not play) in relating salvation to public realities? As we will see in an appendix, I also asked some additional open-ended questions within each of these three categories.

Step Two: Interviewing Ecclesial Leaders and Collecting Data

In order to collect relevant data, I have interviewed about fifteen people. As I belong to one of those grassroots ethnic Christian groups, the interviewees saw me as their compatriot. In having conversation with them, I treated myself both as an outsider (researcher) and as an insider. Since they saw me as their compatriot or insider, they honestly shared with me about their voices. In order for them to express their lived voices without presuppositions, I treated myself as an outsider. I was open to being surprised by hearing a variety of their expressions of faith. I tried not to impose my intellectual voices on them. It is difficult to practice a pure subjectivity, but I tried as much as possible to de-center my subjectivity, giving them the liberty to express their voices. A combination of being an outsider and insider created a helpful space for our friendly conversations on a variety of public issues. I audiotaped the interviews and then transcribed them.

Step Three: Analyzing and Coding Ethnographic Data

I have analyzed the qualitative data. In the process of analyzing data, I have used the method of coding. Some scholars confess that data analysis is the most crucial aspect of qualitative research and coding is one of the most significant processes in organizing raw data into a theoretical narrative.[79] Coding involves managing data, reviewing transcripts, and giving

---

79. Auerbach and Silverstein, *Qualitative Data*, 31; Basit, "Manual or Electronic?, 143–54, at 143.

names to component parts of data. I have used "open coding and selective coding"[80] as the methods for comparing and selecting the issues of data. While open coding tends to manage, compare, and categorize unstructured components of data, selective coding selects, relates core themes of data to each other, and make sense of them. Using these two methods, my coding procedure has six steps within three main phases.[81]

The first phase is "making the text manageable."[82] In this first phase, I have worked at the level of the raw text or data itself. This is a filtering process, in which I have chosen which parts or what kinds of information will be included in my data analysis and which parts will be discarded. The two steps involved in this first phase are: stating my research concerns (step 1) and selecting the relevant text for my data analysis (step 2).

The second phase of data analysis is "hearing what was said."[83] I have gained more access to the subjective experiences of the grassroots Christian interviewees. In this phase of data analysis, what I have done is twofold: "organizing the relevant data into the repeating ideas (step 3) and organizing the repeating ideas into general themes" (step 4).[84] By "repeating ideas," I mean the similar ideas with different words expressed by the interviewees. The third phase is "developing theory."[85] In this phase, I have organized the themes of data into more abstract grouping by fitting them into a theoretical framework. In order to develop theoretical framework from data analysis, I have taken two steps. For one, I have developed theoretical constructs by categorizing the core themes of data into more abstract concepts consistent with my research questions (step 5). For the second, I have used the theoretical constructs to create a theoretical narrative by retelling the grassroots ethnic interviewees' experiences of the ethnic conflict and Buddhist nationalism (step 6).[86]

---

80. Bryman, *Social Research Methods*, 402.
81. I heavily draw the ideas from Auerbach, *Qualitative Data*, 48–49.
82. Bryman, *Social Research Methods*, 402.
83. Bryman, *Social Research Methods*, 42.
84. Bryman, *Social Research Methods*, 54.
85. Bryman, *Social Research Methods*, 43.
86. Bryman, *Social Research Methods*, 67–76.

Conclusion

In this chapter, we have proposed some motivations and methods for engaging grassroots Christian community. We have provided some motivations for why we ought to engage with the grassroots community. The motivations for engaging with some grassroots Christians are based on our transformative understanding of Christianity as a lived religion, a religion of the minorities, a persecuted religion, a flourishing religion, and a storytelling religion. As a lived religion, grassroots Christians do not merely witness Christ in theoretical ways, but in practical ways. Everyday practices of their faith are inherent in their personal and communal experiences. The important motivation that must be emphasized is that Christianity is flourishing among grassroots communities. Their faith is not static, but dynamic. This calls for a fresh methodology that moves beyond the academy and listens to the voices and stories of how grassroots Christians witness their active faith. In the following chapter, we will compose the qualitative data collection and description.

Three

Engaging Grassroots Christian Witnesses of Lived Faith

Introduction

THE AIM OF THIS chapter is to suggest that we cannot construct a relevant Asian public theology without incorporating the voices and experiences of grassroots Christians. Doing an Asian public theology without listening to those voices of grassroots Christians fails to engage with the real life in the Asian contexts out of which an authentic public theology arises. That kind of critique is instinctively known at a local level. One grassroots pastor rightly said in personal conversations that "academic theologians in Myanmar are writing and teaching from their academic perspectives without engaging with the grassroots levels of Christian experiences."[1] Some theologians would also argue that academic theology done without engaging people on the ground is of little account, having limited practical value in the real world.[2]

With this conviction, this chapter will describe the grassroots voices and views, giving them freedom to express their own imaginations. Such a grassroots approach to Asian theology, according to Simon Chan, "assumes that theology arises as much from how being the church is practiced as to

---

1. Interview with a Presbyterian pastor, August 19, 2020.
2. Yung, *Mangoes or Bananas?*, 232. Mbiti, "When the Bull Is in a Strange Land, It Does Not Bellow," 145–70.

how it is understood."[3] Built on this idea, we will study how the grassroots Christians understand their ecclesial identity and how they witness their lived faith. It is *here* that a relevant Asian public theology actually starts—that is, in the ecclesial life of lived worship, preaching, and prayer, rather than by importing a theology from academic life or public life.

How I Engaged the Grassroots Christian Voices

In the past I have conducted online video conversation as a qualitative methodology for engagement with the grassroots Christians. The way participants understood and expressed the role of faith in political and public life is different from one another. Such diversity of voice was due to their different ministerial roles in different locations. Some of the participants work at churches in the small hill towns and rural villages as pastors and church elders; others work among the Bamar Buddhists in the plain areas of the nation as missionaries. Some of them work at the Internally Displaced Persons camps in the villages as the practitioners and philanthropists for the victims of civil war. What they have in common is that all participants identified themselves as devout Christians.

In order to understand these multiple expressions of witness to faith and the gospel, I assembled open-ended questions covering three main areas: (1) church, (2) salvation, and (3) the relationship between salvation and public life. Raising open-ended set of questions allowed participants to make use of their own voices in whatever way they found most helpful. Open-ended questions go like this: (1) How do grassroots Christians understand the church? (2) What is the gospel of salvation? (3) What role can the church (or cannot) play in relating salvation to public realities? As we will see in an appendix, I also asked additional open-ended questions within each of these three categories. In my conversation with them, I also experienced a challenge. The challenge had to do with the theological meaning embedded within my conversations with them. In academic conversations, that is not an issue: we are generally familiar with theological terms. Conversations with grassroots Christians are of a different order. I adjusted our conversations in more accessible ways for those who did not readily understand technical terms.

---

3. Chan, "Grassroots Asian Ecclesiologies," 595.

Grassroots Christian Voices and Expressions

Not surprisingly, the interviews evoked a diverse array of perspectives, as one would expect with participants from three different denominations. My intention now is to describe both similarities and differences found in their expressions, beginning by describing their understanding of what it means to be the church in their lived experiences. In so describing their expressions of the church, I will cover both the internal and the external natures of the church. For the sake of clarity, I will describe them separately. I will begin by describing the internal nature of the church and then I will describe their views of the eternal nature of church when I deal with how the grassroots Christians relate or do not relate their faith to public realities. What are some common components of their understanding of the internal nature of the church?

Grassroots Christian Expressions of the Church

Worship

The overarching theme that has emerged from my interview with grassroots Christians from three different denominations—Baptist, Presbyterian, and Pentecostal—revolves around worship. Grassroots Christians see themselves as the people of worship. Worship is central to their self-imagination. They do not seem to understand the nature of the church doctrinally; but rather they understand the church doxologically. For these grassroots Christians, the church would be meaningless without worship. Corporate worship is held at least three times a week on different days. One service is held for a youth worship, and another is set for women. On Sunday, worship is the main activity for the whole congregation. Grassroots lives and Sunday worship are inseparable. The absence of services was very demanding during Covid. One of the pastors said: "it is hard for us to divorce our lives from Sunday worship during the pandemic. We have been missing Sunday worship."[4]

Although the way they understand the significance of worship for the internal life of the church is similar, the styles of Sunday worship are different from one another due to their different denominations. The Pentecostal churches tend to focus more on the revival form of worship, which consists

---

4. A pastor, interviewed by the author, July 19, 2020.

of dancing with their bodies and the raising of hands during worship. They strongly believe the role of the Holy Spirit in the revival of the church. They do not academically understand the doctrine of the Holy Spirit, but rather they understand the Spirit experientially. They believe in the experiential work of the Holy Spirit. One of grassroots senior Pentecostal pastors helpfully said:

> We did not know much about the doctrine and understood little of the teachings on key aspects of the faith, such as the Holy Spirit or the Trinity. It was only after I had bought my first New Testament in 1978 that the believers and I began to learn more about the gifts and the works of the Holy Spirit.[5]

Grassroots Pentecostals generally understand revival worship in categories of active motion. Dancing in the Spirit, raising their hands is set alongside the singing of contemporary songs rather than hymns. The congregations sing some contemporary revival songs, some of which are Burmese songs, and some of which are translated from the Australian Megachurch Hillsong.[6] Three or four older women left their seats and danced in the altar, waving the Bible. The congregations' posture during the worship is standing with their eyes closed, clasping their hands and voicing out hallelujah so often.[7]

Unlike Pentecostal churches, Baptists and Presbyterians tend to focus more on the traditional forms of worship and liturgy. They normally sing hymns, some of which are Burmese songs, and some of which are translated from the Western songs, such as "How Great Though Art," "Amazing Grace," "The Old Rugged Cross," "I Need Thee Every Hour," "Count Your Blessings," "What A Friend We Have in Jesus," "Trust and Obey," and others. In particular, some of the older generation prefer the traditional structure of worship, singing hymns without much body dancing. The comparison can be made with some younger generation of the congregation who prefer the revival style of worship and the singing some contemporary songs. One of the Presbyterian pastors told me that "the revival style of worship is generally influenced by the surrounding Pentecostal churches, which he also referred to as Hallelujah churches because of their common expressions of Hallelujah during the worship."[8] The same is true for the structure of Bap-

---

5. Ki, *From Darkness to Glorious Light*, 95.
6. A pastor and music leader, interviewed by the author, July 24, and August 1, 2020.
7. I personally experienced this in our hometown in Chin State of Myanmar.
8. A senior Presbyterian pastor, interviewed by the author, July 19, 2020.

tist worship. While some older generation prefer the traditional worship, some younger generation prefer the revivalist form of worship.

A hybrid style of worship is pertinent to the Presbyterian and Baptist practices of Sunday liturgies. They hybridize the traditional and revival styles of Sunday worships, while Pentecostal congregations tend to focus mainly on the revival style of worship. What these three denominations have in common is their understanding and performance of worship as a spiritual encounter with God. Their spiritual encounter with God is demonstrated in terms of clasping their hands and dancing their bodies while singing the worship songs. One of the pastors said, "clasping their hands and dancing their bodies are the key components of worship because these doxological actions echo the Psalmist common expression of praising God."[9]

Most of the congregants I have interviewed disclosed a common understanding to why they worship God. They worship God for His faithfulness, love, and kindness. Sometimes they even sing Psalm 117 composed by a famous Bamar Buddhist artist Htoo Ein Thin as a worship song (*Lumyo a paung toh* in Burmese).[10] God's goodness to their lives in the midst of suffering serves as a motivating power for their praise of God. Sometimes the worship leaders lead the congregation by making the corporate declarations: "God is good for me, God is good for my family, God is good for my job, and God is good for my country." Sometimes, some congregants come up front to the altar and share testimonies on how God is good to their lives. Some testimonies are followed solo songs. Others only share testimonies by reading Bible verses.[11]

Communion

Grassroots congregations consider the rite of communion as an essential Christian ceremony. Although they see the value of communion for Christian ceremony, the sequences of their celebration of communion are different due to different situations. Some congregations celebrate the sacrament monthly: others do so once a year. There are varying reasons for celebrating only once a year. One reason is that bread and wine are not always readily available in some village churches. In order to buy bread and wine, it is necessary to go to a town on foot: that generally takes two or three days or

---

9. A senior Presbyterian pastor, interviewed by the author, July 19, 2020.
10. Psalm 117:1–2 is a popular contemporary song among grassroots Christians.
11. A church elder, interviewed by the author, July 22, 2020.

even three or four days. The other reason is that communion is conducted only by senior ordained pastors. The village congregations must suit his availability.

What is important is that grassroots congregations have a common understanding of the purpose of communion celebration. For them, the key purpose of communion celebration is "to remember the death of Jesus."[12] The sacrificial death of Jesus Christ is meaningful for their purpose of celebrating communion. They commonly recount that Jesus has died for our sin and how gracious he was for us. The celebration of communion is thus a sacred time for grassroots Christians to remember the death of Christ and to confess their sin. The emphasis of the holy communion is not on anticipating the coming of Christ, but on remembering the sacrificial death of Christ. They celebrate communion in an exclusive way rather than in an inclusive way. It is not celebrated by all worship participants. It is only for those who are born again.

Why did this practice of exclusion come from? Did the grassroots Christians adopt the legacy of the Western missionaries? It is possible that some grassroots Christians adopt the practice of exclusion from the legacy of the missionaries. Although they believe that Jesus is present in the rite of the sacrament for the whole congregation, they still hold the belief that the sacrament must be celebrated only by those who believe Jesus as their savior and Lord. For the grassroots Christians, only those who are baptized followers of Christ must participate in a joyful celebration of the sacrament.

Preaching

Preaching is crucial to the grassroots Christian understanding of the church's internal life and work. Worship in grassroots churches is incomplete without preaching. The chairpersons of worship normally say something like this before he or she invited the preachers:

> Those who have fallen asleep, wake up. Stay awake, we are now coming to the most important part of worship. This is an important sermon because the preacher will preach the word of God. "As the Psalmist says, 'as a deer longs for streams of water, so my soul

---

12. A Presbyterian pastor, interviewed by the author, July 19, 2020. A Pentecostal pastor, interviewed by the author, July 25, 2020. A Baptist pastor, interviewed by the author, August 1, 2020.

longs for you, God'" (Ps. 42:2). As you need food for your physical health, so you need the word of God for your spiritual food.[13]

Mostly, senior pastors preach. Sometimes church elders preach. They necessarily remove their shoes before standing on the platform. The preachers' removal of shoes marks respect for the platform as a sacred space. This demonstrates the preachers' resonance with the biblical accounts of removing shoes because of holy ground. Moreover, one of the pastors who works among Buddhists as a missionary, stated that this act could also demonstrate the preachers' attempt to adapt to local Burmese cultural practice of removal of shoes before entering the Buddhist temples.[14] Sermons take up to fifty minutes or an hour. The sermon formats are mostly topical, testimonial, and exhortative rather than expository and exegetical. Some preachers draw the stories from the Bible as the key sources for encouraging the congregations to strengthen their faith amid difficult circumstances.

Other preachers use God's faithfulness to their live as a testimony for encouraging the congregations. Generally, most of the preachers use God's grace, faithfulness, and promise as the main themes for their sermons. The most recurring theme is the message of God's reward for Christian faithfulness. Their understanding of the reward is mostly related to material blessing as a result of exercising faith in God's promise. They often see Job in the Bible as a good example for their achievements of blessings as a result of their faithfulness amid suffering. They use the Bible verse "though your beginning was small, your latter days will be great" (Job 8:7) as the motivating source for their faith and achievement of great blessings. This is one of the texts that some grassroots Christians often use to justify prosperity gospel. They believe that their poverty will be replaced by prosperity if they believe in God faithfully.

Although the prosperity gospel is harmful for some grassroots Christians, they believe that prosperity is possible for them. They do not know how wealthy the prosperity preachers, such as Joel Osteen and others, are, and some grassroots Christians uncritically adopt the messages of some wealthy preachers. For some grassroots Christians, to be Christians means to be wealthy because God's abundant blessings belong to Christians. But some preachers also deal with the need of Christian unity. They do so especially when conflict occurs among church members.[15] Their preaching

13. A Presbyterian pastor, interviewed by the author, July 22, 2020.
14. A pastor interviewed by the author, July 31, 2020.
15. A pastor interviewed by the author, July 19, 2020.

does not address any ethnic or religious conflict outside the church. Their preaching on unity tends to focus on the internal issue of the Christian unity among church members.

Pulpit and Politics

Grassroots Christians have diverse opinions on the external role of the church in political and public life. The level and type of difference is generally inclined to reflect denominational belonging and identity. Regardless of these differences they shared a common conviction that politics should not be preached from the pulpit. Pastors were in agreement, declaring that:

> Pulpit is the place where only the word of God is to be preached. The word of God means the biblical accounts of the salvation, death, resurrection of Christ. It also includes the story of God's dealing with a particular group. The pulpit is not the place where politics is to be preached. Preaching politics at the pulpit may cause division among the church members who have different favors of political parties and interests. For this reason, politics is not to be preached at the pulpit.[16]

They regard the pulpit as a sacred place. Thus, the preachers must remove his or her shoes before he or she stands on the pulpit. They often refer to this policy by echoing God's command to Moses "to remove the sandals from his feet, for the place on which he is standing is holy ground" (Exod 3:5). Lying behind this custom is the deeply held belief that the church is not a *political* community where politics is to be freely preached; it is a *spiritual* community where only the name of God is to be glorified through worship, testimony, dancing, prayer, and preaching the gospel. Understanding faith as a spiritual relationship with God comes with an objection to preaching politics at the pulpit. The pulpit is the sacred place where only the holy word of God is to be preached.[17] The preachers are not encouraged to preach politics.

Prayer

Prayer is a key component of the internal life of grassroots church. Grassroots Christians strongly believe in the power of prayer. They are not just

16. Pastors interviewed by the author, July 19–27, 2020.
17. The pastors interviewed by the author, July 19–27, 2020.

the people of prayer—they are also the believers in the power of prayer. They understand prayer to be a direct communication with God. Prayer is translated in Burmese as *suh-tawng*, which literally means asking God for assistance. In addition to congregational prayer in Sunday worship, there can be weekly and monthly fasting prayers. The normal time for such is Saturday. Some practice dawn prayer every Sunday morning. Most of congregations conduct fasting prayers communally: there are some congregations where some members practice individual fasting prayer. Their different schedules of fasting prayers depend on each congregation. One of the church elders expressed prayer like this:

> Christian life and prayer are inseparable. Just as our breath and air are inseparable, so Christian life and prayer are inseparable. Prayer is like the air we inhale and exhale. Prayer is also like the key. We cannot open the door without the key. When we pray, we do not only speak to God as our Father, but we also open the door of our Father's heart so that we receive something from him.[18]

Interestingly, they have commonality in their understanding of the purpose of fasting prayers. Within the common purpose, they come together and pray for multiple issues: praying for the mission works of the local congregations, for the healing of the sick, for the students' education, for the global missionaries, and for the leaders of the government. Although grassroots Christians are not willing to include politics in their pulpit sermons, they are willing to include political issues in their communal prayers. They pray for the justice and peace of the nation. This will be taken up later.

Bible Study

Bible study plays a key role in grassroots Christian understanding of the internal life of the church. They conduct Bible study corporately and individually. The goal is to equip the disciples of Christ for a deeper knowledge of the Bible and to build up a warmer fellowship. They have a high view of Scripture, placing it at the center of their faith. It is through Bible study that they seek to become more mature disciples whose faith is rooted in the word of God and is transformed into the likeness of Christ. In some congregations, the Bible study is conducted individually for the purpose of personal devotion. This is common among many grassroots Christians.

---

18. A church elder, interviewed by the author, July 22, 2020.

They read Scripture devotionally for enriching faith and spirituality. Most of the interviewees stated that the individual nature of the Bible study is more common for their spiritual lives.

The Bible studies are not necessarily well organized by some academically-trained Christians. There was no one who decided what is to be studied. The Bible studied are normally taken placed at home. One of the Presbyterian elders said:

> I have devotionally read the whole Bible twice. As a lay Christian who has low education, my goal is not necessarily to understand the literal meanings of the Bible. But my primary goal is to read the Bible devotionally in order to nourish my spiritual life. The epistle to the Hebrews is my favorite book in the New Testament because it focuses on the sacrificial role of Jesus Christ as the priest.[19]

This emphasis placed on the priestly and sacrificial nature of Jesus is of particular interest. It is an emphasis that coheres with grassroots Christian understanding of their pre-Christian cultural practice of ritual rites led by the priests in the rural villages. In the following we will describe how the priestly role of Jesus Christ might be central for the grassroots Christian understanding of salvation and atonement.

The Grassroots Expressions of Soteriology

A grassroots Christian understanding of salvation is deeply rooted in the atonement of Christ. When I asked them what salvation is, their common answer is "forgiveness of sin." While the academic Asian liberationist notion of salvation tends to be established in Christ's prophetic ministry of liberating the oppressed and the poor from socio-political oppressions and socio-economic poverties, that is not the case for grassroots Christians. Their understanding of salvation as forgiveness of sin is rooted in the cross of the priestly Christ. The language of the blood shed is of crucial significance in their talk of salvation as atonement. For them, the salvation of Christ is incomplete without the cross where Christ offered himself as a sacrificial victim. This relates back to one of the grassroots church elder who regards the epistle to the Hebrews as his favorite book due to its focus on the priestly and sacrificial role of Jesus Christ.[20]

---

19. A church elder, interviewed by the author, July 22, 2020. The elder passed just two grades.

20. A church elder, interviewed by the author, July 22, 2020.

Some of these grassroots Christians reported that Paul's letter to the Romans is their favorite book: it is so because of its focus on the sinful nature of humanity and the atoning work of Christ through the forgiveness of sin.[21] What these grassroots Christians have in common is their perceptions of salvation as forgiveness of sin through the sacrificial death of Christ. It is quite understandable because grassroots Kachins, Chins, and Karens share the pre-Christian indigenous cultural practices of ritual sacrifices, which are analogous to the Old Testament and New Testament concepts of ritual sacrifices. A Chin spirit-worshiper turned grassroots Pentecostal pastor Tam Ki said:

> Spirit worship was at the very heart of our Chin [K'Cho] culture. Every kind of life event from birth and marriage to death, as well as the annual seasons of seed planting and harvest, were done under the fearful rules of the spirits. Our superstitions were guided by omens, divination, and dreams resulting in numerous ceremonies and feasts involving animal sacrifices to appease the spirits. *Ghun Kho* (mountain spirit), *Ng'yo* (household spirit), *Pakhui Ng'yo* (generation guardian spirit), *Ei Ng'* yo (crops spirit), *Sei Ng'yo* (mountain ox spirit), and *Sa Ng'yo* (animal spirit) were among the hundred spirits, which my people had to appease. The spirits were believed to inhabit homes, springs, paths, rocks, rivers, and mountains. Every individual household had spirit governing them. Each man was believed to have six guardian spirits, whereas each woman had five.[22]

Since there were hundreds of spirits, people did not know which spirits had to be appeased and so they had to consult with the village priest or the mediator who knew the minds of the spirits. Through readings of eggs by the priest, the spirits would demand various animal sacrifices, ranging from the offering of a chicken to a mountain ox. Sometimes, people had to offer many sacrifices to the spirits until the misfortune was removed.[23] Out of some ritual sacrifice commonly found among the Chins, Kachins, and Karens, two ritual practices are crucial. One is the communal and the other individual. Although the way they observed the ritual rites may slightly differ from each of the minority ethnic groups, the concepts and goals of such ritual rites are quite similar to one another.

21. Church pastors, interviewed by the author, July 19–22, 2020.
22. Ki, *From Darkness to Glorious Light*, 5–6.
23. Ki, *From Darkness to Glorious Light*, 6.

The first communal rite is observed at any time when a village has an unnatural death. In such circumstances, a section of the village would be required to make contact with the spirits through the priest of the village as a mediator. The priest would then lead the ritual sacrifices by killing the unblemished animal and offer them to the spirits. A half-burnt extinguished piece of firewood and an old rag are given to the chief priest by each family. Then the chief priest took the sacrificial animals to the center of the village and offered them to the deities, calling them to bless and protect the village. They did this communal rite because they recognized the deities as benevolent and malevolent spirits. The failure to appease the deities through the animal sacrifices would bring harm to the village: appeasing the deities would bring health, prosperity, and success to the community.

The second kind of sacrificial rite has more to do with the bestowing of benefit for the individuals. This kind of rite was performed when a person is seriously sick—and that was reckoned to have been caused by evil spirits. After consulting with the astrologer or medicine person who knew the minds of the spirits, some animals are offered to appease the spirits. The purpose of performing this ritual rite is to ask the spirits for forgiveness and the healing of the sick.[24] These two ritual sacrifices practiced among the minority Chins, Kachins, and Karens, and others pave the way for their grassroots understanding of the sacrificial death of Christ for forgiving sinners.

Central to their understanding of salvation is Jesus's sacrificial and mediatorial role. Just as the unblemished animals were sacrificed for the ritual rites, so was the innocent Jesus sacrificed for salvation. Jesus's mediatorial role for the reconciliation between the Father and sinners is analogous to the way the village priest played a mediatorial role in leading the ritual rites for the reconciliation between people and the spirits.[25] Using 1 Timothy. 2:5, one grassroots pastor said this:

> Jesus is the mediator between the Father and us (sinners). As he is a mediator, Jesus knows the mind of his Father and the condition of us. There is no way for sinners to please God. Only Jesus knows how to please the Father and restores the right relationship between the Father and sinners. It is only through the blood of

---

24. Ki, *From Darkness to Glorious Light*, 3–6.

25. The pastors and elder, interviewed by the author, July 19–22, 2020. See also, Ki, *From Darkness to Glorious Light*, 3–6.,

Jesus's sacrifice that our sin was forgiven and our relationship with God was possible.[26]

These grassroots Christians also related salvation to rescue. The very idea of rescue implies the idea of God's "saving from something." They see God's delivering of the oppressed Israel from the captivity of the Egyptians as a figure for Jesus's rescuing the sinners from the power of sin and the hands of Satan. Grassroots Christians understand that Jesus is not just a sacrificial victim, but he is a *victor*. Jesus was not defeated at the cross as a victim, but rather defeated Satan through the resurrection. They emphasized that Jesus's defeat of Satan and rescuing them from Satan was possible through the power of the Spirit. This is good news. For them, the good news was rooted in Jesus's achievement on the cross. One of pastors provided the following analogy:

> Jesus's rescuing us from the captivity of Satan is comparable to the expert swimmer's rescuing someone from being drought in the river. A person who was draught would die if the swimmer did not save him or her from the river. That would be sad news! Likewise, Jesus has rescued us from the power of sin and the hands of Satan. Jesus's rescuing us from the power of sin and from the hands of Satan is crucial to the meaning of the good news of salvation.[27]

The idea of Jesus's rescuing them from the hands of Satan is crucial to their grassroots notion of the gospel of salvation and to their identity as the children of God. One grassroots Pentecostal pastor and evangelist who was a former spirit-worshiper compares the rule of Christ and the rule of Satan with analogies of light and darkness. In his book *From Darkness to Glorious Light,* Ki told a story of how he experienced God's rescuing of his spirit-worshiping life of darkness to glorious light of Christ.

Born in the village hidden in the jungles of Chin Hills, no foreign missionary had even visited his village. Some of the earliest Baptist converts was a consequence of the work of Adoniram Judson. But this is not the case for the Pentecostals. With no access to the Bible and to salvation from the missionaries, Tam Ki received supernatural visions from God in 1973 and became the earliest Christian convert in his village. He related his understanding of salvation to God's rescuing of his life from evil spirits. For him, Christ's recusing his life from the evil spirits means a total conversion from

---

26. A pastor, interviewed by the author, July 19, 2020.
27. A Presbyterian pastor, interviewed by the author, July 19, 2020.

the old cultural practices of spirit worship and a commitment to sharing the gospel.[28] He preaches the gospel of Christ's rescuing of his life as an example to many people trapped in the darkness of Satan. He preaches the "gospel" (*Htu Ni* in Cho/Muun Chin dialect) to thousands of people.[29]

There is a close relationship between the grassroots Christian understanding of salvation as rescue and Christ's victory over the power of Satan. Victory is the effect of Christ's liberating act of rescue. Again, we have seen this example in the life of a pastor who shares his story about how Jesus has rescued him from evil spirits or fatalism. The Christ of the grassroots Christians is more experienced in liberating people from the fear of evil spirits rather than in liberating people from socio-political oppressions. Moreover, grassroots Christians emphasize the powerful role of the Spirit in Christ's liberating act of delivering their lives from the fear of evil spirits. They believe that the Holy Spirit plays a powerful role not only in Christ's act of rescuing them from evil spirits, but also in protecting their everyday lives. One pastor said, "his prayer is that the Holy Spirit would protect the new converts so that "evil spirits will not snatch them away."[30]

Grassroots Christian expressions and experiences of salvation are not confined to the two aspects of forgiveness of sin and of rescue from Satan; they also relate salvation to healings. While the first two aspects focus on the cross of Christ, their understanding of healings embrace both the atoning work of Christ and the miraculous work of Christ during his social ministry among the poor and sick. Especially within the Pentecostal circles, Jesus's healings and miracles are increasingly recognized as a crucial part of their grassroots ministries. They literally believe in the powerful role of the Spirit in the miraculous act of healing the blind and sick.[31] A Pentecostal pastor who prayed for the healing of the evil spirit-possessed girl and boy said this in his own words:

> We need to be sure of our Salvation and not doubt the power of the Spirit. We could not fight against the enemy in our own strength or with our own understanding. In the unity of Christ, we had to invite the Holy Spirit to fill us with faith and power. Only then, we

---

28. Ki, *From Darkness to Glorious Light*, 53–59. This is common among grassroots Christians.

29. Ki, *From Darkness to Glorious Light*, xxxiii-2; 105–16; 173–84

30. Ki, *From Darkness to Glorious Light*, 45.

31. The Pentecostal pastors, interviewed by the author, July 24–27, 2020. See also Ki, *From Darkness to Glorious Light*, 126–33.

could be successful in the face of spiritual battles. More than thirty people came forward to pray with me over the girl's lifeless body. After praying for about an hour, breath came back into the girl and she sat up. Everyone gave thanks to the Lord. Suddenly, we heard a loud thud. A man in the prayer team had fallen down and become motionless with his eyes wide open, in exactly the same condition as the girl. His breathing had stopped and there was no pulse. This evil spirit must have gone into the man's body. Now even more people ran off. Only six others were left standing with me. We prayed in tongues for more than two hours until sunset. Suddenly, a black mist swirled out of a man and went upwards. The man began to breathe. Since that accident, the man had become a pastor of Ngamai Mission Church, five miles west of Mindat. The girl surrendered her life to the Lord.[32]

In the context where demonic possession that causes psycho-physical sickness is a daily experience, grassroots Christians experience Jesus Christ as their victor and healer.[33] Their expressions of salvation as healing are anthropocentric. Although they did not reject the cosmological idea of environmental healings, they emphasized the anthropological idea of healing. Their expressions of human healings are more individualistic than communal and cosmic (the healing of a broken community and nature).

The ministry of physical healings can also be found among other grassroots Christians beyond the Pentecostal community. While the Pentecostal ministry of healings tends to focus on performing the miracles of healing the sick through prayers, non-Pentecostals tend to focus on healing the sick through the medical facilities. This is not to suggest that Pentecostals are interested only in miraculous healings and non-Pentecostal Christians are interested only in social charity. Some non-Pentecostal pastors and practitioners who work at the refugee camps among the victims of civil war in Kachin and Chin states expressed their ministry focus on social charity of medical facilities, as well as food and school supplies for healing and feeding the victims.[34]

---

32. Ki, *From Darkness to Glorious Light*, 128–29.

33. Ki, *From Darkness to Glorious Light*, 121–40.

34. The pastors and practitioners who work at the refugee camp in Kachin Hills, interviewed by the author, August 1–2, 2020.

Grassroots Witness of Faith and Salvation in Public Life

Do the grassroots Christians witness their faith and salvation in the public life? If yes, how? If no, why? How do they understand the politics of Buddhist nationalism and ethnic discrimination in their own terms? I will begin by describing their answers to the last question. I have chosen to begin with the last question because I assume that grassroots Christian understanding of what Buddhist nationalism means may naturally create the way of witnessing to their faith in public life.

How Do They Understand Buddhist Nationalism?

The academic concept of Buddhist nationalism is not readily familiar to some grassroots Christians. The concept of Buddhist nationalism is more readily familiar to some academic people and political elites. In Burmese terms, Buddhist nationalism is called *lumyo-gyi wada*, which literally means the "domination of the majority race." Some grassroots Christians have different views of Buddhist nationalism, even within the same congregations. Some think of Buddhist nationalism as a myth, while others see it as a reality. For instance, when I asked one grassroots pastor about his personal experience of Buddhist nationalism, his response was that his experience of *lumyo-gyi wada* is natural, but not really problematic. For him, in any context where the majority race rules, the minority's experience of *lumyo-gyi wada* is natural. He said this in his own words:

> Christian experience of marginality is natural throughout the centuries. The disciples of Jesus experienced marginality and persecution. Many Christians in different parts of the world experience marginality and persecution. But they all remained faithful to God in the midst of marginality and persecution. Likewise, ethnic minority Christians in Myanmar experience marginality and persecution. But what is most important for us is to remain faithful to following Christ.[35]

The pastor felt that some politicians are exaggerating about *lumyo-gyi wada*. For him, some Buddhists are even nicer to him than some of his fellow Christians. He observed that some grassroots Buddhists—both his neighborhood friends and those whom he met when he was on the gospel

---

35. A pastor, interviewed by the author, July 24, 2020.

trip for evangelism—were kind and nice to him.[36] Some grassroots Christians, by contrast, see Buddhist nationalism as a reality and as a system. They expressed the reality of Buddhist nationalism from socio-cultural and religio-political experiences. Its reality is identified with the problem of ethnic Christian discrimination and religious persecution. They noted the Buddhist nationalist soldier destruction of Christian crosses as one of the common examples of ethnic Christian discrimination. It is common for the Chin, Kachin, and Karen Christians to erect the crosses at the top of local mountains as their religious symbols.[37] They said that some Bamar Buddhist soldiers demolished some Christian crosses erected in the mountains and replaced them with Buddhist pagodas. In some ethnic minority areas, some church buildings are destroyed and burnt.

Some of them expressed their experiences of discrimination from the perspective of job applications. Some Christians are denied job opportunities for the civic vocations of teaching and medical positions, while some Bamar Buddhist applicants are accepted. One of the Kachin pastors observed:

> The Kachin Christian experience of ethnic discrimination is real. For instance, when the Kachin Christians and Bamar Buddhists apply for the same positions of teaching and medical affairs in society, Kachins are more likely to be rejected. Thus, a few Kachin Christians leave their religion and adopt Buddhism as their new religion in order for them to be accepted for the positions in society.[38]

Not only a few Kachins, but a few Chins and Karens also leave their Christian religion and adopt Buddhism as a new religion in order for them to be accepted into the positions in Buddhist society. Another example of Buddhist nationalism we have learned from grassroots Christians is the Bamar cultural replacement of some ethnic local names with the Burman names. One Kachin pastor gave me an example of naming their local mountain (*machang baw*) a Burmanized term, *machan phu pawh*, which means "it is not cold."[39] One Chin pastor also gave an example of naming their famous local mountain *khawnu tung*, with a Burmanized term, *nat-ma taung*,

---

36. A pastor, interviewed by the author, July 24, 2020.

37. The Chin Presbyterian and Pentecostal pastors, interviewed by the author, July 19–27, 2020. The Kachin Baptist pastors, interviewed by the author, July 27–28, 2020. The Karen pastors, interviewed by the author, July 31–August 1, 2020.

38. A Kachin pastor, interviewed by the author, July 30, 2020.

39. A Kachin pastor, interviewed by the author, July 26, 2020.

which means "the mountain of female spirits." The original meaning of *khawnu tung* in local language is "majestic mountain."[40]

While a few Christians do not have a clear understanding of Buddhist nationalism, some ethnic Christians expressed their experiences of the ethnic persecution. They expressed the ethnic persecution in terms of forced labor and the Buddhist soldiers' brutal practices of raping some ethnic women. One pastor who works among the victims in the Kachin ethnic minority region expressed his personal witness of rape:

> The Bamar Buddhist soldiers often practice ethnic persecution by raping and killing some Kachin ethnic women. The soldiers' brutal practices of Christian persecution and raping the ethnic women are the reality of daily experiences in our Kachin region. Although we witnessed their ethnic persecution and of raping women, they never acknowledge their action. Anyone who speaks truth against their behaviors of raping women would face their persecution.[41]

In the same vein, a Chin pastor, who works in the civil war zone in Paletwa, the Western part of Myanmar reported that "the Bamar Buddhist soldiers' practices of ethnic persecution at the grassroots levels are the daily reality—women are raped and some men are forced into labor for the soldiers."[42] On the other hand, some grassroots pastors tried to be fair by saying "not all Bamar Buddhists necessarily commit the ethnic Christian discrimination and persecution; only a particular group of Bamar Buddhist soldiers commit such violent actions."[43]

Having described some grassroots Christians' diverse expressions and experiences of Buddhist nationalism, I will now explore how they do or do not witness to their faith and salvation in the context of the ethnic discrimination and persecution. Based on what I have observed on their expressions of faith within and outside the church, it might be helpful to make a distinction: that is, between political engagement for grassroots Christian faith and public engagement for grassroots faith.

---

40. A Presbyterian pastor, interviewed by the author, July 19, 2020.
41. A Kachin woman minster, interviewed by the author, July 30, 2020.
42. A pastor interviewed by the author, August 1, 2020.
43. A pastor interviewed by the author, July 26, 2020.

Lived Faith and Political Engagement

Disagreements are present among grassroots Christians about the role of Christian faith in political life. The majority of grassroots Christian leaders spoke in favor of divorcing faith from politics. However, some of them spoke in favor of relating faith to political life. I will begin with those who vote for divorcing faith from politics. Grassroots Christians, especially those represented by the Pentecostals, maintain that the church or Christian faith must stay out of politics. One Pentecostal pastor affirmatively said:

> The church exists for worshiping God and for preaching the gospel or good news (*tha-tin kaung* in Burmese). The church does not exist for politics nor is the church a political community. The church is a holy community of the believers who know Jesus as Savior and Lord. Politics is a secular community made up of a majority of non-believers who do not know Jesus Christ as Savior and Lord.[44]

One of the main reasons for the Pentecostal separation of faith from politics is grounded in their understanding of the sacred-secular divide. They see the church as a sacred community of faith and politics as an area of secular community. As a sacred community, the church must preserve its sacred faith from the secular politics. The task of the church is not to engage in politics. For them, the task of the church is to engage with God through worship, prayer, and preaching.[45] When I asked them, what they would do if some political rulers destroyed their church, their responses were that "they would just pray for them." They quoted Jesus' words: "love your enemies and pray for those who persecute you" (Matt 5:44). They also objected to the street protests against the political rulers.[46]

There are some contrasting voices among the Pentecostals. A few of them noted their views for relating faith to politics. Especially some younger Pentecostals voted for relating the Christian faith to politics when needed. One pastor said:

> There is a reason for relating Christian faith to politics. The reason is rooted in the wide concept of God's kingdom. Since God's kingdom is not confined to the church, but it encompasses political

---

44. A Pentecostal pastor, interviewed by the author, July 24, 2020.

45. The Pentecostal pastors and church leaders, interviewed by the author, July 24–28, 2020.

46. Pentecostal pastors and church leaders, interviewed by the author, July 24–28, 2020.

life, faith needs to engage in politics. Moreover, the politics of the life of Israel is a good example for Christian engagement in politics. What is important is how one engages in politics.[47]

Many non-Pentecostal Christians generally agree with this statement. Some Presbyterians and Baptists spoke in favor of relating Christian faith to politics. They said the life of Israel is inseparable from political engagement. They see Moses as a political leader for the people of Israel and as a role model for their political engagement.[48] Christian faith is to be related to politics. They expressed their willingness to demonstrate on the street if/when the ruling authorities commit some injustices to the church.[49] However, they also expressed their reluctance to engage in politics by street protest against the rulers due to the fear. Their fear has to do with a political arrest as the result of their critique of politics.[50] Thus, some of them expressed the possibility of discussing politics and of criticizing political corruption at their private social gatherings outside the church. What they have in common is the way they see the powerful role of prayer in political life.

Some grassroots Kachin Baptist Christians believe that prayer and private critique of corrupt politics are not enough. The Kachin Christians are more active in resisting political oppression than other ethnic Christians. This is understandable because the Kachins are the most persecuted Christian groups in Myanmar. There are now more than 100,000 Internally Displaced Persons or IDPs at some camps in Kachin state. The Kachin Christians believe that to remain silent in the context of the ethnic persecution and discrimination means taking a side with the oppressors. They have a reputation of saying "to be Kachin is to be Christian. To be faithful Christian is to be resistant warrior." They see their struggle against Bamar domination as a "just war," a fight to defend their ethnic identity.[51] They defend their ethnic identity by demanding for their minority rights. They justify their struggle for political freedom by echoing Moses' prophetic involvement in politics for the liberation of the oppressed Israel. A pastor said:

---

47. A Pentecostal pastor, interviewed by the author, July 31, 2020.

48. See Wildavsky, *Moses as Political Leader*.

49. A pastor, interviewed by the author, July 19, 2020; a Karen Baptist pastor, interviewed by the author, August 1, 2020.

50. The Presbyterian pastors and elders, interviewed by the author, July 19–August 10, 2020; the Pentecostal pastors and leaders, interviewed by the author, July 24–28, 2020.

51. See Lintner, "Burma," https://therevealer.org/burma-faith-and-resistance-in-kachin/ [accessed on August 31, 2020].

Many Kachin Christians believe the whole Bible as the word of God. However, they tend to prioritize the Old Testament over New Testament precisely because the former has some more political implications for their political witnesses of faith. Moreover, the Kachin Christian experiences of socio-political oppression under the Bamar oppressors are similar to those of the oppressed Israel.[52]

In relating their identity to the political freedom of Israel, the Kachin Christians have a political concept of liberation, which they call *Awm-Dawm* in their dialect.[53] The Kachin Baptist Christians believe the holistic concept of salvation, but they prioritize *Awm-Dawm* or political liberation over spiritual liberation. One pastor said:

> We the Kachin Christians prioritize *Awm-Dawm* because we consider it to be more visible and urgent in the current context of Christian persecution. *Awm-Dawm* is a political concept of freedom from oppression. On the other hand, some poor Kachin Christians are more interested in prosperity gospel than in *Awm-dawm*. Prosperity gospel will not last long because it is not biblical.[54]

Seeing themselves as the example of the Israel who eventually entered the promised Canaan land of freedom, the Kachins have their local song *Wunpawng Hkanan*, which represented in the Kachin imagination the promised land of freedom from Bamar domination.[55] In order to achieve realization of *Wunpawng Hkanan*, Kachin Christians boldly resist the Bamar political oppression. Their common goal is to achieve social justice and political freedom from Burman nationalism rather than the reconciliation between the minority Kachin Christians and majority Bamar Buddhists. In light of the former goal, some Kachin Christians even said, "they would not go to heaven if there were Bamar to be there."[56] This bold claim shows that the Kachin Christians' idea of anti-Burmanization is strong.

While many Kachin Christians are explicitly political in terms of resisting the politics of Bamar domination and ethnic discrimination, some grassroots Kachin Christians choose to be involved in the public ministry of social charity for the victims of civil war without confronting the ruling

---

52. A pastor, interviewed by the author, July 27, 2020.
53. Nan, *Awmdawm Hte Anhte A Makam Laknak*.
54. A pastor, interviewed by the author, July 27, 2020.
55. A pastor, interviewed by the author, July 26, 2020.
56. A pastor, interviewed by the author, July 26, 2020.

authorities.[57] This second group of Christians do not use a direct engagement in politics by confronting the unjust state. However, they do relate their faith to the public ministry of social charity in multiple ways. The majority of grassroots ethnic minority Christians witness their lived faith in the public life rather than in the political life as charity workers, pastors, and evangelists.

Lived Faith and Public Engagement

Although some grassroots Christians tend to divorce their faith from politics, they do not necessarily divorce their faith from the public life or society where common people live. They are involved in public engagement in different ways. We will describe two forms of their faith witnesses in the public life: evangelism and charity.

Grassroots Christian Witness and Evangelism in Public Life

Unlike some academics who tend to theorize the concept of evangelism, grassroots Christians just practice evangelism as they understand it. They envisage their church identity as being a gospel people and they understand evangelism as preaching the gospel to non-Christians—the spirit worshipers and Buddhists. They describe the people who particularly preach the gospel in the public life as "evangelists." Although their descriptions of being a gospel people imply entire congregations and their doxological activities of worship, their use of the term evangelists refers specifically to those who believe themselves to be called or sent by the congregations as missionaries.[58] In this regard, grassroots Christians do not necessarily theorize the differences between evangelism and mission: they understand and practice evangelism and mission as two sides of one coin.

Some grassroots Christians use the combined word "evangelistic mission."[59] The task of evangelistic mission is to convert non-Christians, especially Buddhists and spirit-worshipers. Although the majority of Christians in Myanmar are among Chins, Kachins, and Karens, there are still some spirit-worshipers in their neighboring towns and villages. The spirit-worshipers and Bamar Buddhists are, therefore, the two target

---

57. A pastor, interviewed by the author, July 30, 2020.

58. The pastors, interviewed by the author, July 19–August 12, 2020. See also Ki, *From Darkness to Glorious Light*, 121–25

59. Ki, *From Darkness to Glorious Light*, 70–71.

groups of grassroots evangelistic mission. The Chin, Kachin, and Karen Christians focus on evangelizing spirit-worshipers or pre-Christians among their fellow minority ethnic as well as some Buddhists among the Bamar ethnic group.[60]

In reaching out to Buddhists and spirit-worshipers, evangelism is conducted both as the long-term mission activity as well as short-term activity. Either way, grassroots evangelists focus on preaching the gospel of salvation. Because of their focus on preaching the gospel of salvation to non-Christians, they call such activities "gospel trips." On their gospel trips, grassroots evangelists take Bibles, hymnbooks, guitars, and loudspeakers along with them. One grassroots Pentecostal evangelists described such a trip:

> Before I ventured out on any evangelistic trip to the neighboring *pigaw gui* (other religious neighbors), I would pack in my basket enough rice to last me for a week, a change of clothes. My Bible, a hymn book, a notebook, and without fail, my loudspeaker. The loudspeaker—a wet cell battery, an amplifier and a horn—weight a good 22 pounds. I would walk from *pigaw* to *pigaw*, sharing the *Htu Ni* (gospel of Christ) with the loudspeaker until the battery was completely used up.[61]

The loudspeaker is used as a powerful tool for open-air evangelistic rallies to draw the crowds. One evangelist, who preached the gospel in public life said, "Curious onlookers gathered around me just to hear the loudspeakers. The seed of the *Htu Ni* (the gospel) were sown into the hearts of many."[62] In evangelizing Buddhists and spirit-worshipers, grassroots Christians focus on winning lost souls.[63] Winning lost souls arises from their concept of Christ's coming to the world as being for redeeming lost souls. The spiritual aspect of salvation and its futuristic concern is central for grassroots evangelism. They tell non-Christians to confess their sin and to acknowledge Jesus as their Savior. Interpreting John 3:16, one evangelist said: "For God so loved the world that he gave his only begotten son the Lord Jesus, to be born into this world to redeem lost souls who are precious in his sight. He has given eternal life to those who believe in him."[64]

60. A Pentecostal who works among the Bamar Buddhists as an evangelist and church planter, interviewed by the author, July 31, 2020.
61. Ki, *From Darkness to Glorious Light*, 71.
62. Ki, *From Darkness to Glorious Light*, 71.
63. Ki, *From Darkness to Glorious Light*, 121–40.
64. Ki, *From Darkness to Glorious Light*, 41.

For grassroots Christians, those who do not believe in Jesus will surely die in the fires of hell.[65] The redemptive idea of salvation as rescue from Satan or other religious practices is central to the grassroots Christian practices of saving lost souls. Evangelists do not just attempt to win lost souls without planting the churches. Winning lost souls and planting churches go hand in hand. They plant churches as the places for the discipleship of the converts. They then become exposed to the inner life of the church—its Bible study, prayers, and preaching. When the converts become mature in the knowledge of Christ and of the Bible, some dedicate their lives to the evangelistic work of sharing the gospel with the hope of winning lost souls of others.[66]

This is not to say that all the grassroots Christians completely ignore the social significance of salvation. They believe in the holistic concept of salvation, but they do prioritize the spiritual and otherworldly significance of salvation.[67] I will now describe how some grassroots Christians witness to their faith in the public life by practicing the social significance of salvation as social charity for the victims and poor.

Grassroots Christian Witness and Social Charity in Public Life

Unlike some academic liberationists who focus exclusively on the prophetic task of the church as a public critique of political authorities, some grassroots Christians opt for the apostolic task of the church as a public commitment to healing the victims, the sick, and the poor. In other words, they opt for witnessing to their apostolic faith in public life by taking a side with the victims and the poor rather than directly confronting the ruling authorities. The public witness of social charity tends to focus inclusively on the humanitarian work of healing the interreligious community of both Christian and non-Christians in need. One of the pastors and evangelists who work among the Bamar Buddhists said:

> Evangelism and social charity should go hand in hand in the Buddhist context. In the Buddhist context where the Buddhist practice of social charity is a cultural issue, Christian evangelism without social charity is not effective. The Christian practice of social charity and friendship with Buddhists should prioritize

---

65. Ki, *From Darkness to Glorious Light*, xxxviii.
66. A pastor, evangelist, and church planter, interviewed by the author, July 31, 2020.
67. The pastors, interviewed by the author, July 19–August 12, 2020.

over evangelism. This is an effective mission strategy in the Buddhist context.[68]

Grassroots Christians choose apostolic public witness of charity for two main reasons. First, they believe that the witness of social charity in the public life is rooted in the public practices of Jesus's disciples in the first century. For instance, Acts 2:45 says, "the disciples would sell their possessions and goods and distribute the proceeds to all, as they had need." Grassroots Christians, therefore, witness their apostolic faith to the public ministry of charity in the concrete context where medical and educational facilities are extremely basic and, even where there are available, they are often beyond the reach of the poor. Grassroots churches understand social charity as an essential complement to evangelism. They engage in preaching the gospel and practicing charity.

Second, grassroots Christians opt for social charity of healing the poor and victims of the civil war. In the context of civil war, grassroots Christians do not confront the ruling authorities due to fear. Instead, they choose to engage in social charity for the victims of war. This is especially the case for those grassroots Kachin, Karen, and Chin Christians, who find themselves in the civil war zones where there is daily conflict between the Bamar soldiers and the ethnic armed groups occur. Many ethnic Christians live in fear. One pastor who lives in the intense area of civil war said:

> Our faith is often threatened by the Bamar soldiers. Sometimes the internet line is cut off in order not to be able to get in touch with people outside our community. They cut off the internet so that the world would not know what is happening on the ground. Our lives are miserable. We live in fear and in poverty. But what they cannot cut off is our faithful relationship with God who is with us.[69]

Living in such challenging contexts, some grassroots Christians choose not to practice their faith as a public witness of a direct political confrontation against the authorities. Rather, they choose to practice their faith in alternative ways. They practice their faith as a private affair in terms of secret prayers for political freedom and social justice at churches and homes, on the one hand, and they practice faith as a public affair in terms of providing social charity for the wounded victims of war at the Internally Displaced

---

68. A pastor, interviewed by the author, July 31, 2020.
69. Chin pastor, interviewed by the author, August 10, 2020.

People (IDP) camps, on the other.[70] The ministry of charity includes providing some basic humanitarian needs, such as meals, clothes, shelter, medicines, and educational supplies.

Conclusion

This chapter has studied the grassroots Christian expressions of their faith by focusing on three areas of theology: church, salvation, and public witnesses of salvation. We have begun by exploring the similar and different expressions of the grassroots church.

First, their expressions of the church are quite close to each other. Their understanding of the internal life of the church is commonly rooted in the practices of worship. Although the styles of worship differ from one denomination to another, the motivation for their practices of worship are similar to each other. The church exists for the main purpose of worship. Preaching, singing, dancing, prayer, and Bible study are the main elements of grassroots ecclesial worship.

Second, their expressions of salvation are established in the cross of Christ. They are more interested in the cross of Christ than in the social ministry of Jesus. But this decision does not mean that they reject Jesus's ministry of healing and exorcising. The blood language of Christ's death and the power language of Christ's victory over death and devils are central for their understanding of the meaning of salvation. They see salvation in terms of the priestly role of Christ rather than in his prophetic role. As a result, they witness salvation as the spiritual rescue of people from sin and from evils rather than from socio-political oppressions.

Third, grassroots Christian expressions of the faith–public life relation are not the same. While some grassroots Christians tend to object to faith and politics becoming too closely intertwine, others do not. Some Christians who object to faith–politic relations still relate their faith to politics in a private way of praying for political issues of social injustice and conflicts. They have expressed their witnesses of salvation and faith in two ways. One is their public witnesses of proclaiming the gospel and evangelizing non-Christians. The main content of this witness is the spiritual and otherworldly dimension of salvation. The other is their public witness of social charity for the sick, poor, and victims of civil war. In light of the latter, their

---

70. Kachin pastor and practitioner, interviewed by the author, July 30, 2020. Chin minister and humanitarian worker, interviewed by the author, August 10, 2020.

aim is people who encompass the interreligious community of the poor and oppressed. Their public witnesses of spiritual evangelism and social charity in public life are deeply shaped by their lived practices of worship in the private sphere.

Four

Revisiting Asian Public Theology of Religions and Liberation

Introduction

ALOYSIUS PIERIS SUMS UP the context of Asia in a twofold reality: "multi-faceted religiosity" (in which Christianity is a minority) and "mass poverty" (both Christians and other faiths suffer together).[1] This twofold reality calls for the twin praxis of Asian public theology: religiosity calls for interreligious dialogue and poverty calls for the praxis of political liberation. Asian theologians grapple with religions and public life: how do religions play the public role in socio-political liberation of the poor and oppressed?

Asian liberationists commonly use the exodus paradigm (Exod 3:7–14) and the Nazareth public manifesto (Luke 4:18–19) as the biblical sources for engaging with the liberationist sources of other religions.[2] An Asian theology of liberation distinguishes itself from other Majority World liberation theologies.[3] While other liberation theologies are understood as a Christian public engagement with Christians, a distinctive characteristic of Asian public theology of liberation lies in the *inter*religious nature of its

---

1. Pieris, *An Asian Theology of Liberation*, 69–86.

2. See Kim, *Minjung Theology*, xii–xv; Song, *Christian Mission in Reconstruction*, 143–73; Song, *Third-Eye Theology*, 101–23; Pieris, *An Asian Theology of Liberation*, 8–14, 35–68. Pieris, *The Genesis of Asian Theology of Liberation*, 152–67.

3. For a comprehensive study of Third World Theologies, see Abraham, ed., *Third World Theologies*.

public engagement with Asian people of other religions.[4] Asia is religiously diverse, of course, with many variation in its forms of religious pluralism.[5] In this particular case, the focus is on the Southeast Asian Buddhist context.[6] I organize the chapter into three sections.

In the first section, I will show when, why, and how the foundations of Asian public theology were laid and developed before the official rise of the term "public theology" in the West. I will look at two Asian public theologians—Shoki Coe of Taiwan (1914–88)[7] and M. M. Thomas of India (1916–96)[8]—as examples for their pioneering works on Asian public theology. The second section is dedicated to describing fresh perspectives for an Asian public theology. I will proceed through this section into two steps. I will first look at Felix Wilfred of India (1948–).[9] I will then move to a narrower scope of Asian theology of Christian–Buddhist dialogue and liberation. I will engage with the liberationist Aloysius Pieris of Sri Lanka (1934–).[10]

The Origin of Asian Public Theology before the Term Was Invented

Scholars[11] widely acknowledge that the term "public theology" first appeared in 1974 in an article by an American Lutheran historian Martin E. Marty (1928–) in the *Journal of Religion* entitled "Reinhold Niebuhr: Public Theology and the American Experience."[12] While giving credit to Marty for coining the term "public theology," I will argue that the concept of an Asian public theology, without being named as such, had already

---

4. Pieris, *An Asian Theology of Liberation*, 69–86; Balasuriya, "Divergences," 113–19; Wilfred, *Asian Public Theology*, xvii–xxvi.

5. See Phan. eds., *Asian Christianities*; Sunquist ed., *A Dictionary of Asian Christianity*; Ross et al., *Christianity in East and Southeast Asia*.

6. Leukel, *Buddhist-Christian Relations in Asia*, 97–272.

7. Hwang (Shoki Coe), *Joint Action for Mission in Formosa*.

8. Thomas, *The Christian Response to the Asian Revolution*.

9. Wilfred, *Asian Public Theology*.

10. Pieris, *An Asian Theology of Liberation*. Pieris, *Love Meets Wisdom*; Pieris, *Fire and Water*.

11. Kim, *Theology in the Public Sphere*, 3–7; Breitenberg, "Defining Public Theology," 3–20, at 7–10.

12. Marty, "Reinhold Niebuhr," 332–59; Marty, *The Public Church*.

appeared in the late 1950s and early 1960s.¹³ This hypothesis is important in developing an Asian public theology in the context of World Christianity. We should not use a Western public theology as a universal model that can be simply imposed upon a very different kind of cultural context. Rather, we start public theology in the local context and bring it into dialogue with global public theologies. This approach is consistent with my previous suggestion for the third form of dialogue. In his celebrated book *Water Buffalo Theology*, Japanese theologian Kosuke Koyama rightly said:

> Third World Theology [Asian theology] begins by raising local issues, not by digesting First World theologians, namely Saint Augustine, Karl Barth, and Karl Rahner. This is, in short, an attempt to call your attention to some of the Asian theological raw situations that have been on my mind for some time.¹⁴

In his *Subverting Global Myths,* the Sri Lankan public theologian Vinoth Ramachandra also emphasizes the need of developing a local form of Asian public theology. He states:

> There is a great need to develop local theology and missionary practices that receive from all that is best in other cultures and contexts, while being relevant to one's own. In the church we now have a hermeneutical community that is global in scope and character, so we can test the local expressions of Christian faith against one another, thus manifesting the true catholicity of the body of Christ. The way we become truly global Christians is by seriously engaging with our local contexts as members of a global community that has redefined our identities and interests.¹⁵

I regard the inaugural meeting of the East Asia Christian Conference (EACC: now Christian Conference of Asia) held at Kuala Lumpur, Malaysia on May 14–24, 1959, as the origin of local academic Asian public theology.¹⁶ M. M. Thomas, who participated at the meeting, saw the EACC as a point of departure for the origin of an Asian public theology of revolution. He said: "I think the inaugural Assembly of the East Asia Christian Conference

---

13. Christian Conference of Asia statement, "The Confessioning Church in Asia and Its Theological Statement," 199–204; Thomas, *The Christian Response to the Asian Revolution*; Hwang (Coe), *Joint Action for Mission in Formosa*; a collection of articles published in the 1960s republished in *What Asian Christians Are Thinking*, 267–457.

14. Koyama, *Water Buffalo Theology*, 3.

15. Ramachandra, *Subverting Global Myths*, 259.

16. Than ed., *Witnesses Together*, 60–80.

which met in Kuala Lumpur in 1959 gave the clearest expression to what may be called a theology of the Asian revolution."[17] I agree with Thomas, but I would specify that academic Asian public theology was conceptually and contextually formulated at the EACC in Kuala Lumpur, although we might argue that grassroots Asian public theology has long engaged public issues in different parts of Asia.

Put simply, first, the concept of an academic Asian public theology without the official term "public theology" had been developed by Asian theologians before the official rise of the term. Second, a lived Asian public theology had been embodied already by some grassroots Asian Christians without knowing the academic concept. Some grassroots Karen Christians in Myanmar have embodied their lived faith in public life as public preachers and social workers since the 1830–40s under the leadership of American missionaries. The Karens were among the first ethnic minority groups to have received the gospel from an American Baptist missionaries Adoniram Judson and Ann Judson.[18] They did not just preach the gospel in the church, but they were also involved in the social, educational, and spiritual transformation of public society.[19]

There are two reasons for recognizing the EACC as a point of departure for the origins of academic Asian public theology. First, the EACC was the inaugural meeting where a group of pioneer Asian theologians, including Thomas, came together with the common vision of renewing theology in Asia. They renewed the scope of theology by engaging with the public life of socio-political revolution and change.[20] It was during this era that Asian theologians began to re-examine the understanding of Christian mission bequeathed to Asia by Western missionaries and form a new theology that is rooted in what Ramachandra calls "the new Asia" and is relevant for Asian Christian identity and mission.[21] Second, the EACC meeting chose "witnesses together" as a conference theme.[22] The conference theme

17. Thomas, *The Christian Response to the Asian Revolution*, 27.

18. Wa, *Burma Baptist Chronicle*, 67–69. Ko Tha Phyu was the first Karen convert. He was baptized on May 16, 1828 and thereafter he started witnessing the life and work of Christ in public life. Phyu was known as "the first Apostle to the Karens." See Mason, *Memoir of Ko Tha Phyu*, 67.

19. Po, *Burma and the Karens*, 58. See also Augurlion, *Christian Existence*, 45–55.

20. Takenaka, "A New Understanding of the World and the Need of Theological Renewal," 33–42.

21. See Ramachandra, *Church and Mission in the New Asia*.

22. Quoted in Thomas, *The Christian Response to the Asian Revolution*, 24–34. For the report of the meeting of EACC (now CCA); Than ed., *Witnesses Together*, 60–80.

called on the Asian churches to discern Christ's cosmic presence and dynamic work by engaging with people of other religions for witnessing together the common goal of social revolution.[23] It was in the same year, 1959 that *Southeast Asia Journal of Theology* (now *Asia Journal of Theology*) was founded as an academic journal for sharing the public issues of local theology and for exchanging theological insights.

M. M. Thomas and Shoki Coe as Pioneer Asian Public Theologians

Because of their pioneering advocacies for developing Asian public theology in a post-colonial Asia, Coe's and Thomas's legacies were published in the special series "Prophets from the South" sponsored by the Council for World Mission.[24] In a collection of works by pioneer Asian scholars, *What Asian Christians Are Thinking*, editor Douglas Elwood saw Thomas as "Asia's foremost lay [public] theologian."[25] Hwa Yung also said, "Among Asian Christians of his generation, it can be said that he [Thomas] has been peerless in his advocacy of Christian social engagement and involvement in nation building."[26] Hielke Wolters reflected on the pioneering work of Thomas:

> A pioneer is one who explores unfamiliar terrain or initiates a new enterprise, and thus opens up and prepares the way for others. M. M. Thomas has been a pioneer in the area of post-independence Christian theology in India. From the 1930s up to the present day, he has been engaged the search for a meaningful Christian contribution in a completely new situation. Rooted in deep faith, he has been responding to a vision. That response is the subject of our study, and its importance is by no means limited to the Indian context.[27]

---

23. Than ed., *Witnesses Together*, 60–80.

24. See Joseph et al., *Wrestling with God*; Athyal et al., *The Life, Legacy, and Theology of M. M. Thomas*.

25. Elwood ed., *What Asian Christians Are Thinking*, xxviii.

26. Yung, *Mangoes or Bananas?*, 157.

27. Wolters, *Theology of Prophetic Participation*, ix.

Like Thomas, Coe was a pioneer and prophet in developing the foundations of an Asian public theology of liberation. In his tribute for the legacy of Coe, John England concluded:

> It is widely known that Coe's work and writing has been of pivotal importance for every level of Asian theology in recent decades, not least for his pioneering explorations in contextualizing Christian faith and understanding. These were, however, deeply rooted in his own, and his people's historical experience. For the Taiwanese, this included the very long history of its aboriginal peoples, the impact of colonization by Spain and the Netherland, China, Japan, and the endurance of martial law for almost half a century.[28]

Seeing himself as a second-generation Asian theologian, C. S. Song of Taiwan (1929–) regarded his mentor Shoki Coe as a respected pioneer in developing the foundations of Asian theology. Song described "Shoki Coe [as] a respected pioneer in theological education in Asia. Many of us second- and third-generation theologians in Asia are deeply indebted to him for his tirelessly promoting the contextualization of theology."[29]

Put together, Coe and Thomas experienced the contexts of the post-Western missionary and of home-grown nationalism. While Thomas experienced Hindu nationalism in India, Coe experienced Chinese nationalism in Taiwan.[30] Experiencing these contexts, Thomas and Coe had two common concerns in their understanding of liberation: they were committed to a liberation of theology and theology of liberation The "liberation of theology" focused on the erudite liberation from the Western theological captivity;[31] a theology of liberation focuses on political liberation from local political oppression. Their visions of this twofold liberation came out at the height of contextual theologies that were taking the imitative in resisting Western theological captivity and responding to home-grown nationalism in the post-Western mission and post-independence period.

---

28. England, "A Watershed Figure in Asian Theologies," 327–30, at 329.

29. Song, *The Compassionate God*, xiii.

30. See Anderson, *Recollections and Reflections*; Chang, *Shoki Coe*; Wheeler, "The Legacy of Shoki Coe," 77–80. For Thomas, see Athyal et al., *The Life, Legacy, and Theology of M. M. Thomas*, 7–8; Thomas, "Some Notes on a Christian Interpretation of Nationalism in Asia," 16–26; Thomas, "My Pilgrimage in Mission," 28–31.

31. The term "liberation of theology" was coined by Latin American theologian Juan Luis Segundo; see Segundo, *The Liberation of Theology*, 4–6.

M. M. Thomas's Vision of an Asian Public Theology

Thomas was born in a Christian family in 1916 and died in 1996. He was nurtured in the "evangelical and sacramental piety" of the Mar Thomas Syrian Church in which his father was a famous evangelist.[32] Upon graduation from college, Thomas worked several different jobs, which led him into evangelism and social work, interreligious dialogue and politics. He worked as a director of the Christian Institute for the Study of Religion in Society, Bangalore, as a moderator of the Central Committee of the World Council of Churches (1968–75), and as a governor of Nagaland (1990–92), a state with a high population of Christians in Northeast India. He had conferred upon him an honorary doctorate by the University of Uppsala in Sweden 1978.[33]

Thomas was India's most recognized ecumenical leader and self-educated lay theologian (except for a one-year theological training in 1953 at Union Theological Seminary in New York City). As a lay theologian, "Thomas often disclaimed the title theologian."[34] He later came into contact with Gandhianism and Marxism. He aspired to become an ordained minister as well as a member of the Communist Party. But he was rejected both by his church for ordination because he was too Marxist and by the Communist Party because he was a Christian.[35] Thomas reflected on how, "I asked for ordination in my church and for membership in the Communist party. Both rejected me, for opposite reasons."[36]

Despite his acceptance of a double rejection, Thomas's keen passion for integrating faith and social concerns remained. Beginning in the 1930s, Thomas was involved in the public issues of India's national independence and then in the nation-building after the independence from the British in 1947.[37] Thomas's early work went widely unnoticed. He became more globally recognized in the 1960s through his book *The Christian Response to the Asian Revolution* (1966)[38] and through his ecumenical work in the WCC (1968–75). Since Thomas has written widely, it is not easy to summarize his

---

32. Philip, *The Encounter Between Theology and Ideology*, 2.
33. West, "M. M. Thomas," 666–67; Thomas, "My Pilgrimage in Mission," 28–31.
34. Quoted in Wilfred, "Theologies of South Asia," 502–17, at 510.
35. Rajaskekar, "M. M. Thomas," 505.
36. Thomas, "My Pilgrimage in Mission," 30.
37. Wolters, *Theology of Prophetic Participation*, viii; 11–90.
38. Thomas, *The Christian Response to the Asian Revolution*.

thoughts.[39] But the themes of his writings are close to each other within the framework of Asian public theology.[40] I will focus on three main points of his contribution to Asian public theology.

The first point is his basic concept of faith as action in public society. For Thomas, faith must always be active in socio-political involvement for nation-building and theology must articulate such an active faith by grappling with the realities of everyday life. This kind of theology is what Thomas called a "living theology."[41] He did not reflect on theology first and then apply it as an action of faith. He acted on his faith first and then reflected on it theologically. His approach to a living theology was conditioned by his social praxis of engaged faith in public life as a social worker, as a director of the Christian Institute for the Study of Religion and Society, and as a governor of the Nagaland state of India.[42]

For Thomas, theology is not just an academic exercise divorced from the realities of life. It must always be engaged in social revolution as a "living theology." His vision of "living theology" was shaped not merely by the Christian faith, but by a Christian engagement with the revolutionary practices of other religions. In his book *The Acknowledged Christ of the Indian Renaissance* (1969), Thomas showed how Jesus's Sermon on the Mount was practiced by Gandhi for the Indian renaissance and, consequently, a Christian engagement with the Gandhian renaissance was necessary.[43] Thomas uses the cosmic dimension of Christ's public presence in the cultures of other religions as the foundation and as the model for Christian active engagement with the world. He said:

> The church must endeavor to discern how Christ is at work in the revolution of contemporary Asia (it then spells out the various forms of his work), releasing new creative forces, judging idolatry, and false gods, leading people to a decision for or against him, and gathering to himself those who respond in faith to him, in order to send them back into the world to be witnesses in his kingship. The church must not only discern Christ in the changing life, but

---

39. Wolters, *Theology of Prophetic Participation*, 253–329.
40. Thomas, *M. M. Thomas Reader*.
41. Thomas, *The Acknowledged Christ of the Indian Renaissance*, 306.
42. Thomas, *The Christian Response to the Asian Revolution*, 6–8; Thomas, "My Pilgrimage in Mission," 28–31.
43. Thomas, *The Acknowledged Christ of the Indian Renaissance*, 306; Thomas, *The Secular Ideologies of India and the Secular Meaning of Christ*, 10.

be there in it, responding to him and making his presence and lordship known.[44]

Using this cosmic Christology as the foundation and model, Thomas argues that the task of the church is to discern Christ's cosmic and public presence among other faiths and to engage Christ's revolutionary action in dialogue with the revolutionary action of other faiths. In other words, he uses Christ as a meeting point for interreligious people's struggles for sociopolitical revolution in Asia.[45] This agenda leads us to Thomas's idea of salvation.

The second point is his redefinition of salvation as "humanization." Thomas was reacting against the Western understanding and experience of an individual salvation and personal understanding of salvation in which the emphasis fell upon one's vertical relationship with God. Thomas redefined salvation as humanization, which he believed was more of a horizontal relationship leading to social revolution. He redefined salvation in terms of humanization by which the oppressed people find their liberating humanness of inherent rights and dignity.[46] Being the chairperson of the WCC (1968–75), Thomas's grand concept of humanization underlined the WCC meeting in Uppsala, Sweden in 1968 and it eventually influenced the ecumenical Christian leaders to replace "salvation" with "liberation" at the WCC meeting in Bangkok, Thailand (Southeast Asia), December 31, 1972 and January 9-12, 1973.[47]

Third, Thomas's redefinition of salvation as humanization contributed to his realigned perspective on mission. The Uppsala report entitled "Renewal in Mission (1968)" took up Thomas's understanding of humanization in its new approach to mission.[48] Thomas rejected the idea of mission as converting Hindus, because it was the colonial legacy of Western mission that had stimulated Hindu nationalism. Thomas believed there was a relationship between the rise of nationalism and the impact of Western imperial mission.[49] For Thomas, the task of mission in the post-colonial

---

44. Thomas, *The Christian Response to the Asian Revolution*, 28.

45. Thomas, *The Christian Response to the Asian Revolution*, 8–34.

46. Thomas, *Salvation and Humanization*, 40.

47. Thomas, *Salvation and Humanization*, 40. Thomas, "The Meaning of Salvation Today," 158–69. This article was his address given in the opening session of the WCC's Conference on Salvation Today held at Bangkok in 1972.

48. See Goodall, *The Uppsala Report 1968*, 21–38.

49. Thomas, *The Christian Response to the Asian Revolution*, 9.

era was to participate in nation building through "secular fellowship" with Hindus.[50] He saw salvation as a "new humanism," which struggles for the new cultural identity of the Asians in the post-Western mission era.[51] In his article "The World in Which We Preach Christ" (1963), Thomas described mission as:

> Christianity, renascent religions, and secular faiths, are all involved in the struggle of man for the true meaning of his personal and social existence—each in its own terms but together. It seems to me that the relations between Christian faith and other living religions and secular faiths is passing to a new stage, because they not only co-exist in the same society, but also cooperate to build a common secular society and culture. It is within such coexistence and cooperation that we can best enter into dialogue at the deepest level on the nature and destiny of man and on the nature of ultimate Truth. In this form the judgment and salvation of Christ himself can be proclaimed.[52]

In his later essay "My Pilgrimage in Mission" in the *IBMR* (1989), Thomas described how "My journey has taken me through a critique of missions in the narrow sense to the more inclusive concept of the mission of the church in the modern world."[53] For Thomas, mission means a prophetic participation in the public issue of nation building through cooperation with Asian world religions.[54] Paul Rajashekar remarked on how "Thomas's prophetic witness at crucial points where Christian faith and world's religions, cultures, and ideologies intersect made him a truly public theologian."[55] Thomas thus proved himself to be a public theologian by emphasizing the church's interreligious dialogue with Hindus.

---

50. Thomas, *The Christian Response to the Asian Revolution*, 9–65; Thomas, "Some Notes on a Christian Interpretation of Nationalism in Asia," 16–26. Thomas, "Indian Nationalism," 4–26; Thomas and Devanandan, *Christian Participation in Nation-Building*, 266–67; Thomas, "The Struggle for Human Dignity as a Preparation for the Gospel," 356–59; Thomas, *Towards a Theology of Contemporary Ecumenism*, 40.

51. Thomas, *The Christian Response to the Asian Revolution*, 35–92.

52. Thomas, "The World in Which We Preach Christ," 11–19, at 18.

53. Thomas, "My Pilgrimage in Mission," 28.

54. Thomas, *The Christian Response to the Asian Revolution*, 93–126. Thomas, *Salvation and Humanization*, 10–18; 40–60.

55. Rajashekar, "M. M. Thomas," 505.

Evaluating Thomas's Approach

Thomas is a lay public theologian. That said, his theology is quite academic—so much so that he is frequently cited as an example of an Asian theologian. Although he actively worked among some grassroots Christians in India, he did not sufficiently incorporate their ethnographic voices and lived experiences into his theological reflections. It cannot be said, then, his approach qualified as a grassroots Asian public theology. His idea of humanization is limited to a horizontal dimension of social salvation without embracing much of a vertical dimension.[56]

Thomas does not see the church as the starting point for doing Asian public theology. As we will show later, Felix Wilfred adopts Thomas's approach for doing an Asian public theology that starts in public life. This strategy leads us to question Thomas's understanding of ecclesiology. It seems to be an ecclesiology that is confined to its interreligious dialogue with other faiths. He does not ask how the church's internal and sacramental life of praise, prayer, and preaching could shape the church's external life of witness in public life. His understanding of the church is strong in socio-political involvement and is weak in pastoral preaching, evangelism, and social service. Thomas underestimates the church's internal life of prayer, praise, and preaching, reckoning it to be merely "pietistic individualism."[57]

Thomas believes that the church's secular fellowship with other religions for nation-building is the most important example of practicing faith in the post-independence Asia. Such fellowship, according to Thomas, is shaped by Christ's secular fellowship with the outcasts. Thomas does not seem to be interested in preserving the distinctive identity of the church. He regards the church merely as one of the communities of social justice for the oppressed. As such, he depicts the church's direct engagement in socio-political involvement as the only Asian public theology. "Anything else, even if it has had a positive impact on society, is not considered a theology of engagement at all."[58]

Thomas's ecclesiology has been strongly criticized by, among others, Newbigin who worked in India as a missionary teacher and bishop in the Church of South India. The Thomas–Newbigin debates occurred in India in the 1970s, but the issues of the church they raised remain relevant for

---

56. Thomas, *Salvation and Humanization*.
57. Thomas, *Salvation and Humanization*, 12–13.
58. See Chan, *Grassroots Asian Theology*, 35.

the role of the church in society today.⁵⁹ Newbigin argues that Thomas's understanding of the church's secular fellowship is "docetic."⁶⁰ It is so because Thomas emphasizes the church merely as a political community and as a syncretistic community of secular koinonia with Hindus without holding its distinctive identity.⁶¹

Thomas's contextual idea of the church is understandable in the postcolonial context where Christianity was seen by Hindus nationalists not only as a foreign religion, but also as a tool of colonial mission for proselytizing other faiths. While it is necessary for the church to cooperate with other faiths in nation-building, the church does not have to compromise its distinctive nature by breaking religious cultural elements that are "congruent with the Lordship of Jesus Christ."⁶² Thomas's understanding of the church is limited to an interreligious actor in socio-political involvement for humanization.⁶³

Shoki Coe's Vision of an Asian Public Theology

Shoki Coe has two more names, Ng Chiong Hui (Taiwanese name) and Chang Hui Hwang (Mandarin name).⁶⁴ He was born in 1914 during the Japanese colonial rule of Taiwan (1895–1945). The name he later chose to publish under was Shoki Coe, a Japanese version of a Taiwanese name, reflecting the Taiwanese context of his birth during the Japanese rule. He was the son of a Presbyterian pastor.⁶⁵ In 1947, after World War II when Taiwan was finally liberated from fifty years of Japanese rule, he returned to Taiwan from England with his British wife, Winifred Saunders, but only to face a new regime under the Kuomintang from China.⁶⁶ In the 2/28

---

59. Thomas and Newbigin, "Baptism, the Church, and Koinonia," 69–90.

60. Thomas, *Some Theological Dialogues*, 122.

61. Thomas and Newbigin, "Baptism, the Church, and Koinonia, 72.

62. Thomas and Newbigin, "Baptism, the Church, and Koinonia," 80. See also Chan, "Grassroots Asian Ecclesiologies," 598–99.

63. See Yung, *Mangoes or Bananas?*, 160–61.

64. Coe published a book under the name C. H. Hwang, but the rest of his several writings are published under the name Shoki Coe. See Hwang, *Joint Action for Mission in Formosa*.

65. Huang, "Ng Chiong Hui (Shoki Coe, Hwang Chang Hui)," 601.

66. Huang, "Ng Chiong Hui (Shoki Coe, Hwang Chang Hui)," 601.

Incident (February 28, 1947), 20,000 Taiwanese elites were either massacred by Chinese nationalists or ended up missing without a trace.[67]

During this political hardship, Coe served as the first Taiwanese Principal of Tainan Theological College (1947–65). He was also elected twice as the moderator of the Presbyterian Church in Taiwan. During his eighteen years in Taiwan, he encountered Chinese nationalism.[68] Coe's significant writings in the period of 1962–77, during the Chinese nationalist reign, became a basis for Asian theological thinking.[69] In his early articles "Rethinking of Theological Training for the Ministry in the Younger Churches" (1962),[70] "God's People in Asia Today" (1963),[71] and "The Life and the Mission of the Church in the World" (1964),[72] Coe developed an Asian theology as public witness against nationalism. In 1965, Coe left Taiwan and lived in England for security reasons.

After 1965, Coe joined the Theological Education Fund (TEF) of the WCC as assistant and later director during the TEF's Third Mandate (1970–77). He then coined the term "contextualization" in 1972.[73] Coe's coinage of the term contextualization is what Wilbert Shenk called "A true paradigm shift" in rethinking theology that is rooted in local context and is relevant for local Christians.[74] It advances the formation of contextual theology that addresses the public issues of socio-political and socio-economic liberation.[75] This line of interest takes us to the heart of Coe's Asian public theology of liberation.

In order to develop an Asian public theology of liberation in the Asian context of home-grown political nationalism, Coe argued that Asian Christians must first recognize and resist three affections that have been inherited from Western Christendom: "colonialism, denominationalism, and

---

67. Huang, "Ng Chiong Hui, (Shoki Coe, Hwang Chang Hui)," 601.

68. Coe, *Recollections and Reflections*, 244.

69. England, "A Watershed Figure in Asian Theologies," 330.

70. Shoki Coe, "A Rethinking of Theological Training for the Ministry in the Younger Churches Today," 7–34.

71. Coe, "God's People in Asia Today," 5–17.

72. Coe, "The Life and Mission of the Church in the World," 11–38.

73. Fabella, "Contextualization," 58–59; Coe, "In Search of Renewal in Theological Education," 240–43.

74. Shenk, "Contextual Theology," 191–229, at 192–93.

75. Coe, "In Search of Renewal in Theological Education," 233–43. Coe, *Ministry in Context*, 108–15. Fabella, "Contextualization," 240–43. Shenk, "Contextual Theology," 191–93. Bosch, *Transforming Mission*, 430–31.

pietism."⁷⁶ Each of these, according to Coe, creates the problems of religious proselytization, church division, and the church's pietistic isolation from the socio-political involvement in revolution and liberation.

Coe reconstructs the political hermeneutics of salvation as socio-political liberation. Coe does not use the term public theology, but his political hermeneutics of salvation rooted in the *missio Dei* has implications for public theology.⁷⁷ Coe emphasizes that a theology of God's *missio Dei* is manifested in Jesus's incarnational and prophetic engagement with the world.⁷⁸ As the follower of Christ who engages with the world, the church's prophetic engagement with the world in dialogue with other faiths is imperative. Coe emphasized the church's existence between two poles—the relationship with God and with the world is crucial for Coe's social vision of public theology.⁷⁹

Coe argued that the church must be a prophetic agent of social justice. He considered the church's prophetic voice not as a predicator of other-worldly realities, but rather as a social advocate for political liberation in this-worldly life. For Coe, faith without political action is a lifeless faith.⁸⁰ Coe's vision of a public theology and his political involvement are driven by his personal understanding of confessional faith. In his editorial note on "Theology and Church" (1957), Coe boldly said, "A confessional church has inevitably to humble itself and ask, is my confession right? Is my confession in accordance with God's will or is it only my bias? Theology is derived from this sort of self-evaluation of the church."⁸¹ For Coe, the church's social involvement is rooted in the confession of Jesus Christ. Theology is a sort of a critical reflection on faith and its relevance for public life. He asserted:

> I am politically involved because I am a Taiwanese, and I am politically involved because I am a Christian. Taiwanese is the context into which I was born, and in which I was brought up, and which has been and still is very determinative to my whole existence. My political involvements are the outward expression

---

76. Coe, "The Life and Mission of the Church in the World," 11–36.
77. Coe, "The Life and Mission of the Church in the World," 13.
78. Coe, "A Rethinking of Theological Training for Ministry in Younger Churches Today," 10.
79. Coe, "The Life and the Mission of the Church," 13. Coe, "God's People in Asia Today," 37.
80. Joseph, "Context, Discernment, and Contextualization," 6.
81. Coe, "Theology and Church," 1–9, at 5–6.

of a twofold inner wrestling for the meaning of being a Taiwanese and a Christian.[82]

On December 30, 1971, Coe and the Taiwanese Presbyterian leaders made the Public Statement on the Nation Fate against Chinese Nationalism.[83] The Statement declared:

> We oppose any powerful nation disregarding the rights and wishes of fifteen million people and making unilateral decisions to their own advantage, because God has ordained, and the United Nations Charter has affirmed that every people has the right to determine its own destiny.[84]

The church's public statement called for Taiwanese freedom from foreign power.[85] Late in January 1972 in New York, Coe and three other Taiwanese Christian exiles—C. S. Song, Ng Bu Tong, and Lim Chong Gi—organized the Formosan Christians for Self-Determination. Po Ho Huang observed that "Though started outside Taiwan, the Self-Determination movement had a big impact on political developments in Taiwan and was significant to later efforts in constructing contextual theology in Taiwan."[86] One example is the birth of a "homeland theology," a term coined by Wang Hsien-Chih.[87] The task of homeland theology is to resist the Chinese regime and to imagine the Taiwanese cultural identity. Exiled for twenty-two years, Coe returned to Taiwan in 1987 and died in 1988.

Evaluating Coe's Approach

Coe helps us understand the end of one era (the end of Western mission) and the beginning of another era (the new era of Asian Christianity and its new Asian Christian identity). Using contextualization as a methodology, he has grappled with a twofold concern: (1) criticizing a Western understanding of individual salvation and privatizing faith and (2) constructing a new political hermeneutic of salvation that is relevant for the formulation of an Asian Christian identity as well as a public witness of political

---

82. Coe, *Recollections and Reflections*, 234.
83. Quoted in Song, *Third-Eye Theology*, 220.
84. Song, *Third-Eye Theology*, 220.
85. Song, *Third-Eye Theology*, 220.
86. Huang, "Ng Chiong Hui (Shoki Coe, Hwang Chang Hui)," 601.
87. Chih, "Homeland Theology," 185–95.

liberation. While Coe's work advances Asian theological thought at a time when Western theology was dominant,[88] we evaluate his limitations for the sake of a more relevant Asian theology.

Unlike Thomas, Coe takes the church as the starting point for developing Asian public theology. While Coe regards the church as the starting point for developing Asian public theology, he does not incorporate the ecclesial voices of the grassroots Christians in articulating his brand of an Asian public theology. Coe's central understanding of the prophetic role of the church is confined to this-worldly issues of social justice. He emphasizes the prophetic role of the church's interreligious engagement for social justice. It is not clear if Coe recognizes how the doxological practices of the grassroots Christians could shape academic Asian public theology. His notion of the church is strong in its external life for social justice and is weak in its pastoral witness of preaching and social charity.

Coe's understanding of salvation is limited to a social dimension of political liberation and his understanding of sin is confined to political oppression. This bias is understandable in which he developed an Asian prophetic theology as form of a political resistance against the Japanese and Chinese imperial rules. Despite his role as a pastor, as a moderator of the church assembly, and as an educator, Coe failed to integrate pastoral theology into Asian public theology. He did not utilize the lived experiences and voices of the grassroots church as sources for developing Asian public theology of liberation. Overall, his voice has a stronger tendency toward an academic Asian public theology.

An Asian Public Theology in Contemporary Context

If Coe and Thomas have laid the foundations of an Asian public theology, then public theology is not entirely a new concept in Asia. However, some fresh perspectives of an Asian public theology have recently gained its renewal and wide attention from academic circles through the establishment of the Global Network for Public Theology.[89]

---

88. Song, *The Compassionate God*, xiii.
89. Kim, "Public Theology in the History of Christianity," 40.

Felix Wilfred's Vision of an Asian Public Theology

Felix Wilfred is the one who uses the explicit term "Asian public theology."[90] He distinguished his Asian public theology from other Asian public liberationists. Wilfred was born into a Catholic family in 1948. He is emeritus professor and the founding director of the Asian Centre for Cross-Cultural Studies at the University of Madras, Chennai. He is the first Indian to have been appointed by the Pope to be a member of the International Theological Commission of the Vatican. He also serves as an advisor to the Federation of Asian Bishop's Conferences on matters of Christian doctrine.[91] He is the founding editor of the academic journal *International Journal of Asian Christianity* published by Brill. Wilfred helpfully describes the scope of Asian public theology as consisting of four crucial areas:

> In the first place, Asia stands in need of defense of freedom against state despotism of various kinds and grades. The second area of public concern is the defense of the poor from the tyranny of the market. The third important public concern is the creation of harmonious and non-exclusive communities. The fourth concern is that of protecting the environment.[92]

In order to play its public role in this fourfold scope, Wilfred defines an Asian public theology in its broad sense. How does Wilfred define an Asian public theology?

In order to understand what is meant by Asian public theology, it is better to begin by discerning Wilfred's conception of what public theology is not. As we have seen in the work of Sebastian Kim[93] and those of other Asian theologians—Shoki Coe,[94] C. S. Song,[95] Vinoth Ramachandra,[96] Paul Chung,[97] and Hwa Yung,[98] Asian public theology is a discipline that starts

---

90. See Wilfred, *Asian Public Theology*. Wilfred, "Towards an Asian Public Theology," 103–16; Wilfred, *Theology to Go Public*; Wilfred, "Asian Christianity and Public Life," 558–74.

91. For an overview of his life and work, see Gnanapragasam and Fiorenza, *Negotiating Borders*.

92. Wilfred, *Asian Public Theology*, xii–xiv.

93. Kim, *Public Theology in the Public Sphere*, 14–20.

94. Coe, *Joint Action for Mission in Formosa*.

95. Song, *Christian Mission in Reconstruction*, 83–113.

96. Ramachandra, *Subverting Global Myths*, 81–85.

97. Chung, *Public Theology in an Age of World Christianity*, 1–10.

98. Yung, *Mangoes or Bananas?*, 8–10.

in the church life and seeks its public relevance for political liberation. But for Wilfred, doing theology from life within the church and seeking its relevance for public life is not truly Asian public theology.[99] According to him, a theology that starts from the church life and then seeks its faith-movement for public life is not public theology. It is rather a "theology for public life, which is a Western import."[100] He shows how a "theology for public life" and "public theology" is different from each other:

> We need to draw a distinction between theology for public life and public theology. The former speaks about faith-motives and convictions for involving oneself as a believer in the affairs of the world—politics, economy, culture, violence, war, and peace. It is a discourse within the church about the world. On the other hand, in public theology, the concrete life-situation and the questions flowing from it are taken seriously, and an effort is made to respond to them in faith that understands itself in relation to others, and not as a private matter.[101]

He takes public life as the starting point for doing Asian public theology. He argued that an "Asian public theological reflection needs to be open-ended and should begin from the world."[102] Wilfred criticizes the Second Vatican Council's vision of church theology, which moves from the Christian faith to the public society of other faiths.[103] He even criticizes his fellow South Asian theologians Aloysius Pieris and Michael Amaladoss for adopting a Western form of Asian liberation theology that impels the church to engage in public life.[104] Wilfred asserted that "In spite of the innovative character of Asian theology, it is a fact that theological reflections have remained mostly internal to the church and its pastoral needs."[105] In his ambitious *Asian Public Theology*, Wilfred boldly suggests that public life, not the church, should be the starting point for defining Asian public theology.[106] For Wilfred, it is more appropriate to start an Asian public theology in public life because

---

99. Wilfred, *Asian Public Theology*, xvi-xix. Wilfred, "On the Future of Asian Theology."

100. Wilfred, *Asian Public Theology*, xvi.

101. Wilfred, "On the Future of Asian Theology," 35–36.

102. Wilfred, "On the Future of Asian Theology," 35.

103. Wilfred, *Asian Public Theology*, xvii.

104. Wilfred, *Asian Public Theology*, xvii.

105. Wilfred, *On the Future of Asian Theology*, 34.

106. Wilfred, *Asian Public Theology*, xvii-xix. Here Wilfred also quotes Thomas's work, *The Secular Ideologies and the Secular Meaning of Christ*.

non-Christians actually initiate and practice Asian public theology, while Christians are busy with their internal affairs.[107] Wilfred regards Mahatma Gandhi as an example. Wilfred said:

> This kind of Asian public theology originating from the engagement of non-Christians in the field could, perhaps, make the Christian Gospel more relevant and meaningful to the larger public than what hundred years of preaching by Christians and Christian missionaries have succeeded to do.[108]

Wilfred sees the kingdom of God as the foundational source and subalterns or margins as the prime site for doing Asian public theology.[109] Like Sebastian Kim, Wilfred argues against a Christian's narrow concept of God's reign within the church and urges Asian Christians to see the wider scope of God's reign beyond the church. For Wilfred, the broad vision of God's reign opens up a larger horizon of doing Asian public theology with immense possibility to dialogue and interact with other religions on public issues of socio-political oppression, ethnic marginalization, and economic poverty.[110] He has argued that:

> Public theology is strongly based on God's creation and on God's reign which have no boundaries. Besides, in public theology we try to create a discourse and language that is understandable to others, and therefore can be shared with them. This new language breaks forth when we hold aloft the truth of creation and the great vision of the Kingdom of God.[111]

Wilfred describes a distinctive characteristic of Asian public theology as its interreligious public engagement with people of other religions. He notes that:

> Asian public theologies must be developed in the various religious traditions and there be continuing dialogue and exchange among these theologies. Christian theology is challenged to become truly a partner among the various public theologies of the continent sharing the same historical, social, political, and cultural situation

---

107. Wilfred, *Asian Public Theology*, xix.
108. Wilfred, *Asian Public Theology*, xix.
109. Wilfred, *Asian Public Theology*, xxiv. See also Felix Wilfred, *Margins*.
110. Wilfred, "On the Future of Asian Theology," 36–55. Wilfred, *Asian Public Theology*, 134.
111. Wilfred, "On the Future of Asian Theology," 36.

and turn into a force of transformation for justice, peace, and harmony with the entire creation.[112]

The cosmic concept of God's reign in the public domain provides the meeting point of religions for their interreligious struggle and the goal is for the liberation of the margins.[113] Wilfred emphasizes that an Asian public theology of religions is "in service of liberation."[114] In order to achieve liberation, Christians and people of other religions have to struggle together against political powers. Wilfred sees the Philippines and Korea *minjung*'s achievement of political liberation through their struggles as the examples.[115] Public theology and liberation are teleologically related, but the two are methodologically different from each other. Liberation theology starts in the church, and it moves to public life, while public theology starts in public life, and it struggles for the common good in public society. Wilfred suggests that the two are mutually beneficial.[116]

Evaluating Wilfred's Approach

Unlike many Asian public theologians, Wilfred proposes to start an Asian public theology in public life. He justifies this approach by seeing the world as the reign of God where people of other religions practice public theology, while Christians remain busy with their internal affairs of worship and divorce their private faith from socio-political involvement. For Wilfred, public theology originating from the engagement of non-Christians in the field could, perhaps, make the Christian gospel more relevant and meaningful to the larger public.[117] Wilfred's approach seems to be attractive, but such an approach is problematic.

It seems problematic from the missiological perspective of *missio Dei*. *Missio Dei* means God's sending of the Son into the world as a missionary by the power of the Spirit. Mission (*missio* in Latin or *apostellein* in Greek) means commissioning the church into the world as embodying God's sending of Jesus into the world (John 20:21–22; Acts 1:8).[118] The identity

---

112. Wilfred, *Asian Public Theology*, 326.
113. Wilfred, "On the Future of Asian Theology," 37.
114. See Wilfred, "Public Theology in Service of Liberation," 485–504.
115. Wilfred, *Asian Public Theology*, 322.
116. Wilfred, "On the Future of Asian Theology," 37.
117. Wilfred, *Asian Public Theology*, xix.
118. See Bosch, *Transforming Mission*, 398–402; Köstenberger, *The Mission of Jesus and the Disciples According to the Fourth Gospel*, 27–37.

of the church is rooted in God's calling of the church out of the world for doxological relationship with God. God then commissions the church to the world to witness his life and action. The church's identity is rooted in this dialectical relationship between calling and commissioning. Starting public theology in public life weakens the identity of the church as a doxological community. Starting public theology in public life is problematic in contexts where the public space is dominated by other religions. In such contexts, it is more appropriate to start in the life of the church and empower its marginal faith to resist the dominant culture.

Wilfred's approach is thus ecclesiologically problematic. Over-appreciating socio-political actions done by other faiths, Wilfred does not recognize the grassroots Christians' ecclesial internal practices of doxology, priestly prayer, pastoral preaching, and their external practices of evangelism and social charity. He recognizes a theology of direct engagement in political life as the only public theology relevant in Asia. In this regard, Wilfred is inspired by Thomas' vision of public theology.[119] Their theology is strong in political involvement but weak in pastoral engagement. Their understanding of the public praxis of faith is confined to its socio-political involvement in dialogue with people of other faiths who practice public theology in the non-ecclesial life.[120]

In reaching out to public life, the church must not see people of other faiths as the objects of conversion. This likelihood is Wilfred's concern.[121] Wilfred suggests that an Asian public theology should take a shift in "understanding mission not in terms of salvation or damnation or not in opposition to other religious traditions, but in terms of relationship with them."[122] It is necessary for Christians to co-operate with other faiths for the liberation of those on the margins. But this way of engagement does not mean that the church should limit its mission to dialogue. Dialogue is one of the actions of mission, but not the end goal. Wilfred's understanding of the mission of the church is confined to the church's public practices of interreligious dialogue. He rejects the role of evangelism in mission. Paul practices interreligious dialogue in Athens and its impacts on the conversion of some dialogue partners (Acts 17:23–34).

---

119. Wilfred, *Asian Public Theology*, xix.
120. Wilfred, *Asian Public Theology*, xix.
121. Wilfred, *Asian Public Theology*, xviii-xix.
122. Wilfred, "Theology of South Asia," 502–17.

Wilfred's understanding of salvation is limited to political liberation. He does not address the significance of the cross of Christ for an Asian public theology of reconciliation. For him, social justice is the only soteriological need in Asia. While political liberation of the oppressed is urgent in Asia, where the minority Christians and other minority groups suffer at the hands of political powers, we cannot limit the broad concept of God's salvation to political liberation. God's salvation encompasses a comprehensive concept of reconciliation, healing, forgiveness, and so on. Our concern is to address how these soteriological terms integrate God's broad drama of salvation in the world.

Aloysius Pieris's Asian Public Theology of Religions and Liberation

I have chosen Aloysius Pieris of Sri Lanka (1934–) as one of the interlocutors because he is one of the most eminent of Asian liberation theologians and his commitment to Christian–Buddhist dialogue is significant.[123] Pieris first studied at Sacred Heart College in India (1959) and earned a B.A degree in Sanskrit and Pali from the University of London (1961), and an STL degree from the Pontifical Theological Faculty in Naples, Italy (1966). He taught Asian religions at the Gregorian University in Rome for a year and explored the possibility of a doctorate in Buddhist studies at a Western university. However, his zeal for developing Asian theology in dialogue with Asian Buddhism at an everyday level led him to pursue a PhD in Buddhism at the University of Sri Lanka. In 1972, he became the first Asian Christian to gain a PhD in Buddhism under the supervision of a monk. He is the founding director of the Tulana Dialogue Centre at Gonawala-Kelaniya.[124]

It was Pieris who first proposed the thesis that a serious theological inquiry in Asia should deal with its twofold reality: religious diversity and mass poverty. In his landmark book *An Asian Theology of Liberation*,[125] Pieris states how the Second Vatican Council (1962–65) shaped his vision for theologizing an Asian theology of liberation:

> The Second Vatican Council was for me a point of departure rather than a point of arrival, as I joined my Asian colleagues over

---

123. Sugirtharajah, *Frontiers in Asian Christian Theology*, 141.

124. Crusz et al., *Encounter with the World*, 643–69. See also Pieris, "Two Encounters in My Theological Journey," 141–46.

125. Pieris, *An Asian Theology of Liberation*.

twenty years ago in the challenging task of applying the conciliar teachings to our Asian context and of trying to give concrete Asian form to the spirit of the council.[126]

In theologizing an Asian public theology of liberation, Pieris takes seriously the twin poles of Asian realities: religious diversity and mass poverty. The first pole calls for interreligious dialogue (Christian–Buddhist dialogue) and the second pole calls for liberation through interreligious dialogue. These twin poles are the driving forces for Pieris's distinctive contribution to Asian public theology of interreligious engagement and liberation. Pieris's dialogue with Buddhism is principally related to his main theological concern to develop Asian political/public theology of religions and liberation.[127]

A "liberating Christology of religions"[128] is the foundation for Pieris's vision of Asian public theology of religions and liberation. His conception of liberating Christology of religions is rooted in two related images: "Christology of liberation" (the liberating person of Christ) and "liberation of Christology" (the liberating act of Christ).[129] While the former image focuses on the Synoptic Gospels conveying the historical event of humanity of Christ's identification with the poor for their liberation and the latter focuses on Christ's cosmic solidarity with the interreligious community of the poor, Pieris brings Christ's political act of liberation into dialogue with the Buddha as a liberator.[130] Central to Pieris's vision is that Christ's and the Buddha's ethical praxis of resistance against social injustices shape the public role of Christians and Buddhists in the liberation movement.

Pieris suggests that there are two ways of witnessing to the prophetic role of the liberating Christ in the Asian context of poverty and religious diversity. One is a "Christo-struggle to be poor and the other is a Christo-struggle for the poor."[131] Pieris refers to the "struggle to be poor" as a Christian spiritual embodiment of Christ's solidarity with the poor in terms of renunciation of the world. Pieris calls this "voluntary poverty," which

---

126. Pieris, *An Asian Theology of Liberation*, xv.

127. Pieris, "Political Theology in Asia," 256–70. See also Fleming, *Asian Christian Theologians in Dialogue with Buddhism*, 201–65.

128. Pieris, *The Genesis of Asian Theology of Liberation*, 169.

129. Pieris, *Love Meets Wisdom*, 124. See also Tombs, "Liberating Christology," 173–88, at 179.

130. Pieris, "The Buddha and the Christ," 162–77.

131. Pieris, *An Asian Theology of Liberation*, 15.

Christians should act out through the spiritual renunciation of the comfortable ecclesial life.[132] On the other hand, Pieris refers to the "struggle for the poor" as the Christian social public embodiment of Christ's prophetic struggle against political powers.[133] Pieris calls this "forced poverty."[134] The two are interrelated to each other for performing public theology.

The interrelated idea of Christ's struggle to be poor and Christ's struggle for the poor is rooted in God's public reign of liberating action for all suffering human communities.[135] Rejecting a narrow view of Christ's exclusive solidarity with the suffering churches, Pieris emphasizes Christ's cosmic solidarity with all victims of poverty. This move opens up into the Christian–Buddhist social involvement in the liberation movement.[136] Vietnamese Buddhist activist Thich Nhat Hanh (1926–2022) inspires Pieris's vision of the role of Buddhism in socio-political engagement.[137] Hanh is often cited for his approach to Buddhism as an engaged religion.[138] Hanh coined the term "engaged Buddhism" in the 1960s to show how Buddhism plays a role in social engagement.[139] In *Engaged Buddhism: Buddhist Liberation Movements in Asia*, Christopher Queen and his colleagues state how the term "engaged Buddhism" characterizes a paradigm shift in seeing Buddhism not just as a meditative religion, but as an engaged religion.[140] Hanh's creative approach to Buddhism as an engaged religion shaped the Christian transformative understanding of Buddhism.[141]

Thus, Pieris argues that the Christian praxis of Christo-struggle to be poor through the spiritual renunciation and of Christo-struggle for the poor through the social action is complementary to the Buddhist spiritual struggle to be poor in terms of renunciation of the world and of the prophetic struggle for the poor in terms of social resistance against political powers. Pieris cites some engaged Buddhists and activist Christians in Sri

---

132. Pieris, *An Asian Theology of Liberation*, 20–23.
133. Pieris, *An Asian Theology of Liberation*, 15.
134. Pieris, *An Asian Theology of Liberation*, 20–23.
135. Pieris, *God's Reign for God's Poor*, 1–18; Pieris, *The Genesis of Asian Theology of Liberation*, 211–16.
136. Pieris, *The Genesis of Asian Theology of Liberation*, 168–88.
137. Pieris, *An Asian Theology of Liberation*, 28; 35–68.
138. Quoted in Queen, "Introduction," 1–44.
139. Queen, "Introduction," 2.
140. Queen, "Introduction," 2.
141. Pieris, *An Asian Theology of Liberation*, 28; 35–68.

Lanka as prime examples due to their spiritual and social struggles against political powers.[142]

Pieris envisions the interreligious practice of the struggle to be poor and of the struggle against political powers leading to the liberation of the poor from socio-political oppression. Pieris emphasizes that liberation can be achieved only through the interreligious struggle against political powers or societal sin, which deprive those on the margins. He criticizes as inadequate the pastoral work of social charity and preaching, which is mobilized in the struggle against societal sin. The goal of the Christo-praxis to be poor and the praxis for the poor against political powers is to liberate the oppressed from the oppressors.

Evaluating Pieris's Approach and Influence

Pieris's Asian public theology of religions and liberation is deeply rooted in Christology. Christ is the key for Pieris's vision of Asian public theology of religions and liberation. His understanding of Christology is demonstrated in the liberating praxis and cosmic Lordship of Christ. He sees Christ as the cosmic liberator of all humans. He then brings the liberating praxis of the cosmic Christ into dialogue with the Buddha as a liberator. He sees Jesus and the Buddha as liberators. Pieris does not accept Jesus's divinity.[143] For Pieris, the uniqueness of Jesus lies in his praxis for liberation of the poor. For Pieris, the cosmic Lord and the historical Jesus who labored among the poor in the Gospels are the one and the same, sharing identical purpose. According to Pieris, Buddhists also have a liberating gnosis in the liberating praxis of the cosmic Lord.

Pieris's creative approach to Christian–Buddhist interreligious dialogue for the public vision of political liberation of the poor inspires several contemporary Asian liberation theologians in the Buddhist-dominant contexts. Saw Hlaing Bwa from Myanmar (1955–2022) is one of them. Building on Pieris's theory, Bwa utilizes Christo-praxis as the basis for a Burmese public theology. In his essay, "Mission: Christo-Praxis in Myanmar," Bwa employs Christo-praxis as the model for the Christian praxis of liberation.[144] Bwa's theological understanding of Christo-praxis is rooted in the cosmic

---

142. Pieris, *The Genesis of Asian Theology of Liberation*, 197–201. Pieris, "The Buddha and the Christ," 163. Pieris, "Religion and Politics in Sri Lanka," 113–16.

143. Pieris, *An Asian Theology of Liberation*, 15–23

144. Bwa, "Mission," 1–26 at 7.

idea of Christ's liberating work for the oppressed in the public sphere beyond the church. He claims that "Christo-praxis as God's salvific-liberative work can be discerned throughout the religio-political context in Burma and Christians are called to participate in this public arena."[145]

Since political liberation can be promoted only through dialogue, Bwa believes that the future of a peaceful public society in Myanmar depends on Christian–Buddhist dialogue.[146] Bwa explores the public role of religions in conflict resolutions. He said:

> Political solutions alone cannot resolve a century of political suppression. This is where religions can enter, playing a vital role for the embodiment of human rights. Religious beliefs are a fundamental way in which people organize their life and their personal and social development. By reducing the role of religion and restricting it, society could miss an essential element of being human.[147]

For Bwa, religious peace cannot be promoted against religions, but only with them. To that end goal, he has promoted Christian–Buddhist dialogue through the Judson Research Center (JRC) since 2003. The JRC has promoted what Bwa calls the "academic Christian–Buddhist dialogue" in collaboration with some international universities: the International Theravada Buddhist Missionary University and the Program on Peace Building and Rights of Columbia University.[148] The JRC conducted the forums on these themes: "A Critical Appraisal of Reconciliation from the Buddhist and Christians Perspectives" (August 28, 2015); "Loving Kindness" (August 29, 2014); "Interfaith Dialogue: The Religious Roots of Social Harmony (January 19, 2014); "Towards a Better Harmonious Society through Buddhist-Christian Dialogue" (October 30, 2011), and others.

While praising the Buddhist liberation movement, Bwa criticizes Christians who rely on the Western-financed development projects for charity toward the poor.[149] He also criticizes some Christians who see conflict as the sign of the end time. Bwa asserts that political suffering in

---

145. Bwa, "Mission," 13.

146. See Bwa, "Why Interfaith Dialogue is Essential for Myanmar's Future," 71–78; Bwa, "Myanmar," 179–95, at 191. Bwa's approach to religious peace is also inspired by Han Küng's dictum: "there is no world peace without religious peace;" see Hans Küng, *Global Responsibility*, 76; 89; 105.

147. Baw, "Why Interfaith Dialogue is Essential for Myanmar's Future," 74.

148. Bwa, "Myanmar," 191.

149. Bwa, "Mission," 12.

Myanmar is caused by "moral evils."[150] For Bwa, the task of the church is not about the salvation of lost souls but about political liberation. He claims that a common journey toward political liberation is possible only through Christian–Buddhist dialogue.[151] While Bwa's commitment for promoting Christian–Buddhist interreligious dialogue is admirable, his failure to engage with his own grassroots Karen minority congregations is questionable. Being the pioneer receivers of Christianity from missionaries, Karen ethnic minority Christians' public and private witnesses to their faith is remarkable from the colonial past to the post-colonial present.[152] It is noted that Bwa's vision for the interreligious dimension of political liberation and peace in Myanmar is deeply inspired by Pieris's approach to cosmic Christology and its liberating praxis in Asia.

While I appreciate Pieris's emphases on the cosmic Lordship and liberating praxis of Christ and find them insightful for developing Asian public theology of religions and liberation, I am not satisfied with his understanding of Christ merely as a human liberator. In order to meet for the interreligious exchanges of liberating praxis, Pieris increases the status of the Buddha and diminishes Jesus by rejecting his divinity. It is indispensable for the church to discern and recognize Christ's cosmic presence and liberating activity in the pluralistic contexts, but we cannot limit Jesus to being only a liberator. Jesus can holistically be seen as a reconciler, redeemer, and healer. Pieris's soteriology is limited to socio-political liberation.

With his overemphasis on Christ's liberation of the poor, Pieris rejects the possibility of reconciliation. He makes a claim: (1) "the irreconcilable antagonism between God and mammon, and (2) the irrevocable covenant between God and the poor (i.e., a defense pact against their common enemy: mammon)."[153] While Jesus takes a stand with the poor, we should also accept the fact that he resists the oppressive systems and opens the door for reconciliation between victims and oppressors. Since Jesus serves as a reconciling victim between God and humanity by the power of the Spirit, he stands in solidarity with the victims and resists their oppressors. The goal of Christ's resistance is to restore justice and reconciliation between the victims and the perpetrators. While Pieris's view of Christ's solidarity with the poor of all faiths and his commitment to their socio-economic

---

150. Bwa, "The Problem of Evil," 169–76.
151. Bwa, "Mission," 21. See also Bwa, "Journey Together," 1–13.
152. Naw, *The History of the Karen People of Burma*, 129.
153. Pieris, *An Asian Theology of Liberation*, 120–21.

liberation is admirable, he does not address the reality of how some majority religious and ethnic groups could become another's oppressor of the minority ethnic and religious groups.

His home country of Sri Lanka is notorious for the majority Sinhalese ethnic Buddhist nationalism and discrimination against the minority Tamil ethnic Christians and Hindus. However, Pieris fails to address what Sugirtharajah calls "a plurality of oppressions."[154] Although masses may be economically poor in many parts of Asia, some religiously dominant groups are political oppressors of minority ethnic and religious groups. Pieris fails to address how the economically poor but religiously and ethnically majority groups could be oppressors of minority ethnic groups. Pieris's writings fail to critique the root causes of Sinhalese Buddhist nationalism, and he only praises Buddhism as a liberating religion. If the true vision of public theology is not just for one public aspect of socio-economic liberation but also for the larger aspect of the common good, Asian Christians should reconsider the larger public issues of Buddhist nationalism and ethnic conflict.

Conclusion

This chapter has attempted to accomplish three goals. First, I have revisited the origins and foundations of an Asian public theology of religions and liberation. I have shown how the concept of academic Asian public theology was developed by Asian public theologians without the term "public theology" before the official rise of public theology in the West. I have demonstrated how the 1959 EACC should be understood as a point of departure for an Asian public theology. I have selected Thomas and Coe as two examples, who have laid the conceptual foundations of Asian public theology of religions and liberation. I have described their key contributions to the conceptual and contextual development of Asian public theology.

I have explored the current state of Asian public theology. I have looked at how Wilfred has approached to some fresh perspectives and methodologies of Asian public theology of religions and liberation. His radical proposal for seeing public life rather than the church as the starting point for an Asian public theology has been highlighted. Then I have engaged with Pieris who focused on an Asian public theology of Christian–Buddhist dialogue and interreligious liberation. I have highlighted Pieris's

---

154. Sugirtharajah, *Postcolonial Criticism and Biblical Interpretation*, 120.

distinctive contributions to the development of an Asian public theology of Christian–Buddhist dialogue and his influence on contemporary Asian liberation theologians. Pieris and contemporary Asian liberation theologians have seriously considered the cosmic Christology as the foundation and model for developing an Asian public theology of religions and liberation.

I have also described how liberation and public theologians utilize the prophetic and kingly role of Christ as foundations for doing an Asian public theology of religions and liberation. With the focus on the cosmic Christopraxis, they do not develop the role of the Spirit in an Asian public theology. Their conception of soteriology is confined to political liberation. They focus on political powers and ignore spiritual powers. Ordinary people in Asia experience both political and spiritual powers. There is another contrast between liberation theologians and some grassroots Christians. While some grassroots Christians tend to focus on personal sin as an alienation from God, liberation theologians tend to focus on structural sin of sociopolitical oppression.[155] Their understanding of salvation is also different. Liberation theologians tend to focus on liberation from political oppression, while some grassroots Christians focus on salvation as forgiveness of sinners. In the context of political oppression, seeing salvation as restricted to forgiveness of sinners is problematic because the oppressors would take it for granted and injustice would be likely to be perpetuated.

There is a need to reconsider a comprehensive understanding of salvation and sin in concrete contexts. These contrasts call for reconsidering the holistic dimension of sin and salvation as liberation, reconciliation, redemption, and healing of the bodies. Liberation theologians' conception of the church is reduced to its functional role for interreligious dialogue without balancing it with its ontological role. There is also the need of balancing the political and pastoral role of the church in public witness. In the next chapter, we will reformulate a lived Asian public theology of religions that bridges some gaps between academic liberationist voices and grassroots Christian lived voices.

---

155. See, for instance, Park, *The Wounded Heart of God*, 69.

FIVE

Synthesizing Academic–Grassroots Voices for Lived Public Theology of Religions

Introduction

IT IS NOW TIME to put the academic and grassroots Christians voices together in conversation. This integrative interpretation is a consequence of my own firsthand cultural experiences as a participant observer in local grassroots churches and of my qualitative interviews with the grassroots Christians. I will interpret the embodied public theology that emerges from the grassroots Christian voices. Although some theologians criticize grassroots Christians' uncritical adoption of the legacy of Western missionary dualism, some liberationists themselves fall into a dualistic idea of thought. They dichotomize social justice and social charity, spiritual salvation and social liberation, personal sin and societal sin. Their ideas of sin and salvation are reduced to structural sin and liberation from political powers, while some grassroots Christians focus on personal sin and spiritual liberation from spiritual powers.[1]

It is not my intention to adopt some form of replacement model where the lived experience is overcome by a Western public theology or a liberation theology. Using a synthesis model, I will integrate two different voices by recognizing each distinctive contribution to a lived Asian public theology of religions.

---

1. See Ramachandra, *The Recovery of Mission*, 52–60; Chan, "Evangelical Theology in Asian Contexts," 225–40; Ki, *From Darkness to Glorious Light*.

Performing Lived Public Theology as Everyday Theology

A lived public theology should be understood and performed as an everyday theology. Public theology is not only about academic reflection in the academy as a "weekday theology" and not only about a doxological singing, praying, and preaching in the church as a "Sunday theology," but it is also about the performative witness of everyday theology. There must be an inseparable connection between confessional faith and everyday practice. As the apostle James reminds us, "faith without works is dead" (Jas 2:14). In order to keep faith active, one must perform belief in God every day.

In his edited book *Everyday Theology*, Kevin Vanhoozer described how "Everyday theology is faith seeking understanding of everyday life. Nothing should be easier to understand the notion of the everyday for the simple reason that it is so commonplace. What is most familiar to us, however, is often the hardest thing to understand."[2] Vanhoozer's understanding of everyday theology is rooted in Anselm's traditional definition of theology as "faith seeking understanding." Everyday theology is faith seeking understanding of God and making sense of that faith for all of everyday life by actually engaging everyday life.[3] Everyday theology is not just "faith seeking understanding of God," but also "faith speaking performance for God" in everyday life.

In one of his other texts, *The Drama of Doctrine*, Vanhoozer introduces the idea of God's trinitarian mission as a drama performance in everyday life. He uses the church and public life as an analogy to theater, with the Scripture as the script, the triune God as the director, and Christians as actors.[4] As Christians participate in the drama of God's public mission, we must relate the Bible and newspaper. Karl Barth's dictum, "Holding the Bible in one hand, and the newspaper in the other,"[5] as the vocation of Christians is helpful for reflecting everyday public theology. The Bible and newspapers are informative sources, though not equally, for discernment of God's speech in performing public theology as everyday theology. When we read newspapers, we learn some everyday trends and issues as the *kairos*

---

2. Vanhoozer, "What Is Everyday Theology?" 15–60, at 17.

3. Vanhoozer, "What Is Everyday Theology?" 16; see also Vanhoozer, *Faith Speaking Understanding*.

4. Vanhoozer, *The Drama of Doctrine*, 57–75.

5. Though frequently credited to Barth for this dictum, no authoritative source is found yet for this citation. Probably the clearest statement on the record from Barth regarding these maters can be seen in *Time Magazine*, published on Friday, May 31, 1963.

for our ethical responses from the perspective of the Bible. To make sense of a lived Asian public theology as an everyday theology, one needs to consider the public role of the Bible and digital media.

Like Vanhoozer, Volf regards public theology as everyday theology. Volf has a stronger vision of interreligious engagement that serves the common good. In *For the Life of the World*,[6] Volf states that the aim of theology is "to discern, articulate, and commend visions of flourishing life."[7] "As Christians, we seek to think and speak plausibly about our journeys with Christ into our own and the world's fullness to make the practice of faith coherent. Call this "everyday theology."[8] Volf criticizes academic theology for its detachment from real life. Knowledge generators and scholars are too detached from life as it is lived on the ground.[9] The task of a public theology is to discern the everyday trends of God's worldly home (John 1:14; 6:15; 10:40); it is to articulate theology for all people, and to commend a vision of human flourishing.[10] It is in this sense that Volf brings theology in dialogue with other faiths for the common good. Volf is clear:

> We need to revive a sustained truth-seeking cultural conversation about the flourishing life. We live in a globalized world where partly overlapping and partly contradictory visions of flourishing life coexist in the same public space. People of many diverse perspectives, religious and nonreligious, will need to participate in that conversation. Christian theology ought to become one such voice. If it does, it may be able to help both religious and educational institutions to make the true life their central concern.[11]

Although Volf and Vanhoozer may have popularized the term "everyday theology," Asian theologians had already developed analogies for such an idea.[12] C. S. Song, for instance, has suggested that we must relate faith and theology to the everyday lives of people politics and stories in action.[13] In his *Third-Eye Theology*, Song noted that "Active theology is thus a theology that grows out of the life of people. This was well stated by participants of

---

6. Volf and Croasmun, *For the Life of the World*.
7. Volf and Croasmun, *For the Life of the World*, 11.
8. Volf and Croasmun, *For the Life of the World*.
9. Volf, "On Being a Christian Public Intellectual," 8.
10. See also Volf and Ryan McAnnally-Linz, *The Home of God*.
11. Volf and Croasmun, *For the Life of the World*, 32.
12. See Than ed., *Witnesses Together*.
13. Song, *The Tears of Lady Meng*, 43–48.

the 'Theology in Action' workshop held in Manila in the Philippines and Kuala Lumpur in Malaysia in 1972 and 1973 under the auspices of the Christian Conference of Asia."[14] We now turn to the grassroots–academic voices in conversation.

Grassroots–Academic Voices in Conversation: Bridging the Ecclesial Ontology and Function

While Christology has been a dominant theme in Asian public theology of liberation,[15] ecclesiology is a neglected theme. Asian theologians tend to articulate theology *for* the grassroots church as the recipient, but they do not do adequately a theology *of* the church, with the grassroots Christians as collaborator.[16] Asian liberationists use the cosmic and prophetic Christology as the model for the function of the church's political and interreligious witnesses. If the cosmic Christology addresses God's universal reign and public presence in the public squares, the prophetic Christ calls for the church's prophetic witnesses of social justice and peace together with the people of other religions.[17] Public theologians focus on the prophetic model of public theology.[18] If a public theology reconsiders the whole nature and action of God as its model for the church's participatory engagement in political and public life, then Asian theologians should also recognize the priestly and healing role of Christ in performing a lived Asian public theology of religions.

The two most pressing issues facing Christians in Asia are how to rethink the church and salvation for the public mission of God. The church has two crises: one is the privatization of faith without taking the public

---

14. Song, *Third-Eye Theology*, 82.

15. For a comprehensive study of Christology in Asia, see Sugirtharajah, *Asian Faces of Jesus*.

16. Simon Chan is one of the strongest Asian proponents of grassroots ecclesiology or a theology of the church. See Chan, *Liturgical Theology*; Chan, *Grassroots Asian Theology*, 157–202.

17. Than ed., *Witnesses Together*, 60–78. Thomas, *The Christian Response to the Asian Revolution*, 27–65; Wilfred, *Asian Public Theology*, xix–xx. For a comprehensive summary of academic Christology in ecumenical context, see Levison and Levison, "Toward an Ecumenical Christology for Asia," 3–17; Levison and Levison, *Jesus in Global Contexts*, 55–88.

18. See Moltmann, *God for a Secular Society*, 5. Kim, *Theology in the Public Sphere*, 3; Koopman, "Public Theology as Prophetic Theology," 117–30.

issues of social justice and salvation seriously; the other is the publicization of faith in terms of interreligious dialogue without taking the internal life of faith seriously. Another crisis has to do with salvation. The problem is a one-sided emphasis on the doctrine of salvation: while the liberationists tend to focus on the social dimension of salvation as social justice, grassroots Christians tend to focus on the spiritual dimension of a vertical relationship with God.[19] Their opposing perception of human salvation becomes a kind of partial salvation rather than a holistic salvation. By holistic salvation, I mean God's holistic act of human physical and spiritual salvation and eco-salvation—*shalom*.

A *shalomic* concept of holistic salvation is expressed by the apostle Paul as holding all things, both anthropos and cosmos, together in Christ (Col 1:20). Salvation is not just for humans, but for all creatures. Jürgen Moltmann is right to say that justice and peace means a blessed life in Christian communion with God, with humans and with other creatures. Justice and peace are communal and integrative, not limited to individualistic salvation.[20] However, there are some contrasts. While liberationists tend to focus on the social ministry of Christ and read Luke 4:18–19 as a key text for liberation theology, grassroots Christians focus on the atonement of Christ and read the Hebrews and the epistle to the Romans—what N. T. Wright calls "Paul's greatest letter"[21]—as key texts for their understanding of salvation as an anthropocentric justification and forgiveness. Although Romans 8 talks about a cosmos dimension of salvation and "the groaning of the Spirit" (Rom 8:22–27), grassroots Christians emphasize an anthropocentric salvation.

Central to an authentic Asian public theology is the question of how the church is to be rightly understood in relation to the triune God and the world. But when it comes to the Trinity, theologians tend to emphasize the economic Trinity as the functional model for the church's engagement with the world. What is often neglected is the significance of the immanent Trinity for the church. If a lived Asian trinitarian public theology is to be celebrated in the church, then we should reconsider the role of the internal life of the church seriously. My inquiry is how the immanent Trinity serves as the model for the internal life of the church.

---

19. Ki, *From Darkness to Glorious Light*, 23–30.
20. Moltmann, "Political Theology and the Ethics of Peace," 31–42, at 38.
21. See Wright, *Into the Heart of Romans*.

Cappadocian fathers, especially Gregory of Nyssa, are the most important early advocates of employing communal images for the Trinity.[22] While Nyssa advocated for a social model, Augustine was committed to a "psychological model of the Trinity." Nyssa's social model of the Trinity offers a more significant role for the church's internal and external communion.[23] Holding the inseparable unity between the immanent Trinity and the economic Trinity, we will explore the significance of their internal and external distinctions for the internal life and the external life of the church.[24] While the immanent Trinity refers to the image of the internal communal relationship within the triune God, the economic Trinity refers to the image of God's external act of salvation for the world. My aim is to show how the immanent Trinity and economic Trinity serve as models for the internal and external life of the church.

The Immanent Trinity and the Doxological Church

The church could be like any other social community in terms of being the instrumental champion of charity for the poor, which other non-church charity communities or NGOs could also do, but worship, according to Simon Chan, distinguishes the church from other communities.[25] Grassroots Christians believe that the church's distinctive identity is to be demonstrated in its worship. Grassroots worship demonstrates the church's witness of God's salvation as reconciliation among Christians and as God's communal life inside and outside the church. We should see the church's internal witness of salvation as communion with God in terms of what Nicholas Wolterstorff calls "the primary justice in the life of the Trinity."[26] By primary justice Wolterstorff has in view the inner trinitarian relationship marked by reciprocal love. "Primary justice consists of treating three persons with due respect for their worth."[27] Primary justice and secondary or restorative justice must come together; the latter being grounded in the former. The triune God is inherently just, executing restorative justice for the world through Jesus Christ. Wolterstorff writes:

22. Volf, "Being as God is Trinity and Generosity," 2–13, at 5.
23. Volf, "Being as God is Trinity and Generosity," 6.
24. Moltmann, *The Spirit of Life*, 290–305.
25. Chan, *Liturgical Theology*, 42–47.
26. Wolterstorff, "Is There Justice in the Trinity?," 177–87, at 187.
27. Wolterstorff, "Is There Justice in the Trinity?," 185.

God's doing of secondary/restorative justice reflects the primary justice internal to God's own life; God's love of justice in human affairs reflects the justice that incorporates love that is internal to the immanent life of the Trinity. Primary justice within the Trinity is caught up within love for each other.[28]

For Wolterstorff, primary and secondary justice are grounded in two kinds of love. One is *erotic love*, and the other is *agape love*. "The former grounded in the latter."[29] He refers to *erotic love* as the love within the Trinity because it "seeks one's own well-being" within the Trinity, while he refers to *agape love* as the love, which seeks the well-being of the other or restorative justice between God and the world through the "sacrifice of one's own life in Christ."[30] Our notion of the church's internal and external witness of salvation as the communal life and the loving action of the Trinity is built on this fresh approach.

Worship, Witness, and Withness: The Church as the Image of the Trinity

First, we see worship as a joyful witness of mission. As a community of worship (1 Tim 2:10; Heb 12:28), the church's ontological witness should not be underestimated for the sake of its functional role.[31] Centering our ontological relationship with the Trinity, "doxology cannot be an end in itself."[32] Orthodox Christians consider doxology as mission and they call it "liturgy before liturgy."[33] Mission is the church's breathing: "we inhale in worship; we exhale in public witness."[34] Protestants do not often see worship as mission due to their overemphasis on the church's functional witness of the Great Commission (Matt 28:19–20). "Mission is not just from inside to outside, but also from outside to inside."[35] We bring public issues

---

28. Wolterstorff, "Is There Justice in the Trinity?," 187.
29. Wolterstorff, "Is There Justice in the Trinity?," 187.
30. Wolterstorff, "Is There Justice in the Trinity?," 185.
31. Chan, *Liturgical Theology*, 21–24; Hastings, *Worshiping, Witnessing, and Wondering*.
32. Schroeder, *What Is the Mission of the Church?*, 115.
33. Schroeder, *What Is the Mission of the Church?*, 115.
34. Coorilos, "Mission as Liturgy Before Liturgy and as Contestation," 175.
35. Schroeder, *What Is the Mission of the Church?*, 116.

into liturgy and reflect them in preaching and prayers (1 Tim 2:2).[36] Mission does not merely come to us from God, but mission may also go to God by way of our ontological and joyful witness in participatory communal worship.

Second, we consider public mission as a humble *with*ness. By withness, I mean the church's dialogical engagement with people of other faiths in witnessing together to the public mission of the care of creation and nurturing the common good without losing the church's distinct identity as a worshiping community. The task of the church is not only to witness *to* people of other religions, but also to witness *together with* them as conversation partners. This kind of witnessing the life and work of God in a dialogical way is needed in the post-colonial era.

The grassroots Christians' joyful witness of worship is rooted in their imagination of the church as the chosen people. The grassroots Christians' imagination of the church carries three main images: "the chosen people of God (1 Pet 2:9), the body of Christ (1 Cor 12:27), and the holy temple of the Spirit (1 Cor 6:19)."[37] Especially the first image is the strongest point for their identity imagination in relation to the Israel.[38] They use 1 Peter 2:9 as a source for justifying their identity as the chosen people. Peter said: "But you are a chosen race, a royal priesthood, a holy nation, God's own people, in order that you may proclaim the mighty acts of him called you out of darkness into his marvelous light." They emphasize the idea of "chosen from darkness"[39] and "chosen for." While the term "chosen from darkness" refers to their notion of Christ's calling the church out of the world as a holy temple, the term "chosen for" refers to Christ's calling the church for worship. Worship embodies what Jürgen Moltmann calls a "trinitarian doxology."[40] He notes that:

> In the trinitarian doxology, we adore God for himself and glorify him because he is what he is. The trinitarian figure for this is therefore the immanent Trinity. Of course, in human doxology the Trinity becomes an unfathomable mystery which excels

---

36. Schattauer, *Inside Out*, 1–21.

37. Interviews with some grassroots Christians by the author, July 19–20, 2020. See also, Chan, *Liturgical Theology*, 24–40.

38. For the analogical relation between the Israel's identity-nation imagination and the Christian identity imagination, see Brett, *Locations of God*, 46–68.

39. See Ki, *From Darkness to Glorious Light*.

40. Moltmann, *The Spirit of Life*, 304.

all imaginings and concepts. For anyone who enters the wonder, the be-wondered counterpart becomes an inexhaustible source of always wider and every deeper wonderment. How could we ever stop and where could we ever come to an end of the marveling?[41]

When Jesus came to the world by the power of the Spirit, the Father is the receiver of glory from the Son and the Spirit. When Jesus ascended into heaven, the Father, the Son, and the Spirit were the receivers of honor from the church.[42] In his book *Being as Communion*, the Orthodox ecclesiologist John Zizioulas develops the significance of the Trinity for the life of the church.[43] Central to Zizioulas' idea of trinitarianism is his notion of the being of the Trinity as communion and personhood. It is his conviction that a "person cannot exist without communion, but every form of communion, which denies the personhood is inadmissible."[44] The three perichoretic persons in one God is communion in Godself, communion with the church and with the world. He sees the trinitarian communion as the model for the Christian communion and the human communion. Our view of monotheism (Deut 6:4) without communion is challenging. It can be misunderstood as individualism, not personalism.

Zizioulas's notion of the trinitarian perichoretic personalism without individualism and divine communion without uniformity is helpful for envisioning a communitarian Trinity from an Asian perspective. In his *Towards a Theology of the Concord of God*,[45] Japanese theologian Nozomu Miyahira argues against a Western individualistic view of the Trinity and takes the Asian communal culture as a way for embodying the Trinity.[46] A communitarian view of the Trinity enables the Asian church to embrace one another as the Christian communion of one faith with different gifts for glorifying the Trinity (John 17:1–26; 1 Cor 12:27–31; Eph 4:4–6) and as the human communion who represent God's image with equal rights and different gifts for imagining God's creation care (Gen 1:28).

---

41. Moltmann, *The Spirit of Life*, 304.
42. Moltmann, *The Spirit of Life*, 302–4.
43. Zizioulas, *Being as Communion*, 15–26.
44. Zizioulas, *Being as Communion*, 18.
45. Miyahira, *Towards a Theology of the Concord of God*, 48–65.
46. Miyahira, *Towards a Theology of the Concord of God*, 48–65, 223–25. See also Jung Young Lee, *The Trinity in Asian Perspective*, 22–24.

Built on Zizioulas's idea, Volf sees the "church as the image of the Trinity."[47] Volf's notion of the relation between the Trinity and the church is rooted in two theological assumptions: "there is no church without the reign of the Trinity and there is no reign of the Trinity without the church."[48] By the former, Volf means the "church lives from and toward something that is greater than the church itself."[49] Volf refers to the latter as the church's witness of the reign of God. The Trinity forms the church not simply to be the church for itself, but to be God's image. How should the church be God's image?

In order for the church to be the image of God, Volf emphasizes the analogical relation between the inner communion of the triune God and the communal identity of the Christian community. Just as "three persons in one divinity exist so intimately with, for and in one another by the power of the eternal love," so also is the church as a community with different gifts exists by the power of reciprocal love (Eph 4:15; 1 Cor 12:1–31).[50] The triune God's mutual abiding in one another is the model for the church's mutual participation in the life of God. The church does not exist only through the narrow offices of ordained ministers and elite leaders, but through the life of all its members. The Spirit does not constitute the church exclusively only through ordained pastors and elite leaders, but through all grassroots members who share different gifts (1 Pet 4:10–11).[51] Just as the triune God treats each other member justly, so must the church members treat each other equally.

Grassroots Christians do not articulate the doctrine of the Trinity, but they embody the communal life of the Trinity. One grassroots pastor said, "We did not know much about doctrine and understood little of the teaching on key aspects of the faith such as the Holy Spirit or the Trinity."[52] They prefer an experiential embodiment of the Trinity through the communion of the church rather than a doctrinal reflection on faith.[53] Participating in the interim mission of Jesus's incarnation and *parousia*, the role of the

---

47. Volf, *After Our Likeness*.
48. Volf, *After Our Likeness*, x.
49. Volf, *After Our Likeness*, x.
50. Volf, *After Our Likeness*, 210.
51. Volf, *After Our Likeness*, 152.
52. Ki, *From Darkness to Glorious Light*, 95.
53. Ross, "Hybridity among the Chin of Myanmar," 167–85; at 176–77.

church is "to keep alive the memory of the crucified Christ and to anticipate His coming again."[54] Volf writes:

> To believe means to enjoy communion with God. Faith is not, however, merely the flight of the lonely to the lonely. Because the Christian God is not a lonely God, but rather a communion of the three persons, faith leads human beings into the divine communion. One cannot, however, have a self-enclosed communion with the triune God—a "foursome," as it were—for the Christian God is not a private deity. Communion with this triune God is at once also communion with those others who have entrusted themselves in faith to the same God. Hence one and the same act of faith places a person into a new relationship both with God and with all others who stand in communion with God.[55]

While Volf focuses on the analogical relationship between the communion of the Trinity and the communion of the church, Yong focuses on the relationship between different gifts of the Spirit and multiple witnesses of the Christ-like and Spirit-led church. Yong describes how:

> From a Pentecostal perspective, we have already seen that there is no one form of political, economic, or social engagement in global Pentecostalism. Rather there is a multiplicity of pentecostalisms in the global south, with distinct orientation toward the political, broadly construed. The preliminary biblical explorations provided in this chapter suggests that the many tongues of Pentecost, precisely because they represent a diversity of ethnic, linguistic, and cultural experiences, also imply the redemption of many political practices.[56]

The task of the church is not only to gather for the ontological communion with God, but also to scatter for the public and prophetic witness of God in public life. Just as the immanent and the economic Trinity are inseparable, so must the church hold its inner vocation or doxological identity and its dialogical or external vocation in tension.[57] We will explore how the

---

54. Volf, *After Our Likeness.*, x.
55. Volf, *After Our Likeness.*, 173.
56. See Yong, *In the Days of Caesar*, 99–111; Yong, *The Spirit Poured Out*, 110.
57. Martin Luther argues that all Christians have a twofold vocation—"spiritual vocation in the church and external vocation in society," see Max Weber, *The Protestant Ethics and the Spirit of Capitalism*, 80.

economic Trinity serves as the model for the church's dialogical witness of social engagement (withness) in public life beyond the life of the church.[58]

The Economic Trinity and the Engaged Church

John 20:21–22 and Matthew 18:19–20 may be taken as the touchstones for the relation between God's economic mission to the world through the Son and by the power of the Spirit and the apostolic public mission of the church for and to the world.[59] When the economic trinity turns to the world, Jesus is the witness of God (John 14:9–10; Col 1:15). When Jesus calls and commissions his disciples, they become the witnesses of Jesus. Acts 1:8 indicates the cross-cultural and public dimension of the apostolic witness.[60] In this text, Jesus said, "But you will receive power when the Holy Spirit comes on you; and you will be my witnesses in Jerusalem, and in all Judea and Samaria, and to the ends of the earth." This text stresses two things: (1) the Holy Spirit empowers the disciples of Jesus, and (2) the Spirit-empowered disciples witness about the life and work of Jesus.

In fact, Jesus had first sent women to tell the good news of his resurrection before he sent his male disciples. After his resurrection, Jesus appeared first to Mary Magdalene and other women to tell his male disciples about his resurrection (Matt 28:5–9; Mark 16:9). The gospel was carried out by Jesus' disciples who were Jewish. They witnessed to Jesus across ethnic barriers. In my approach to the church's public witnesses in Asia, I emphasize the inclusive roles of males and females. Darrell Guder said, "what God has accomplished through Christ by the Spirit remains connected with how he will accomplish through the church."[61] Now the question is no longer *why* the church should engage with the world, but *how* it should engage with the world where God is at work.

Spiritual Powers: Pastoral Public Witness of Anthropos-Healing

Overemphasizing political powers, Asian theologians, like their counterpart Western theologians, do not address spiritual powers and their

---

58. See, for instance, Volf, "The Trinity Is Our Social Program," 403–23.

59. Keener, *The Gospel of John*, 1203–6; Moe, "The Word to the World," 68–85.

60. Bosch, *Transforming Mission*," 9–50; Walls, *The Cross-Cultural Process in Christian History*, 3–26.

61. Guder, *Be My Witness*, 20.

implications for the pastoral public witness of healing the spirit-possessed sick. The pastoral witness of prayer and healing plays a key role in a priestly response to spiritual powers in Asia.[62] I am proposing that we should reconsider "pastors as public theologians."[63] Public theology is not confined to those who academically theologize about public issues, but it encompasses lay pastors who experientially witness to the healing gospel.[64] If a lived public theology is to be done at the grassroots level, we must rethink seriously the priestly role of pastoral witness in healing the sick from spiritual powers (Mark 13:22; Matt 7:22f; 2 Thess 2:9).

The grassroots pastoral witness of healing the spirit-possessed sick in the twenty-first century echoes Jesus's public mission of exorcising and healing the sick in the first century (Matt 10:8; Luke 4:31–37). Jesus' public ministry of healing the sick becomes what Craig Keener calls "the credibility of the New Testament accounts of Miracle."[65] As an American New Testament scholar, Keener is writing to his fellow Western people who do not believe in the miracles of healing the spirit-possessed sick. In his book *From Darkness into Glorious Light*, a grassroots Pentecostal pastor Tam Ki provides evidence of his pastoral witness of healing the spirit-possessed sick in the remote villages of Myanmar. Ki was both the victim of the spirit and later the healer of the spirit-possessed sick.[66]

While public theologians tend to focus on the prophetic role of Jesus for their political witness of social justice, grassroots Christians focus on the priestly and atoning role of Jesus. A grassroots notion of salvation is rooted in Christ the victor and the reconciler models (Rom 4:25; 1 Cor 15:3–5; Heb 9:23–28).[67] A pastor explained:

> During the [Easter] gathering, Pa Za Mung, preached using these words, for God so loved the world that he gave his only begotten Son, the Lord Jesus, to be born into this world to redeem lost souls who are precious in his sight. He has indeed given eternal life to those who believe in him (John 3:36). At this Easter, we celebrate the resurrection of Christ. Easter! It was a completely new festival

---

62. See, for instance, Yung, *Mangoes or Bananas?*, 230.
63. Stackhouse, "Pastor as Public Theologian," 106–29.
64. Interview with grassroots Christian leaders, by the author, July 19–21, 2020.
65. Keener, *Miracles*. See also Fox, *Disability and the Way of Jesus*.
66. See Ki, *From Darkness to Glorious Light*.
67. Grassroots Christian leaders, interviewed by the author, July 19–August 25, 2020.

for us. During this first Easter, we learned about the Lord's works of redemption for sinners on Good Friday.[68]

Grassroots Christians' understanding of the gospel is centered in the atoning work of Jesus. The gospel for them is good news because of what Jesus has done on the cross. Their notion of the gospel as good news resonates with N. T. Wright's theological definition of the gospel. Why is the gospel good news and what makes the gospel good? In his popular book *Simply Good News*,[69] Wright states the early Christian concept of the gospel as good news:

> The Messiah died for our sins in accordance with the Bible; he was buried; he was raised on the third day in accordance with the Bible; he was seen by Cephas, then by the Twelve; then he was seen by over five hundred brothers and sisters at once, most of whom are still with us, though some fell asleep (1 Cor 15:3–6). Yes, the good news is indeed about Jesus, and about his death and resurrection in particular. Yes, this is good news does indeed open up a vision of an ultimate future beyond death, so that we live in hope and joy meanwhile.[70]

Grassroots Christian witnesses to the gospel of salvation have more to do with proclaiming the power of Jesus's victory over spiritual powers, the power of healing the sick, and the gospel of salvation as forgiveness of sinners.[71] They refer to God's power as the consequence of Jesus's victory over devils and as the Holy Spirit's empowering act of miracles in their lives.[72] Sometimes, they focus too much on their own power of healing the sick rather than the power of the true healer (Jesus). Nevertheless, they rightly see themselves as the public witnesses of the gospel of healing in the context of spiritual powers. A grassroots pastor who shared the gospel of healing in the public rallies said:

> As I became more accustomed to venturing into the nearby *pigaw* [villages] to share the *Htu Ni* [Good News], I realized that a loudspeaker was a powerful tool for open-air evangelistic rallies. Too many people living in remote *pigaw gui* [village compatriots] located deep in the mountains of South Chin State, the loudspeaker

68. Ki, *From Darkness to Glorious Light*, 40–41.
69. Wright, *Simply Good News*.
70. Wright *Simply Good News*, 5, 23.
71. Ki, *From Darkness to Glorious Light*, 23–30.
72. Ki, *From Darkness to Glorious Light*, 44–45.

was a completely foreign invention. I would rent one to take a long with me on my trips. Curious onlookers gathered around me just to hear the loudspeaker. The seeds of the *Htu Ni* were sown into the hearts of many.[73]

The goal of sharing the gospel in the context of spiritual powers, according to grassroots Christians, is to heal and convert people. They are inclined to treat spirit-worship as a mere negative religious practice and attempt to replace it with Christianity. Their understanding of Christ and spiritual culture echoes H. Richard Niebuhr's first typology of "Christ against Culture."[74] A lay pastor who was converted from the spiritual culture said:

> One day, there was a spirit worship ceremony near my home. When it came to offering the animal sacrifice, the *pigaw* (village) elders wanted me to perform the role of *tai gui tung* [priest]. I flatly rejected them. So, they forced Mana Ling Mana, another distant uncle, to undertake the ritual. He took it on grudgingly, afraid of putting his family under threat from the unpredictable spirits. But he held me responsible for his predicament. After the ceremony, it was suggested that this proxy high priest should approach me to some kind of donation to the costs of the ceremony. He angrily marched to my home and sensing that there was going to be a confrontation, the crowd followed. Mana Ling called out, "Tam Ki, come out! We have come to collect a donation." I refused to donate anything, saying I am now a servant of God and I don't belong to the spirits anymore.[75]

Grassroots Christians' notion of the spirits needs to be reformulated from the perspective of contextual imagination. The gospel is to be built on culture, not to be built against it. There are both negative and positive elements in spirit-worship or *nat*-worship. *Nat* came from the Sanskrit word *nath*, which means spirit or lord.[76] The negative element is that people worship spirits out of fear. There are malevolent spirits and benevolent spirits.[77] People worship the spirits for their mundane lives. *Nat*-worship is seen as a primal religion because it is native in Asian soil prior to the arrivals of Christianity, Islam, Buddhism, and other world religions. When Buddhism

---

73. Ki, *From Darkness to Glorious Light*, 70–71.
74. Niebuhr, *Christ and Culture*, 45–82.
75. Ki, *From Darkness to Glorious Light*, 43–44.
76. Aung, *Folk Elements in Burmese Buddhism*, 2.
77. En, *Nat Worship*, 67–69.

was introduced to Southeast Asian countries from India during the first, second, and third centuries, spirit-worship was already a native religion across Southeast Asia.[78]

When Buddhism was introduced to Myanmar from India through the Indian emperor Ashoka, Anawrathar (1014–77), the first king of Myanmar, forced people to replace *nat*-worship with Buddhism as a national religion. They were unwilling to abandon spirit-worship. They chose to integrate Buddhism into *nat*-worship.[79] Bamar Buddhists worship both the Buddha and *Nat*. They worship the Buddha for their future and *Nat* for their mundane lives. Buddhists put Buddha shrines alongside the *Nat* shrines at their houses. Ethnic minorities have more negative perception of spirit-worship. They have no interest in integrating Christianity into *nat*-worship.[80] Some grassroots people in Asia have a lot to say about the spirits. They live in a religious community where the spirits and they share space. The spirits are known as *bons* in Tibet, *devas* in India, *nats* in Myanmar, *phis* in Thailand, Laos, and Cambodia, *kami* in Japan, and *kalash* in Pakistan.[81] Two positive things about the primal religion could be applied for lived public theology of religions.

Primal Religion and Public Witness of Eco-Healing

First, a primal religion shapes an Asian holistic worldview. Western ways of thinking are dualistic in terms of a "spiritual–material and a God–creation dichotomy,"[82] while Asian ways are non-dualistic.[83] Yet not all Asian religions are non-dualistic. Buddhism is a dualistic religion in terms of its dimension of this-worldly and otherworldly existence.[84] Only a primal religion is non-dualistic. If an Asian public theology's task is to engage personal and public life, a primal religious worldview could transform Asian Christians' uncritical adoption of Western dualistic worldview of sacred–secular dichotomy and anthropos–cosmos salvation dichotomy. Salvation is not

---

78. Lester, *Theravada Buddhism in Southeast Asia*, 1–8.

79. Aung, *Folk Elements in Burmese Buddhism*, 1.

80. Moe, "Paul Tillich and Nat-Worship," 123–36.

81. See Haire, "Stories in Animism and Christian Pneumatology," 119–35.

82. Smith, *The Faith of Other Men*, 74. Smith acknowledges that "we in the west presume that an intelligent must choose either this or that."

83. Lee, "The Yin-Yang Way of Thinking," 81–88. Chan, *Grassroots Asian Theology*, 9.

84. Pieris, *An Asian Theology of Liberation*, 71–81.

merely one dimension of human redemption but interconnected between anthropos and cosmos healing (Rom 8:19–22; Col 1:20).

Second, a primal religion plays a key role in an Asian public theology of eco-healing. Christians should reconsider seriously the public mission of creation care in light of God's first commission of humans (Gen 1:28). If we do so, we would appreciate the role of Christians and the primal religious adherents in eco-healing. The primal religion plays an ethical role in veneration of creation.[85] Since nature-spirits are powerful in their jurisdiction, they do not tolerate human trespass.[86] Neither shooting animals nor cutting trees is permissible in the vicinity. Farmers must first give an offering to the spirits, asking permission for their undertakings. The failure to appease the spirits brings misfortunate to those who trespass. Even after asking permission from the spirits to use natural resources, no one is allowed to take more than necessary. This is relevant for Asian peasants.[87]

It is a challenge to tell the peasants about the ecological issues. They think of all creation as God's gifts to be used by humans at any time for any purpose related to farming. To convince them, we need to engage their grassroots understanding of the spirits as the guardians of creation. There are spirits everywhere with their territorial names, such as *taw-sauk nat* (forest guardian), *le-sauk nat* (farm guardian), *myit-sauk nat* (river guardian), *thitpin-sauk nat* (tree guardian), and *ein-sauk nat* (house guardian).[88] This naming of guardians is analogous to the purpose of God's creation of humans as the guardians of creation not as the destroyers. God gives humans the authority of dominion over creation, but after the fall (Gen 3), they become sinful destroyers of creation. Spirit-worship should be utilized as source for the preservation of creation. Spirits have no power to create the world, but their benevolence is analogous to the Spirit's continued work of sustaining the groaning nature (Rom 8:21).

Political Powers: Prophetic Witness of Speaking Truth

In their book *Jesus and the Powers*, N. T. Wright and Michael Bird explore the global politics of powers in different forms of nationalism, totalitarianism, and dictatorship, and suggest creative ways how the church should

---

85. Haire, "Stories in Animism and Christian Pneumatology," 120–30.
86. Spiro, *Burmese Supernaturalism*, 42.
87. En, "Nat-Worship," 43–53.
88. En, "Nat Worship," 46. See also Aung, *Folk Elements in Burmese Buddhism*, 2–5.

become the prophetic voice for confronting political powers. They argue that building for Jesus's kingdom requires the church's engagement in confronting political powers.[89] Their suggestion is a kingdom-centered biblical political/public theology that sees political powers as opposition to Jesus's kingdom of justice and peace. Using Jesus's kingdom as a theological foundation and the Bible as source, they demonstrate how the prophets in the Old Testament and Jesus and his disciples in the New Testament faithfully resist political powers.[90] Wright and Bird wrote:

> The Christian vocation is neither pious longing for heaven nor scheming to make Jesus king by exerting force over unwilling subjects. Instead, Christians should be ready to speak truth to power, being concerned with the righteous exercise of government, seeing it bent towards the arc of justice and fulfilling the service that God expects of governing authorities.[91]

Wright and Bird emphasize that "Jesus is King, and Jesus's kingdom is the object" of the church's prophetic witness of speaking truth to powers or evils that combat Jesus's kingdom of justice, truth, and freedom. Speaking truth to powers is central for Christian political witness.[92] The prominent Old Testament scholar Walter Brueggemann also observes that speaking truth to powers is central for the prophetic witness. In his book *Interrupting Silence*,[93] Brueggemann states that the ancient prophets are the "silence breakers." According to him, God's command to the prophets is to break silence and speak truth to powers.[94] The Hebrew Bible is filled with stories where marginalized people break repressive silence and speaking against it. Since maintaining silence allows the powers to keep control, prophetic Christians must break silence and speak out against powers.

Developing the prophetic witness of speaking truth to power in the Western context, Brueggemann, Wright, and Bird, encourage the prophetic church's direct confrontation against powers. They do not pause to ask how the church should cooperate with people of other faiths in speaking out

---

89. Wright and Bird, *Jesus and the Powers*, 122–49.

90. Wright and Bird, *Jesus and the Powers*, 64–65.

91. Wright and Bird, *Jesus and the Powers*, xv.

92. Wright and Bird, *Jesus and the Powers*, 64–65; Wright, *God in Public*; Wright, *Evil and the Justice of God*.

93. Brueggemann, *Interrupting Silence*.

94. Brueggemann, *Interrupting Silence*, 84. For the role of political theology in the Hebrew Bible, see Brett, *Locations of God*.

together against powers. I will emphasize the interreligious prophetic witness in the context of Asia.

In order to speak truth to powers and seek justice, it would be helpful to learn how political powers cause the politics of economic exploitation and poverty. Take Myanmar for an example. Myanmar is a rich country, blessed with natural resources, such as jade, timber, and rice. The Burmese historian Thant Myint-U unlocked the hidden history that "in the 1920s, Myanmar was richer than the rest of British India. The Burmese were healthier and better fed, enjoyed far higher rates of literary, and commanded bigger incomes than the average person in India."[95] For a period in the 1920s, millions of people from some neighboring nations (India and China) migrated to Myanmar for a new and better life—not just laborers but businessmen and professionals as well. Some returned to their nations, but many stayed on. Because of its welcoming millions of immigrants into the nation, Myanmar was known as "first America" in the words of Indian-American writer Mira Kamdar.[96] Yangon once rivaled New York as the biggest immigrant port in the world.[97]

But after the first regime took powers in 1962, the nation became poor. Ordinary people suffered from extreme poverty, and suffering (*dukkha*) has become a commonly spoken word of people to express their experience. *Pyithu-dukkha* is a combination of two Burmese words—*Pyithu* (mass) and *dukkha* (suffering). Put together, it means the "suffering mass of people."[98] The term *dukkha* has no boundary, and it can be heard and seen in every economic milieu. Melford Spiro stated:

> *Dukkha* is the most frequently used term in the Burmese context; it is on everyone's lips at work, at school, in the house, on a trip. For the Burmese, as for the rest of humankind, the notion that life involves suffering is not an article of faith; it is datum of everyday experience.[99]

The term *dukkha* leads us to a theological question of why ordinary people in Myanmar are economically poor if the country is rich in natural resources. In her book *Freedom from Fear*,[100] Aung San Suu Kyi, the Noble

95. Myint-U, *The Hidden History of Burma*, 18.
96. Kamdar, *Motiba's Tatoos*, 123.
97. Myint-U, *The Hidden History of Burma*, 18.
98. For a full definition of this term, see Moe: *Pyithu-Dukkha Theology*, 4–9.
99. Spiro, *Buddhism and Society*, 74.
100. Suu Kyi, *Freedom from Fear*.

Beyond the Academy

Peace laureate, gives us an answer. She argues that the ordinary people and the country's economic poverty are not to be understood as the result of their own *karma* or fate (the link between act and consequence), but as the result of the regime's misuse of powers. For her, "the people's economic suffering results much from the consequence of bad government."[101] If this is so, then what is the role of the church? Is it not one of speaking truth to corrupt powers by cooperating with ordinary Buddhists who share the same experience of economic corruption?

Religion and Resistance

There is an analogical relation between prophetic Christianity and engaged Buddhism under religion and resistance. People often misperceive Buddhism and Christianity as anti-political religions. The German sociologist Max Weber is known for his misperception of "Buddhism as an anti-political status religion" that divorces itself from political engagement.[102] Weber's view of Buddhism is unacceptable from the perspective of the anti-coup political movement in Myanmar. Buddhism is not merely a spiritual religion, but it is a political religion. The Vietnamese monk and activist Thich Nhat Hanh is credited for his coinage of the term "engaged Buddhism" in the 1960s.[103] His term "engaged Buddhism" describes the Buddhist political movements in Vietnam, India, and other parts of Asia.[104] Today some Gen-Z Burmese Buddhists echo "engaged Buddhism" in their ongoing quest for liberation movement from the Buddhist military coup as *adharma* (evil).[105]

On the other hand, some grassroots Christians in Asia focus more on their spiritual relationship with God. Brueggemann's *The Prophetic Imagination* serves as a correction for a balanced understanding of Christianity as a prophetic religion.[106] Brueggemann argues that the first task of the prophetic church is to provide a prophetic imagination; its second task is to actualize that prophetic imagination into a prophetic implementation. Prophetic imagination and the embrace of pathos must come first before

---

101. Suu Kyi, *Freedom from Fear*, 170.
102. Weber, *The Religion of India*, 206.
103. See Queen, "Introduction," 1–44.
104. Queen, "Introduction," 2.
105. Jordt et al., *How Generation Z Galvanized a Revolutionary Movement against Myanmar's 2021 Military Coup*, 7.
106. Brueggemann, *The Prophetic Imagination*.

the implementation. Linking Moses to Jeremiah and Jesus, Brueggemann observes that the prophetic imagination not only embraces the pathos of the people, but it resists powers.[107] Although grassroots Christians recognize the prophetic element of Christianity, they focus more on a foretelling prophecy rather than a forthtelling prophecy.

When regime rulers misuse their powers, truth is the victim. Thus, the task of the prophetic church is to speak truth to powers with courage. Courage is what it takes to stand up and speak out against powers. The goal is to expose the deceptions of powers and to transform the unjust systems they cause. Speaking truth to powers in the context of the regime is not without challenges. There is the challenge of preforming the public witness of prophetic faith. In Western democratic contexts, it is easier to critique political powers publicly. That is not the case in Myanmar and other dictatorial nations. In non-democratic contexts where life is highly risky, the public witness of faith is not the only option. A public theology is not just about the public and open witness of faith, then: it is also about the hidden and symbolic witness of faith.

In his influential book *Domination and the Arts of Resistance*, Yale political scientist and Southeast Asianist James Scott, coined the term "hidden transcript," to describe hidden resistance as an alternative witness of faith under the regime.[108] It was during his fieldwork among the peasants in a Malay village (1978–80) that Scott observed the hidden resistance by subjugated groups. He observed how:

> Every subordinate group creates, out of ordeal, a hidden transcript that represents a critique of power spoken behind the back of the dominant. The powerful, for their part, also develop a hidden transcript representing the practices and claims of their rule that cannot be openly vowed. A comparison of the hidden transcript of the weak with that of powerful and of both hidden transcripts to the public transcript of power relations offers a substantially new way of understanding resistance to domination.[109]

Scott insists that there is no single form of resistance. There are various forms of everyday resistance—some are open, and others remain hidden.[110] New Testament scholars find Scott's theory helpful for their transformative

---

107. Brueggemann, *The Prophetic Imagination*, 40–41.
108. Scott, *Domination and the Arts of Resistance*, 1–16.
109. Scott, *Domination and the Arts of Resistance*, xii.
110. Scott, *Weapons of the Weak*, 37–41.

understanding of how Jesus, Paul, and the disciples witnessed to their faith under the empire. Richard Horsey, who edited *Hidden Transcripts and The Arts of Resistance* that engages Scott's work, acknowledges that "Scott's analysis of resistance is not only innovative and insightful, but opens to view aspects of resistance that previously went unnoticed in academic investigation."[111]

Using Scott's theory, I suggest that Paul's Rom 13:1–7 be read as a "hidden transcript of public theology." What is hidden in this text is that Paul did not say anything about the role of the church when the state misused its powers. Paul just said, "be subject to the ruling authorities" (13:1). There is debate about Paul's attitude toward the empire. We should read Romans 13:1–7 through the lens of Romans 12:9 ("love what is good, hold fast to what is evil"). This way of reading enables us to see Paul not as a political quietist who blesses the empire, but rather a hidden sort of a prophetic theologian who resists the empire in a hidden way. Horsley argues that "just because Paul did not organize attacks on Roman officials does not mean that he was a social conservative with regard to the Roman imperial order."[112] Similarly, N. T. Wright argues that Paul remains indirect with his anti-imperial attacks so as not to encourage his congregations to an outright revolution.[113]

Scott's theory is relevant to the Christian–Buddhist's everyday resistance to the coup. Their resistances are hidden, public, symbolic tattooing, and open forms of social movements, ranging from the private and public prayers through online blessings to singing of the protest Christian and non-Christian songs. *Kabar Ma Kyay Bu* (translated as "We will not forget until the end of the world"), has become one of the most popular anti-coup songs and "three-finger salute" from "The Hunger Games" movies, has become a symbol of resistance at protests in Myanmar. *Kabar Ma Kyay Bu* is a song commemorating Myanmar's 1988 revolutionary movement. Anti-coup protesters across the nation sang this anthem and chanted democracy and justice for Myanmar.[114]

111. Horsley, "Introduction—Jesus, Paul, and the Arts of Resistance," 1–28.

112. Horsley, "Introduction—Jesus, Paul, and the Arts of Resistance," 7; Horsley, *Paul and Politics*.

113. Wright, *Paul and the Faithfulness of God*, 13–15; Wright, "Paul's Gospel and Caesar's Empire," 42–65.

114. Bociaga and Regan, "Myanmar protesters getting permeant symbols of resistance—tattoos," in *CNN*, March 9, 2011, https://www.cnn.com/style/article/myanmar-tattoo-protest-intl-hnk/index.html [accessed March 14, 2024].

They struggle for removing the coup from political leadership and for restoring democracy as freedom. Myanmar was once one of the "fastest-developing [sic] nations in Southeast Asia" before the first regime took power in 1962.[115] In order to take back its early promise as one of the most energetic nations in Asia, people must struggle for democracy.[116] Before the new coup, Suu Kyi had sought to think through the ethical role of Buddhism in defining the moral duties of the rulers. The ten duties of the rulers are:

> *Liberality*, which demands the rulers' generous contribution to the welfare of the people and nation; *morality*, which demands the rulers' moral character to win the respect and trust of people; *self-sacrifice*, which demands the rulers' removal of their egocentric mind for the service of their fellow citizens; *integrity*, which demands the rulers' government with truth both in public and private official affairs; *kindness*, which demands the rulers' compassionate concern for the poor and marginalized in society; *austerity*, which demands the rulers' spiritual discipline; the seventh, eighth, and ninth roles of the rulers are *non-anger, non-violence, and patience*, and the tenth role of the rulers is *non-opposition* to the public consent of the "ordinary people who may oppose to the government rulers at any time if the rulers fail to practice the previous nine duties.[117]

A reading of these duties makes it clear that Buddhism is not a religion that endorses selfish and power-hungry action in society. Buddhism has a democratic vision of personal and communal well-being and peace.[118] In the context where the rulers misuse religion, we must approach religion paradoxically: the amoral role of Buddhism in oppression and violence and a moral role of Buddhism in democracy and peace. In order to achieve a religion-shaped democracy of justice, peace, and freedom, we must understand the Buddhist and Christian moral concepts of democracy and peace. The Sri Lankan Buddhist R. S. S. Gunewardene declared that Buddhism is democratic and that its emphasis on self-reliance supports democratic values:

> Democracy is not something new in Asia and is not Western-imposed as many people in the West used to think. . . . Democracy is inherent in the very principles of Buddhism. . . . Tolerance,

---

115. Suu Kyi, *Freedom from Fear*, 168–73.
116. Suu Kyi, *Freedom from Fear*, 168.
117. Suu Kyi, *Freedom from Fear*, 170–73. Italics are original.
118. Harris, "The Cost of Peace," 149–62.

> individual freedom and responsibility, the spirit of understanding, the value of individual and collective service, all these constitute a part of the Buddhist philosophy of life.[119]

Our concern here is not with how we impose Buddhism on democracy, but with how we save moral Buddhism by rediscovering its ethics for shaping a public vision of democracy in a Buddhist nation.[120] Using Buddhism as a source for shaping a moral vision of democracy is helpful in speaking truth to the regime who misuse their powers to cause suffering and poverty. The aim of using Buddhist ethics is to transform Buddhist undemocratic systems and behaviors from within their religious ethics. Instead of adopting a Western liberal democracy model, we use the Buddhist ethics of compassion as a local source for a democratic vision of liberation that is aimed not just at the political elite but at the grassroot levels.

The Apostolic Public Witness of Social Charity

Theologians limit the scope of Asian theology to a prophetic and liberative paradigm of social justice and often ignore social charity. For them, the church's political engagement in confronting powers is the only relevant paradigm of Asian public theology. "Anything else, even if it has an impact on social transformation in society is not explicitly considered a theology of social engagement."[121] R. S. Sugirtharajah criticizes pastoral charity work:

> In its overzealousness to represent the poor, liberation hermeneutics has ended up as a liberation theology of the poor rather a theology of liberation by the poor. The goal now is not social change, but pastoral concern. Political activism is replaced with the church's traditional concern for good work and charity projects.[122]

While the prophetic witness of resisting political powers for social change is imperative in the context of domination, we cannot ignore the apostolic witness of social charity for the victims. The church has a twofold task of social engagement: the prophetic witness of resistance to the oppressors and the apostolic witness of social charity for the victims. As a prophetic and apostolic voice, the church must stand in solidarity with the victims

---

119. Gunewardene, "South and Southeast Asia Look at the United States," 21.
120. See, for instance, Turner, *Saving Buddhism*, 106–9.
121. Chan, *Grassroots Asian Theology*, 35.
122. Sugirtharajah, *Postcolonial Criticism and Biblical Interpretation*, 115.

and resist their oppressors. The prophetic witness of resistance speaks truth to power with courage for social change, while the apostolic witness of social charity extends hands of compassion to the victims. Social change takes time, but social charity requires immediate action. We cannot wait for social change. Otherwise, victims would die.

The public mission of social charity is rooted in both the Old Testament and the New Testament. Psalm 10:5–9 states the conditions of people who need charity. Likewise, Matthew 25:35–36 is known for Jesus's teaching about social charity. Jesus said: "for I was hungry, and you gave me food, I was thirsty, and you gave me something to drink, I was a stranger and you welcomed me, I was naked, and you gave me clothing, I was sick and you took care of me, I was in prison and you visited me." Seeing himself as the victim, Jesus emphasizes that what we did to the needy is tantamount to what we did to him (25:40–41).

This shows the relationship between orthodoxy (personal faith in Jesus) and orthopraxy (public action for Jesus). Social charity was central to the apostolic faith and action of the early Christian community. Acts 2:45 said, "the disciples of Jesus Christ sold property and possessions to give to anyone who had need." In his commentary on *Acts*,[123] Keener noted that "The sharing of possessions is a central (perhaps because so distinctive) feature of Luke's vision of the early Christian community formed by the Spirit, leading to a wide impact on the society around them."[124] For Keener, a core part of Luke's portrait of the faith of the early church is its sharing of possessions with those in need. Luke focuses on the healing aspect of social charity.[125] Above all, the Lukan account of the Good Samaritan's act of social charity and of crossing ethnic barriers (10:25–37) indicates the concept that Christian individuals and communities must practice public witness of social charity.

Social charity is central not only to the Christian tradition, but also to the Buddhist tradition. In her comparative study of *Karma* and *Grace*, the Sri Lankan scholar Neena Mahadev explores their cultural practice of social charity. According to Mahadev, there are some similar and distinct kinds of charity among Buddhists and Christians.[126] One distinction about the act of charity between Buddhists and Christians is this: Buddhists practice

---

123. Keener, *ACTS*.
124. Keener, *ACTS*, 992.
125. Keener, *ACTS*, 1012.
126. Mahadev, *Karma and Grace*, 79–82.

charity as a path toward salvation, while Christians practice charity as the result of receiving God's grace from an external force. While Christianity teaches that salvation comes through the gracious act of Jesus, Buddhism teaches that people must work out their salvation (enlightenment) through their own efforts.

Buddhism teaches men and women to trust themselves and summon their powers within them to achieve their goals in life. Meditation and donation (*dana*) become two of the most important efforts in their salvation. For their better future Buddhists must accumulate merit in the present life, such as almsgiving to the monks, donations to the poor, abstaining from immorality, and protecting others from harm.[127] In a contemporary example, some anti-coup Buddhists generously extend social charity to thousands of the victims. Despite extreme poverty, Burmese Buddhists are rich in social charity. In her book *Culture of Giving in Myanmar*, Hiroko Kawanami helpfully explores how the Buddhist religious doctrine of compassion shapes their charitable practices for the society.[128]

Like Buddhists, some grassroots Christians are also among the most charitable people. The work of some grassroots church leaders performing the mission of charity in slum areas is scarcely noticed. And their works of charity are likely to have made a much greater impact on healing many wounded victims than the work of liberation theologians in the academy.[129] Among those whom I interviewed are those working at the Internally Displaced People (IDPs) camps. Some of them perform their apostolic and generous faith by visiting the victims at the camps and prisoners by providing food, drink, clothes, medicine, and shelter.[130]

The first response to the humanitarian crisis is not about debating the doctrine of God in abstract ways[131] but about embodying the compassionate heart of God by extending social charity to wounded victims. Many grassroots Christians extend social charity to those who are the victims

---

127. Lorgunpai, "The Book of Ecclesiastes and Thai Buddhism," 155–62.

128. See Kawanami, *Culture of Giving in Myanmar*.

129. Yong recognizes the church's charity works of what he calls "subsidiary and solidarity" for the well-being of people as contributions to political/public theology, Yong, *In the Days of Caesar*, 389–95.

130. Pastors and practitioners interviewed, by the author, July 19, 2020, March 9, 2021.

131. Wee, "Thousands Flee Myanmar for India amid Fears of a Growing Refugee Crisis," in *The New York Times*. https://www.nytimes.com/2021/10/19/world/asia/myanmar-refugees-india.html, [accessed January 17, 2022].

of the coup. They donate money to individuals and families of those who have lost their work through their participation in the Civil Disobedience Movement (CDM). The *CDM* is the first effective strategy of prophetic resistance to the coup. Hundreds of thousands of civil servants, such as medics, engineers, nurses, schoolteachers, and general workers in the train stations joined the *CDM* with the high commitment of refusing to get salaries from the illegitimate military. The *CDM* is not only an anti-coup social campaign, but a potential foundation from which to replace the coup-controlled administration.[132]

The Intercultural Witness of Reconciliation and Hospitality

The gospel of reconciliation is at the heart of Jesus's kingdom mission and Paul's cross-cultural mission among Jews and Gentiles (2 Cor 5:18–20).[133] Karl Barth, for instance, places the doctrine of reconciliation in a central role of Christian theology.[134] Public theologians focus on the kingdom of God as the main foundation for their public witness of political liberation, while grassroots Christians focus on the gospel of reconciliation as the key content of their public witness. As we have seen, their grassroots witness of reconciliation has more to do with proclaiming the spiritual and vertical aspect of reconciliation rather than the social and horizontal aspect of ethnic reconciliation. We need to witness to the relational dimensions of reconciliation, liberation, and hospitality from interreligious perspectives.[135]

In his book *Reconciliation and Liberation*, Jan Lochman argues that a one-dimensional view of salvation needs to be challenged for the purpose of applying reconciliation and liberation in contexts of conflict and hostility.[136] In order to illustrate this view, the Lukan parable of the good Samaritan (Luke 10:25–37) can be seen as a paradigm for a lived public theology of ethnic reconciliation, liberation, and hospitality.[137] In his *Jesus*

---

132. Anonymous, "The Centrality of the Civil Disobedience Movement in Myanmar's Post-Coup Era," in *Mandala*, https://www.newmandala.org/the-centrality-of-the-civil-disobedience-movement-in-myanmars-post-coup-era/ [accessed December 1, 2021].

133. See Keener, "Some New Testament Invitations to Ethnic Reconciliation," 195–213; Constantineau, *The Social Significance of Reconciliation in Paul's Theology*; Porter, "Reconciliation as the Heart of Paul's Missionary Theology," 169–79.

134. Barth, *Church Dogmatics*.

135. See Gort et al., *Religion, Conflict, and Reconciliation*.

136. Lochman, *Reconciliation and Liberation*.

137. See, for instance, Marshall, "Parables as Paradigms for a Public Theology," 23–44.

through Middle Eastern Eyes, Kenneth Bailey, who had a rich personal experience and ethnographic knowledge of the peasant culture where Jesus delivered his parables said, "the parable of the good Samaritan is famous for its ethics."[138] This study will now turn to the key implications of the ethics of this parable.

The methodological reading of the parable reveals some contrasts. While Asian liberationists, such as *minjung* theologians Ahn Byung-Mu and Suh Nam Dong depict the victim in the parable as the primary agent who embodies Jesus's suffering,[139] grassroots social charity workers and Asian intercultural theologians see the Samaritan as the primary agent who embodies Jesus's cross-cultural ministry.[140] I argue against emphasizing only one agent without embracing the other.[141] I wish to reconsider the neglected role of the third agent, that is the innkeeper in the parable. In order to apply a full contextual meaning of the parable for our contemporary Asian context, I argue that we should use a fresh methodology that rethinks the equal role of three agents in witnessing reconciliation, solidarity, and hospitality. The parables' setting within the question, "who is my neighbor?" and its exemplary witness of compassion allow it to become a "touchstone text" for reimagining neighbors and an intercultural ethics of ethnic reconciliation and solidarity.[142]

Since cross-cultural dimensions are involved in the parable, one should not confine it to the Christian tradition. It should be interpreted within a multicultural society. First-century Christian exhortation to the witness of ethnic reconciliation among majority Judeans and minority Samaritans remains relevant for our public vision of ethnic reconciliation in Asia, especially in Myanmar's conflictual context. In this concrete context, my approach is that the parable can be read through a paradigmatic method[143] that serves as a model for ethnic reconciliation, religious solidarity,

---

138. Bailey, *Jesus through the Eastern Middle Eyes*, 284.

139. Suh, *Exploring Minjung Theology*, 107; Ahn, *Talking about Minjung Theology*, 117–18.

140. See, for instance, Phan, *In Our Own Tongues*, 136–52; Phan, "Crossing the Borders," 8–19.

141. This first appeared in Moe, "A Cross-Cultural and Liberative Hermeneutics of Luke 10:25–37 in Asian and Asian-American Perspectives," 439–49.

142. See Powery, *The Good Samaritan*; Spencer, *The Political Samaritan*; Carter and Wells, *Who Is My Neighbor?*

143. For the paradigmatic readings, see Wright, *The Old Testament Ethics for the People of God*, 64; Gowler, *Host, Guest, Enemy, and Friend*, 246.

and generous hospitality.¹⁴⁴ It can then be interpreted through the contextual lenses of three social performers: the good Samaritan (a cross-cultural model for reimagining ethnic reconciling with neighbors), the wounded victim (a liberating model for social healing), and the welcoming innkeeper (a hospitable model for accepting the religio-ethnic other). This fresh reading of the parable represents a moral challenge to those whose experience has led them to draw religio-ethnic boundaries around the care and level of solidarity they are prepared to bestow.¹⁴⁵

The first model reads the parable through the lens of the good Samaritan. As George Forbes and I. Howard Marshall observed, the Samaritan was not only ethnically marginal, but he is also a despised indweller and religious other in the Jewish-dominant context.¹⁴⁶ His marginal identity shares similarity with the ethnic minorities in the context of Bamar Buddhist domination. E. P. Sanders and Brendan Byrne argue that compassion is central for a transformative relationship between the Samaritan and the victim. In the parable that Jesus uses to illustrate who is the neighbor is the one who shows compassion to the victim (10:34).¹⁴⁷ The religious elites—Levite and the Priest—saw the victim, but they did not help him because they lacked compassion (10:32–33). It was the Samaritan who crossed the ethnic barriers and extended the helping hand to the victim. The compassion-based reconciliation requires a transformative recognition of the other as neighbor by crossing one's religio-ethnic boundaries. In his *What the Buddha Taught*, Walpola Rahula said:

> According to Buddhism for a human to be perfect there are two qualities that he or she should develop equally: compassion (*karuna*) on one side, and wisdom (*pana*) on the other. Here compassion represents love, charity, kindness, tolerance, and such noble qualities on the emotional side, or qualities of the heart, while wisdom would stand for the intellectual side, or qualities of the mind. If one develops only the emotional neglecting the intellectual, one may become a good-hearted fool; while to develop only the intellectual

---

144. Moe, "A Cross-Cultural and Liberative Hermeneutics of Luke 10:25–37 in Asian and Asian-American Perspectives," 439–49.

145. I first presented this version at the meeting of Society of Biblical Literature's session of Asian and Asian American Hermeneutics Seminar, November 19, 2018, Denver, CO, USA. I also preached the sermons on this parable at Yale Divinity School's iconic Marquand chapel, on March 10, 2023.

146. Forbes, *The God of Old*, 63–64; Marshall, *Commentary on Luke*, 450.

147. Sanders, *The Historical Figure of Jesus*, 6; Byrne, *The Hospitality of God*, 101.

side neglecting the emotional may turn one into a hard-hearted intellect without feeling for others. Therefore, to be perfect one has to develop both equally. This is the aim of Buddhist way of life: in it wisdom and compassion are inseparably linked together.[148]

The Tibetan Buddhist monk and activist Dalai Lama also emphasizes that compassion (*karuna*) should be the key motive for responding to human suffering. It is his conviction that "living in society, we should share the sufferings of our fellow citizens and practice compassion and tolerance not only towards our loved ones but also towards our enemies."[149] In the past, religion played an exclusionary role in the politics of Myanmar. For example, when the Rohingya Muslims faced a crisis in 2017, some Christians did not share compassionate solidarity with them. However, the rise of the 2021 coup created an unexpected opportunity of witnessing to ethnic reconciliation and religious solidarity among the anti-coup protesters. Christians, Muslims, and other religio-ethnic communities reconciled their religious and ethnic differences to resist the violent coup as a common enemy.

Ethnic reconciliation and religious solidarity are not confined to religious leaders and elites: they can also be found among non-state ordinary people from the villages, towns, and cities. Christians were witnesses to ethnic reconciliation by extending charity to railroad workers across different religious and ethnic barriers when the military expelled them from their residences for joining the Civil Disobedience Movement. In Monywa, a Buddhist fruit seller embodied the good Samaritan by distributing her fruits to the protesters who joined sit-up protests. A Buddhist in Yangon donated her watermelons to thirsty protesters. In Yangon, a Hindu seller of fritters donated her food to protesters. In front of the Central Bank of Myanmar, a Hindu well-wisher donated her coconut juice to the protesters.[150]

The second model reads the parable through the lens of the one who was left on the side of the road "half dead" (10:30). He has undergone suffering. Moltmann wrote:

> The sufferings of Christ on the cross are not just His sufferings; they are the sufferings of the poor and the weak, which Jesus shares in His own body and His own soul, in solidarity with them (Heb. 2:16–18; 11:26; 13:13). Because of this, the sufferings of Christ are open for the sufferers still to come, both the men and women

148. Rahula, *What the Buddha Taught*, 46.
149. Cited in Pui-Lan, *Postcolonial Politics and Theology*, 169.
150. See Frydenlund, et al., "Religious Responses to the Military Coup in Myanmar," 77–88, at 79.

who suffer with Christ (Col. 1:24) and those with whom Christ will suffer—open for the sufferings of the martyrs for His new and kingdom, and for the coming apocalyptic sufferings which will fall upon all vulnerable creatures.[151]

According to Moltmann, the God who was in the crucified Christ is present among the suffering people. In a similar vein, Asian liberation theologians, such as C. S. Song, argue that the compassionate God is present among the suffering people.[152] In the parable the victim has no name; he is "a certain man" and there is no distinguishing reference to his ethnicity and religion. The Samaritan does not care about the victim's identity. His concern is to see the victim as a human neighbor in need.[153] One Karenni Christian expressed how "The challenge for the Karenni Christians is their exclusive act of extending charity to fellow Christians. They are less willing to extend charity to Buddhists."[154] The Samaritan's act of ethnic crossing to reach out to the victim as neighbor serves as a model for Christians' acts of ethnic crossing. For Joel Green, the Samaritan's act of neighborly love for the victim by crossing ethnic barriers is the main feature of the parable. Such neighborly love, he argues, "knows no boundary."[155] Likewise, Keener invites us to see the Samaritan's ethic of ethnic crossing as a model for the vision of contemporary ethnic reconciliation.[156]

We now turn to the third model. The relative neglect of the role of the innkeeper leaves the paradigmatic reading of the parable incomplete. The Greek word *pandocheion* is central for reading the parable through the lens of the innkeeper. *Pandocheion* has two meanings. One is that *pandocheion* states the generous act of charity. In a generous act of charity, the innkeeper healed the wounded victim by taking care of him (10:35–36). The other is that *pandocheion* describes a safe space.[157] This can be applied to the innkeeper's act of providing a hospitable space for the victim. The innkeeper's generous act of welcoming the vulnerable victim-stranger into his space is

151. Moltmann, *The Spirit of Life*, 130–31.

152. Song, *Jesus, the Crucified People*; Ahn, "Jesus and the Minjung in the Gospel of Mark," 136–51.

153. Green, *The Gospel of Luke*, 429.

154. A Karenni Christian activist, interviewed by the author, November 26, 2021.

155. Green, *The Gospel of Luke*, 426.

156. Keener, "Some New Testament Invitations to Ethnic Reconciliation," 195.

157. Constable, *Housing the Stranger in the Mediterranean World*, 25–26. See also Longenecker, "The Story of Good Samaritan and the Innkeeper (Luke 10:30-35)," 422–47.

actually risky. It embodies Jesus's double identity as a vulnerable guest and a generous host. According to Christine Pohl, extending hospitality to the other, including strangers, defines the identity of Christians as the followers of Christ. She said:

> In His life on earth, Jesus experienced the vulnerability of the homeless infant, the child refugee, the adult with no place to lay His head, the despised convict. This intermingling of guest and host roles in the person of Jesus is part of what makes the story of hospitality so compelling for Christians. Jesus welcomes and needs welcome; Jesus requires that followers depend on and provides hospitality. The practice of Christian hospitality is always located within the larger picture of Jesus's sacrificial welcome to all who come to Him.[158]

The innkeeper's exemplary act of hospitality not only embodies Jesus' act of hospitality, but also echoes the Christian–Buddhist interreligious ethics of hospitality and healing to wounded neighbors in the aftermath of the coup. That is, despite Myanmar being one of the poorest countries. Hiroko Kawanami describes this culture of generous giving:

> Myanmar has topped a global generosity list for the past few years, despite having at one time been listed by the World Bank as one of the poorest countries in the world in GNP terms, and more than 90 percent of the population is not reported to engage in giving activities, offering donations to charity and to a large extent to the Buddhist monastic community. Generally speaking, the country's people are known to be exceedingly hospitable and generous even towards strangers, and as an indication of this there are earthenware water jars placed at almost every street corner offered to quench the thirst of anyone who passes by. You can never outdo a Myanmar person with generosity. They never stop giving.[159]

The politics of hospitality, healing, and reconciliation by opening hearts, hands, and houses for friends and strangers in Myanmar's post-coup embody the innkeeper. There are many such individual acts in the post-coup. One example was that a pregnant Buddhist woman in Mandalay who opened her house for protesters to seek refuge. She was a protester and a protector, an act for which she was shot dead by the military. Some Christians opened their houses for protesters to seek safety. Many religious practitioners serve

---

158. Pohl, *Making Room*, 17.
159. Kawanami, *The Culture of Giving in Myanmar*, 21.

not only as political protesters against the military coup but also as social protectors for each other in the post-coup. Millions of minority Christians and majority Buddhists raised funds for healing the victims and supporting people who joined the Civil Disobedience Movement (CDM). Such actions bear testimony to Naim Ateek's reading of the parable.

> The question posed by the young lawyer to Jesus, "who is my neighbor?" (10:29) is, as relevant today as it was two thousand years ago. So long as we define the neighbor negatively as a person who is foreign and alien, our humanity is in jeopardy. So long as we divide the world and our own communities into friends and enemies, neighbors, and strangers, we feel no moral obligation toward those whom we have already designated as outsiders. This distinction between us and them creates a binary society that shuts the door on viewing the other as a neighbor that deserves to be loved.[160]

The parable of the good Samaritan provides a source for a lived Asian public theology of religions that crosses ethnic and religious barriers. The virtues it privileges—reconciliation, solidarity, and hospitality—resonate with the Buddhist and Christian moral practices of compassion and courage. They lay the foundations for a lived public theology of religious solidarity and ethnic reconciliation in a violent context. However, we should also raise a question: how deep is ethnic reconciliation and religious solidarity that quickly arose after the coup? There is no easy answer for this question. Reconciliation is a process.

Relational Identity, *Anatta,* and Mutual Embrace

How does religion shape an interethnic co-existence among different religious and ethnic groups?[161] How should the ethnic minority Christians witness to their prophetic and apostolic faith and the gospel of reconciliation in the context of ethnic conflict and political domination? These questions are often raised among Christian theologians and political scientists. The Catholic theologian Robert Schreiter suggests that establishing a shared identity is critical in the healing of traumatic memories and the pursuit of justice and reconciliation.[162] I suggest that minority Christians have two moral options: the prophetic struggle for their minority rights (a liberation

---

160. Ateek, "Who Is My Neighbor?", 156–65, at 156.
161. See, for instance, Weiner, "Coexistence Work," 13–26.
162. Schreiter, "Establishing a Shared Identity," 7–20.

model) and the gracious willingness to relate themselves to out-groups or to embrace them in their community (a reconciliation model).

In his influential book *Exclusion and Embrace*, Volf addresses this type of task from the perspective of a public theologian. The question is: "What kind of selves do we need to be in order to live in harmony with the other?"[163] Volf argues that the cross of Christ plays a key role in shaping the way Christians should relate to the other. It is "God's reception of hostile humanity into divine community that should be a model for how humans should relate to the other."[164] For Volf, the cross is not only its political witness to Christ's solidarity with the victims, but also the fact that he gave up his life for his enemies that they too can be reconciled to God (Rom 5:8–10; 2 Cor 5:18–20).[165]

Using embrace as a metaphor of reconciliation, Volf argues that embrace must be initiated by victims in their relation to perpetrators. Volf's approach to embrace is set in the context of the victim-perpetrator relationship. In some contexts, the victims represent the majority groups but that is not the case in Myanmar where Bamar are trying to embrace ethnic minorities within their dominant culture in the name of national integration. Volf calls this analogy a "bear-hug."[166] Volf insists that Christians should take the initiative of embrace. Volf's thesis is that justice cannot be done without mutual embrace. Justice must be accompanied by embrace. He argues, "To agree on justice in conflict situations you must want more than justice; you must want embrace. There can be no justice without the will to embrace. It is, however, equally true that there can be no genuine and lasting embrace without justice."[167] Volf's concern is for a relational justice: the justice that is sought must be beneficial for the other so that true reconciliation can be achieved.

In contexts where ethnic minorities are dominated and marginalized, it is essential for them to resist the dominant for the vision of restorative justice. While struggling for justice, it is important for the minority groups to open their hearts and arms for reconciling with the other. Debates range

---

163. Volf, *Exclusion and Embrace*, 9–10.

164. Volf, *Exclusion and Embrace*, 98. See also Boersma, *Violence, Hospitality, and the Cross*.

165. Volf, *Exclusion and Embrace*, 11–15. See Grenz, *The Social God and the Relational Self*, 162–82.

166. Volf, *Exclusion and Embrace*, 46.

167. Volf, *Exclusion and Embrace*, 202.

among scholars about the priority of justice over reconciliation or reconciliation over justice. It is fair to say that it depends on the context. In some concrete contexts, such as in Myanmar, it is difficult to reconcile (political reconciliation) with the state-military in the face of their evil commission of political violence.[168] Yet it seems possible for "ethnic reconciliation" among non-state people. For example, non-state people from different religious and ethnic backgrounds can reconcile their divisions to confront the coup as a common enemy. A transformative recognition of each identity in the aftermath of the state-coup opens up for a vision of ethnic reconciliation.

It is in this context that religious ethics have become crucial for deepening ethnic reconciliation and mutual embrace. The Christian doctrine of *kenosis* and the Buddhist doctrine of *anatta* serve as potential religious sources for the vision of deep reconciliation and mutual embrace. The Japanese Buddhist scholar Masao Abe saw this potential.

Abe admits that "The Epistle to the Philippians (Phil. 2:6–11) is one of the most impressive passages in the Bible."[169] There are two reasons for Abe's appreciation of the Pauline passage. The first is the abnegation of Christ, the other is Jesus Christ's self-giving love for human beings. The ethics of abnegation and of self-giving love are inseparably interlaced for practicing mutual embrace. Through self-giving love, God reaches out to human community. By abnegating, God makes a space in himself for human beings to be embraced.[170] The Christian doctrine of *kenosis* (self-emptiness) does not compete against but completes the Buddhist doctrine and ethics of *anatta*. *Anatta* is an opposite of *atta*. According to the Buddha, *atta* means egocentrism, while *anatta* means non-egocentrism. People often misunderstand Buddhism as a religion that fosters an exclusive vision of individualism. The Buddha taught about the relational and communal identity of humanity. The Buddha declared, "consider others as yourself" (*Dhammapada* 10.1).[171]

This Buddhist teaching emphasizes a hospitable relationship between the self and the other. Compassion (*karuna*) is the bridge between the self and the other and conflict and peace. It is in this sense that *anatta* (non-egocentrism) plays a hospitable role in building the ethics of an ethnic and

168. For the ethic of political reconciliation, see Philpott, *Just and Unjust Peace*.

169. Abe, "Kenosis and Emptiness," 5–25. *Anatta* in Theravada Buddhism is *Sunyata* in Zen Buddhism.

170. Abe, "Kenosis and Emptiness," 12–15.

171. Borg ed., *Jesus and the Buddha*, 23.

religious relationship between the self and the other. *Anatta* is the boundless openness to the other.[172] The interreligious ethic of *kenosis* and *anatta* teach two things. In the first instance, there is the need to embrace the other by rejecting the egocentrism of the self. In the second, there is the need to make an open space for the other to come into one's community. This twofold ethic of *anatta* invites ethnic minority Christians and ethnic majority Buddhists to change their exclusionary dimensions of nationalism and tribalism to one of building a new multicultural society where ethnic minorities and ethnic majorities would recognize each other as relational neighbors.

Ethnic and religious differences are not the problem: but the problem is the failure to recognize such ethnic identity and differences as gifts from God. God is the originator of human identity and differences.[173] Buddhist nationalism and Christian tribalism distort our differences with the sinful notion that our differences are misperceived as the problem. Instead of diversifying and maintaining cultural differences as identity makers, tribalists and nationalists misuse those differences as amoral factors for dividing each other.[174] The Christian doctrine of *kenosis* and the Buddhist doctrine of *anatta* should be reconsidered as interreligious sources for a transformative recognition and reception of each identity and otherness as beautiful strengths for building a multicultural society.

Conclusion

Using the church's practices of worship, preaching, and prayer as the primary means of public witnesses, I have shown how a lived Asian public theology of religions should be developed. The church's internal witness of worship, preaching, and prayer should not be underestimated. The reason is that the church's internal witness embodies the immanent Trinitarian communal life. The church should embody the economic Trinity by witnessing its public faith to the world. In order to perform public theology as everyday theology, a confessional faith in Christ and a public commitment to witnessing Christ should go hand in hand.

---

172. Abe, "Kenosis and Emptiness," 20–22. See also Volf, *Exclusion and Embrace*, 98–99; Friedlander, "Conflict and Peace in Buddhism," 79–95.

173. See Hiebert, *The Beginning of Difference*; Russell, *Just Hospitality*.

174. For the idea of maintaining cultural difference as an identity marker, see Barth, *Ethnic Groups and Boundaries*.

There is a diversity in how the church manifests its public witnesses. These varied expressions include the church's pastoral witness of *anthropos*-healing in the context of spiritual powers; the church's public witness of eco-healing through dialogue with adherents of primal religion; the church's prophetic witness of speaking truth to political powers; the church's apostolic witness of social charity; and the church's intercultural witness of ethnic reconciliation and hospitality in the context of ethnic conflict. It is desirable that the Buddhist doctrine of *anatta* and the Christian doctrine of *kenosis* be utilized as interreligious sources for envisioning a transformative notion of relational identity, cultural otherness, and mutual embrace.

Conclusion

THIS STUDY HAS BEEN about the invitation to rethink the methodology of Asian public theology. With that simple sentence I have invited all of us to rethink the current state of Asian theology with the spirit of appreciation and appropriation. The aim of my invitation is not to replace the existing Asian theology, but to renew and appropriate it. While Asian public theology has several strengths, its tendency is toward engaging with people of other faiths and academics as primary dialogue partners, and not sufficiently engaging with grassroots Christian voices. An Asian public theology that emerges from engaging with other religions and academicians does not sufficiently meet the needs of grassroots Christian communities. In order to meet their needs, I have suggested that we should reimagine the paradigm shifts in developing a lived Asian public theology that recognizes the voices of lived communities. There is an embodied theology in their lived practices.

My invitation is to do a lived Asian public theology with grassroots Christian communities as dialogue partners rather than doing public theology on their behalf. It is urgent that we listen to and recognize their lived practices as the primary sources for creating a relevant Asian public theology. Doing theology is not a dichotomic work, but a dialogical work between grassroots Christians and academic Christians. Doing a lived Asian public theology in this way enables us to realize that all Christians—both grassroots and academic persons—are participating in God's kingdom mission. The result of the academic–grassroots dialogue makes it clear that we ought to integrate and overcome the dichotomies between public and private, vertical reconciliation and horizontal reconciliation, social justice and social charity, personal sin and structural sin, the social ministry of Christ and the cross of Christ, spirituality and social engagement.

I have sought to reveal the grassroots Christians' distinctive contribution to Asian public theology. Asian public theology has been mainly treated as the church's prophetic and direct engagement in politics for political liberation. This type of theology is popular among more theologically progressive Asian Christian communities. They tend to see the church's direct and prophetic confrontation against politics as the only effective theology in Asia. But, if we start public theology from the life and work of the lived Christian communities, we will recognize their *multiple* witnesses in public life, going beyond the prophetic type of witness. As noted in chapter three, grassroots Christians witness to their lived faith not only as the prophetic, but also as the priestly, apostolic, and healing people of God. The significance of such a bottom-up approach is that it focuses on the internal life of the church and then examines how the ecclesial life of worship, prayer, and preaching shapes the church's public engagement as public preachers, priestly people of prayer for the nation, apostolic proclaimers of the gospel of salvation, and pastoral healers and social charity workers for healing the victims of both political powers and spiritual powers.

Although the way we understand public theology may share general commonality, the way we perform that theology can differ due to the context. We need to reconsider relevant options. Using the lived Christians' multiple witnesses of their faith in the political context of a military dictatorship as an example, I have sought to reframe the nature of the publicness of public theology. Public theology is not just about the church's public and open witness of faith in public life: it is also about the church's private and hidden witness of faith. This kind of public theology is relevant in the dictatorial context where the public witness of faith is not safe or noticeable. Faithful witness of Jesus is grounded in both public and hidden forms of multiple witnesses.

I have explored the relationship between the vertical dimension of reconciliation and the horizontal dimension of reconciliation in the context of Buddhist nationalism and ethnic conflict. In response to Buddhist nationalism, I have suggested the need of an alternative imagination that approaches religion (Buddhism) paradoxically: that is, I have sought to discern and engage with both the moral and amoral sides of religion. While the amoral side of religion causes conflict and discrimination, its

CONCLUSION

moral counterpoint transforms and effects reconciliation. Ethnic-minority Christians cannot overcome Buddhist nationalism by themselves. It is more effective for a dialogical interaction with those moral Buddhists who confront their religion's embrace of an exclusivist nationalism. I also have emphasized the idea that a Christian's interaction with interreligious resistance to the political powers is more effective than the marginal church's confrontation against state.

While the church's direct engagement with politics and the state may be possible in some contexts where Christianity is a majority religion, I have argued that such a public engagement is not readily relevant in some Asian contexts where Christianity is a minority religion. A better option is that the church should first engage with the people of other religions in the society and then resist political powers in the name of interreligious solidarity. There is the prior need of interreligious solidarity among the people at the grassroots levels before their prophetic resistance to political powers. This kind of interreligious engagement and public witness of social charity would be more meaningful for resisting political powers and for standing in solidarity with the political victims. I also have demonstrated how the church in Asia should practice its pastoral public witness of social healing and public witness of eco-healing in the context of spiritual powers.

Finally, this study finds that the failure of the Buddhist majority to recognize the distinctive otherness of the minority Christians is the root of minority–majority conflict. If the healing word of the gospel needs to be heard today in such a context, I have suggested that a public theology must address a threefold aspect of reconciliation: transformative, restorative, and relational reconciliation—all three aspects of reconciliation are grounded in the life and work of Christ. While a transformative reconciliation tends to focus on a new perception of the religio-ethnic other by crossing their ethnic boundaries, restorative reconciliation focuses on seeking the restorative justice for liberation of the minorities who are being marginalized. Restorative justice is not the end goal. There is the need of a relational aspect of reconciliation that demands recognizing relational identity, mutual embrace, and a harmonious coexistence between Buddhists and Christians. A twofold ethic of a mutual recognition of one's ethnic identity and otherness and of making a hospitable space for one another is crucial for the public vision of reconciliation and liberation in Asia.

Appendix

Interview questions with the Grassroots Ethnic Christians

A. Background Questions

    1. Could you introduce yourself, please? (education level, family, and role at church)

    2. When and how did you start working as church pastors, elders, music leaders, Sunday school teachers, missionaries, or social charity workers?

    3. If you are converted from other religious backgrounds, can you tell me about your conversion story and your journey of new faith?

B. Research Questions

    I. Ecclesiology: What is your understanding of the church?

        1. Which of the following are the most defining characteristics of the church?

            a. The people of God

            b. The body of Christ

            c. The followers of Christ

            d. The temple of the Spirit

            e. Others (if any)

Appendix

2. Describe what defines the people of God
3. Describe what defines the body of Christ
4. Describe what defines the temple of the Spirit
5. Describe what makes the church distinctive from other religious communities?
6. What are the main internal tasks of the church?

    a. How important is worship to you?

    b. How many times do you hold church worship a week?

    c. How important is preaching to you?

    d. What are the main messages of preaching?

    e. Did anyone ever mention politics at the pulpit? How and why?

    f. How important is prayer/fasting prayer to your faith?

    g. How important is holy communion to you?

    h. How important is Bible study for the church?

II. Soteriology: What is your understanding of salvation?

    a. The concept of salvation

    b. The scope of salvation

    c. The goal of salvation

    1. How important is the death of Christ for salvation?
    2. How important is the forgiveness of Christ for sinners?
    3. How important is Jesus's ministry of exorcism for salvation?
    4. How important is Jesus's solidarity with the oppressed for salvation?
    5. How does the gospel of salvation play a role in your faith?

III. What is your understanding of mission?

    1. How does your church understand and practice mission?
    2. What is the key biblical source for the mission of your church?

3. How is Jesus's last commission important for your church's mission?
4. How do you relate your faith to public life?
5. How does the church preach about the gospel of salvation among other religions?
6. How does the church preach and practice salvation among the poor?
7. How does the church preach about the gospel of salvation among ethnic conflict?
8. Do you experience Buddhist nationalism (*lumyo gyi watha*)?
9. Can you identify some characteristics of Buddhist nationalism?
10. How does your church react to Buddhist nationalism and ethnic conflict?
11. What are some challenges in your reactions to Buddhist nationalism?

Bibliography

Abe, Masao. "Kenosis and Emptiness." In *Buddhist Emptiness and Christian Trinity*, edited by Roger Corless and Paul F. Knitter, 5–25. Mahwah, NJ: Paulist, 1990.

Abraham, K.C, ed. *Third-World Theologies: Commonalities and Divergences*. Maryknoll, NY: Orbis, 1986.

Ahn Byung-Mu, "Jesus and the Minjung in the Gospel of Mark." In *Minjung Theology: People as the Subjects of History*, edited by Kim Yong-Bock, 136–51. Singapore: CCA, 1981.

———. *The Story of Minjung Theology*. Seoul: Korea Institute of Theology, 1990.

———. *Talking about Minjung Theology*. Seoul: Korean Theological Study Institute, 1990.

Ammerman, Nancy T, et al. *Studying Congregations: A New Handbook*. Nashville: Abingdon, 1998.

Anderson, Benedict. *Imagined Communities: Reflections on The Origin and Spread of Nationalism*. New York: Verso, 1983.

———. *The Spectre of Comparisons: Nationalism, Southeast Asia, and the World*. New York: Verso, 1998.

———. "Western Nationalism and Eastern Nationalism: Is There a Difference That Matters?" *New Left Review* 9 (2011) 31–41.

Anderson, Boris, ed. *Recollections and Reflections*, 2nd ed. New York: Rev. Dr. Shoki Coe's Memorial Fund, 1993.

Anonymous, "The Centrality of the Civil Disobedience Movement in Myanmar's Post-Coup Era." *New Mandala*, October 19, 2021. https://www.newmandala.org/the-centrality-of-the-civil-disobedience-movement-in-myanmars-post-coup-era/.

Ateek, Naim. "Who Is My Neighbor?" *Interpretation* 62. 2 (2008) 156–65.

Athyal, Jesudas M, et al. *The Life, Legacy, and Theology of M. M. Thomas: Only Participants Earn the Right to be Prophets*. London: Routledge, 2016.

Augurlion, Saw. *Christian Existence and Issues Related to Nationalism and Religious Identity in Postcolonial Myanmar*. Yangon, Myanmar: Tin Tin Chit, 2017.

Aung, Maung Htin. *Folk Elements in Burmese Buddhism*. Oxford: Oxford University Press, 1962.

Bailey, Kenneth E. *Jesus through Middle Eastern Eyes: Cultural Studies in the Gospels*. Downers Grove, IL: IVP Academic, 2008.

———. *Poet and Peasant and through Peasant Eyes: A Literary-Cultural Approach to the Parables in Luke.* Grand Rapids: Eerdmans, 1976.
Balasuriya, Tissa. "Divergences: An Asian Perspective." In *Third-World Theologies: Commonalities and Divergences*, edited by K. C. Abraham, 113–19. Maryknoll, NY: Orbis, 1986.
Barth, Fredrik. *Ethnic Groups and Boundaries: The Social Organization of Culture Difference.* Oslo: Universitesforlaget, 1969.
Barth, Karl. *Church Dogmatics: The Doctrine of Reconciliation.* IV. 2. Translated by T. F. Torrance and G. W. Bromiley. Edinburgh: T&T Clark, 1958.
———. *Community, State, and Church: Three Essays.* Reprint, Eugene, OR: Wipf & Stock, 2004.
Basit, Tehmina N. "Manual or Electronic? The Role of Coding in Qualitative Data Analysis." *Educational Research* 45.2 (2003) 143–54.
Battung, Mary Rosario. "Commonalities: An Asian Perspective." In *Third World Theologies*, edited by K. C. Abraham, 95–99. Maryknoll, NY: Orbis, 2000.
Bociaga, Robert Bociaga, and Helen Regan. "Myanmar Protesters Getting Permeant Symbols of Resistance—Tattoos," *CNN*, March 9, 2011. https://www.cnn.com/style/article/myanmar-tattoo-protest-intl-hnk/index.html
Boersma, Hans. *Violence, Hospitality, and the Cross: Reappropriating the Atonement Tradition.* Grand Rapids: Eerdmans, 2004.
Borg, Marcus. *Jesus and the Buddha: The Parallel Sayings.* Pleasantville, NJ: Ulysses, 1999.
Bosch, David J. *Transforming Mission: Paradigm Shifts in Theology of Mission.* 20th anniversary ed. Maryknoll, NY: Orbis, 2011.
———. "Reflections on Biblical Models of Mission." In *Towards the Twenty-First Century in Christian Mission: Essays in Honor of Gerald H. Anderson*, edited by James M. Philips and Robert T. Coote, 175–92. Grand Rapids: Eerdmans, 1993.
Breitenberg, E. Harold. "Defining Public Theology." In *Public Theology for a Global Society: Essays in Honor of Max Stackhouse*, edited by Deirdre King Hainsworth and Scott R. Paeth, 3–17. Grand Rapids: Eerdmans, 2010.
Brett, Mark G. *Locations of God: Political Theology in the Hebrew Bible.* Oxford: Oxford University Press, 2019.
Brueggemann, Walter. *Interrupting Silence: God's Command to Speak Out.* Louisville, KY: Westminster John Knox, 2018.
———. *The Prophetic Imagination.* 40th anniversary ed. Minneapolis: Fortress, 2018.
———. *Texts That Linger, Words That Explode: Listening to Prophetic Voices.* Minneapolis: Fortress, 2000.
———. *Theology of the Old Testament: Testimony, Dispute, Advocacy.* Minneapolis: Augsburg, 1997.
Bryman, Alan. *Social Research Methods*, 2nd ed. Oxford: Oxford University Press, 2004.
Butwell, Richard. *U Nu of Burma.* Stanford, CA: Stanford University Press, 1963.
Bwa, Saw Hlaing. "Journey Together: Toward a Community of Peace for All." *RAYS: MIT Journal of Theology* 8 (2007) 1–13.
———. "Mission: Christo-Praxis in Myanmar." *Missio Dei: Journal of Mission and Evangelism* 2 (February 2008) 1–26.
———. "Myanmar: Religious Presence in the Public Space and Interreligious Relations." In *Interactive Pluralism in Asia: Religious Life and Public Space*, edited by Simone Sinn and Tong Wing-Sze, 179–95. Geneva: WCC, 2016.

———. "The Problem of Evil: A Theological and Scientific Assessment." In *Doing Theology in a Global Context: A Festschrift for Rev. Prof. Dr. Hans Schwarz*, edited by Craig L. Nessan and Thomas Kothmann, 169–76. Bangalore: ATC, 2009.

———. "Why Interfaith Dialogue Is Essential for Myanmar's Future." *The Review of Faith & International Affairs* 13.4 (2015) 71–78.

Bryne, Brendan. *The Hospitality of God: A Reading of Luke's Gospel*. Collegeville, MN: Liturgical, 2000.

Cady, Linell E., and Sheldon W. Simon, eds. *Religion and Conflict in South and Southeast Asia*. London: Routledge, 2007.

Cartledge, Mark J. "Public Theology and Empirical Research: Developing an Agenda." *International Journal of Public Theology* 10.2 (2016) 145–66.

Carter, Richard., and Samuel Wells, eds. *Who Is My Neighbor? The Global and Personal Challenge*. London: SPCK, 2018.

Chan, Simon. *Grassroots Asian Theology: Thinking the Faith from the Ground Up*. Downers Grove, IL: IVP academic, 2014.

———. "Asian Christian Spirituality in Primal Religious Context." In *Walking with God: Christian Spirituality in the Asian Context*, edited by Charles R. Ringma and Karen Hollenbeck-Wuest, 32–52. Manila: OMF Literature, 2014.

———. "Evangelical Theology in Asian Contexts." In *The Cambridge Campion to Evangelical Theology*, edited by Timothy Larsen and Daniel J. Treier, 225–40. Cambridge: Cambridge University Press, 2007.

———. "Grassroots Asian Ecclesiologies." In *The Oxford Handbook of Ecclesiology*, edited by Paul Avis, 595–614. Oxford: Oxford University Press, 2018.

———. *Liturgical Theology: The Church as Worshiping Community*. Downers Grove, IL: IVP Academic, 2006.

———. *Spiritual Theology: A Systematic Study of the Christian Life*. Downers Grove, IL: IVP Academic, 1998.

Chang, Jonah. *Shoki Coe: An Ecumenical Life in Context*. Geneva: WCC, 2012.

Cheesman, Nick, and Nicholas Farrelly, eds. *Conflict in Myanmar: War, Politics, Religion*. Singapore: ISEAS, 2016.

Chia, Edmund. "Receptive Ecumenism through Asia's Triple Dialogue Theology." *Pacifica* 28.2 (2015) 126–36.

Chelvadura, Manogaran. *Ethnic Conflict and Reconciliation in Sri Lanka*. Honolulu: University of Hawaii Press, 1987.

Chih, Wang Hsian. "Some Perspectives on Homeland Theology in the Taiwanese Context." In *Frontiers in Asian Christian Theology: Emerging Trends*, edited by R. S. Sugirtharajah, 185–95. Maryknoll: Orbis, 1994.

Christian Conference of Asia Statement. "The Confessing Church in Asia and Its Theological Statement." *International Review of Mission* LV.218. (1966) 199–204.

Clooney, Francis X. *Comparative Theology: Deep Learning across Religious Borders*. Hoboken, NJ: Wiley-Blackwell, 2010.

Clooney, Francis X., and Klaus von Stosch, eds. *How to Do Comparative Theology*. New York: Fordham University Press, 2017.

Coe, Shoki. "God's People in Asia Today." *South East Asia Journal of Theology* 5.2. (1963) 5–17.

———. [Hwang, C. H]. *Joint Action for Mission in Formosa. A Call for Advance into a New Era*. Commission on Mission and Evangelism. New York: WCC 1968.

BIBLIOGRAPHY

———. "The Life and Mission of the Church in the World." *South East Asia Journal of Theology* 6.2 (1964) 11–38.

———. *Ministry in Context: The Third Mandate Programme of the Theological Education Fund (1970–977)*. Bromley: TEF, 1972.

———. "A Rethinking of Theological Training for the Ministry in the Younger Churches Today." *South East Asia Journal of Theology* 4.2 (1962) 7–34.

———. "In Search of Renewal in Theological Education." *Theological Education* (Summer 1973) 233–43.

———. "Theology and Church: Editorial." *Theology and Church* 1 (1957) 1–9.

Constable, Olivia R. *Housing the Stranger in the Mediterranean World: Lodging, Trade, and Travel in Late Antiquity and the Middle Ages*. Cambridge: Cambridge University Press, 2004.

Constantineanu, Corneliu. *The Social Meaning of Reconciliation in Paul's Theology: Narrative Readings in Romans*. London: T&T Clark, 2010.

Coorilos, Geevarghese Mor "Mission as Liturgy before Liturgy and as Contestation." In *Orthodox Perspective on Mission*, edited by Patros Valiliadis, 175–85. Oxford: Regnum, 2013.

Cordell, Karl, and Stefan Wolff. *Ethnic Conflict: Causes—Consequences—Responses*. Malden, MA: Polity, 2010.

Crider, Donald M. "The Work among Kachins." In *Burma Baptist Chronicle*, edited by Genevieve Sowards and Erville Sowards, 372–73. Yangon, Myanmar: Burma Baptist Convention, 1963.

Crusz, Robert, et al. *Encounter with the World: Essays in Honor of Aloysius Pieris S.J*, 643–69. Colombo, Sri Lanka: The Ecumenical Institute for Study and Dialogue, 2004.

Dahfred, Karl. "History of Christianity in Thailand." In *Missions in Southeast Asia: Diversity and Unity in God's Design*, edited by Kiem-Kiok Kwa and Samuel Ka-Chieng Law, 119–38. Carlisle, UK: Lanham Global Library, 2022.

Deegalle, Mahinda, ed. *Buddhism, Conflict, Violence in Modern Sri Lanka*. London: Routledge, 2006.

Eilers, F. J. *For All Peoples of Asia: Federation of Asian Bishops' Conferences: Documents from 1997 to 2002*. 3. Quezon City, Philippines: Claretian, 2002

Elwood, Douglas J., ed. *What Asian Christians Are Thinking: A Theological Source Book*. Quezon City, Philippines: New Day, 1976.

En, Simon Pau Khan. *Nat-Worship: A Paradigm for Doing Contextual Theology*. Yangon. Myanmar: Judson Research Center, 2012.

———. "Nat-Worship: A Paradigm for Ecumenical Theology in Myanmar." *Asia Journal of Theology* 8.1 (1994) 43–53.

Endres, Kirsten W., and Andrea Lauser, eds. *Engaging Spirit World: Popular Beliefs and Practices in Modern Southeast Asia*. New York: Berghahn, 2011.

England, John C. "A Watershed Figure in Asian Theologies: The Very Rev. Dr. Hwang Chiong-Hui (Shoki Coe, C. H. Hwang) 1914–1988." In *Wrestling with God: Revisiting The Theology and Social Vision of Shoki Coe*, edited by M. P. Joseph et al., 327–30. Minneapolis: Fortress, 2019.

Esman, Milton J. "Communal Conflict in Southeast Asia." In *Ethnicity: Theory and Experience*, edited by Nathan Glazer and Daniel P. Moynihan, 391–419. Cambridge: Harvard University Press, 1975.

Fabella, Virginia. "Contextualization." In *Dictionary of Third World Theologies*, edited by Virginia Fabella and R. S. Sugirtharajah, 58–59. Maryknoll, NY: Orbis, 2000.

Farrelly, Nicholas. "Myanmar's Conflicted Politics." In *Conflict in Myanmar: War, Politics, and Peace*, edited by Nick Cheesman and Nicholas Farrelly, 3–24. Singapore: ISEAS, 2016.

Fleming, Kenneth. *Asian Christian Theologians in Dialogue with Buddhism*. 201–65. New York: Peter Lang, 2002.

Forbes, George W. *The God of Old: The Role of the Lukan Parables in the Purpose of Luke's Gospel*. London: Continuum, 2000.

Friedlander, Peter. "Conflict and Peace in Buddhism." In *The Ashgate Research Companion to Religion and Conflict Resolution*, edited by Lee Marsden, 79–95. Burlington, VT: Ashgate, 2012.

Frydenlund, Iselin, et al. "Religious Responses to the Military Coup in Myanmar." *The Review of Faith and International Affairs* 19.2 (2021) 77–88.

Fukuyama, Francis. *Identity: The Demand for Dignity and the Politics of Resentment*. New York: Picador, 2018.

Furnivall, J. S. *Colonial Policy and Practice: A Comparative Study of Burma and Netherlands India*. New York: New York University Press, 1956.

Geertz, Clifford. *The Interpretation of Cultures*. New York: Basic, 1973.

Gier, Nicholas F. *The Origins of Religious Violence: An Asian Perspective*. Lanham, MD: Lexington, 2014.

Glazer, Nathan, and Daniel Moynihan, eds, "Introduction." In *Ethnicity: Theory and Experience*, edited by Nathan Glazer and Daniel Moynihan, 1–28. Cambridge: Harvard University Press, 1972.

Gnanapragasam, Patrick, et al. *Negotiating Borders: Theological Explorations in the Global Era: Essays in Honour of Prof. Felix Wilfred*. Delhi: ISPCK, 2008.

Goodall, Norman, ed. *The Uppsala Report 1968: Official Report on the Fourth Assembly of the World Council of Churches, Uppsala July 4–20, 1968*, 21–38. Geneva: WCC, 1968.

Gort, Jerald D, et al., eds. *Religion, Conflict, and Reconciliation: Multifaith Ideals and Realities*. New York: Rodopi, 2002.

Gowler, David B. *Host, Guest, Enemy, and Friend: Portraits of Pharisees in Luke and Acts*. New York: Peter Lang, 1991.

Gravers, Mikael. *Nationalism as Paranoia in Burma: An Essay on the Historical Practice of Power*. 2nd ed. London: Curzon, 1999.

———. "Tatmadaw's Coup in 2021: The Return of Totalitarian Rule." In *Ethnic and Religious Diversity in Myanmar: Contested Identities*, edited by Perry Schmidt-Leukel et al., 249–56. London: Bloomsbury Academic, 2022.

Green, Gene, et al. *Majority World Theology: Christian Doctrine in Global Context*. Downers Grove, IL: IVP Academic, 2020.

Green, Joel B. *The Gospel of Luke*. The New International Commentary on the New Testament. Grand Rapids: Eerdmans, 1997.

Grenz, Stanley J. *The Social God and the Relational Self: A Trinitarian Theology of Imago Dei*. Louisville, KY: Westminster John Knox, 2001.

Guder, Darrell L. *Be My Witnesses: The Church's Mission, Message, and Messenger*. Grand Rapids: Eerdmans, 1985.

———. *Called to Witness: Doing Missional Theology*. Grand Rapids: Eerdmans, 2015.

Gunewardene, R. S. S. "South and Southeast Asia Look the United States." In *Nationalism and Progress in Free Asia*, edited by Philip W. Thayer, 16–28. Baltimore: The Johns Hopkins University Press, 1956.

Gutiérrez, Gustavo. *On Job: God-Talk and the Suffering of the Innocent*. Translated and edited by Sister Caridad Inda and John Eagleson. Maryknoll, NY: Orbis, 1987.

———. *A Theology of Liberation: History, Politics, and Salvation*. Translated and edited by Sister Caridad Inda and John Eagleson. 50th anniversary ed. Maryknoll, NY: Orbis, 2023.

Hainsworth, Deirdre King, and Scott R. Paeth, eds. *Public Theology for a Global Society: Essays in Honor of Max L. Stackhouse*. Grand Rapids: Eerdmans, 2010.

Haire, James. "Stories in Animism and Christian Pneumatology." In *Doing Theology with the Spirit's Movement*, edited by John C. England and Alan T. Torrance, 119–35. Singapore: ATESEA, 1991.

Harris, Elizabeth J. "The Cost of Peace: Buddhist and Conflict Transformation in Sri Lanka." In *Can Faiths Make Peace? Holy Wars and the Resolution of Religious Studies*, edited by Philip Broadhead and Damien Keown, 149–62. New York: Macmillan, 2002.

Hastings, Thomas J. *Worshiping, Witnessing, and Wondering: Christian Wisdom for Participation in the Mission of God*. Eugene, OR: Cascade, 2022.

Hauerwas, Stanley. *A Community of Character: Toward a Constructive Christian Social Ethic*. Notre Dame, IN: University of Notre Dame Press, 1991.

Hector, Kevin W. *Christianity as a Way of Life: A Systematic Theology*. New Haven, CT: Yale University Press, 2023.

Heer, Jeet, "Benedict Anderson, Man without a Country." *The New Republic*, December 13, 2015.

Herman G. Tegenfeldt, *A Century of Growth: The Kachin Baptist Church of Burma*. Pasadena, CA: William Carey Library, 1970.

Hiebert, Theodore. *The Beginning of Difference: Discovering Identity in God's Diverse World*. Nashville: Abingdon, 2019.

Horsley, Richard A. "Introduction—Jesus, Paul, and the Arts of Resistance: Leaves from the Notebook of James C. Scott." In *Hidden Transcripts and The Arts of Resistance: Applying the Work of James C. Scott to Jesus and Paul*, edited by Richard A. Horsley, 1–28. Semeia Studies 48. Atlanta: SBL, 2004.

———. *Paul and Politics: Ekklesia, Israel, and Imperium, Interpretation* Harrisburg, PA: Trinity, 2000.

Huang, Po Ho. "Ng Chiong Hui (Shoki Coe, Hwang Chang Hui)." In *A Dictionary of Asian Christianity*, edited by Scott W. Sunquist, 601. Grand Rapids: Eerdmans, 2001.

Hunsberger, George. "The Missional Voice and Posture of Public Theologizing." *Missiology: An International Review* 34.1 (2006) 15–28.

Huntington, Samuel P. "The Clash of Civilizations?" *Foreign Affairs* 72.3 (1993) 22–49.

———. *The Clash of Civilizations and the Remaking of World Order*. New York: Simon & Schuster, 1996.

Hutchinson, John, and Anthony D. Smith, eds. *Ethnicity*. Oxford: Oxford University Press, 1996.

———. "Introduction." In *Nationalism*, edited by John Hutchinson and Anthony D. Smith, 3–13. Oxford: Oxford University Press, 1994.

Jenkins, Philip. *The Next Christendom: The Coming of Global Christianity*, 3rd ed. Oxford: Oxford University Press, 2011.

Johnson, Robert G. "The Church in the Chin Hills." In *Burma Baptist Chronicle*, edited by Maung Shwe Wa, 383–97. Rangoon, Myanmar: Rangoon University Press, 1963.

Johnson, Todd, and Gina Zurlo, eds. *World Christian Encyclopedia*. 3rd ed. Edinburgh: Edinburgh University Press, 2020.
Jones, Julie Scott., and Sal Watt, eds. *Ethnography in Social Science Practice*. London: Routledge, 2010.
Jordt, Ingrid, et al. *How Generation Z Galvanized a Revolutionary Movement Against Myanmar's 2021 Military Coup*. Singapore: ISEAS, 2021.
Joseph, M. P, et al. *Wrestling with God: Revisiting the Theology and Social Vision of Shoki Coe*. Minneapolis: Fortress, 2019.
Judson, Edward. *The Life of Adoniram Judson*. New York: Randolph, 1883.
The Kairos Theologians. *The Kairos Document: A Theological Comment on the Political Crisis in South Africa*. London: The Catholic Institute for International Relations, 1985.
Kamdar, Mira. *Motiba's Tatoos: A Granddaughter's Journey into Her Indian Family's Past*. New York: Public Affairs, 2000.
Kawanami, Hiroko. *The Culture of Giving in Myanmar: Buddhist Offerings, Reciprocity and Interdependence*. London: Bloomsbury Academic, 2020.
Keener, Craig S. *ACTS: An Exegetical Commentary. Introduction 1:1—2:47*. Grand Rapids: Baker Academic, 2012.
———. *ACTS: An Exegetical Commentary. Introduction 3:1—14:28*. Grand Rapids: Baker Academic, 2013
———. "The Gospel and Racial Reconciliation." In *The Gospel in Black and White: Theological Resources for Racial Reconciliation*, edited by Dennis L. Okholm, 117-30. Downers Groves, IL: IVP Academic, 1997.
———. *The Gospel of John: A Commentary*. Grand Rapids: Baker Academic, 2003.
———. *Miracles: The Credibility of the New Testament Accounts*. 2 vols. Grand Rapids: Eerdmans, 2011.
———. "Some New Testament Invitations to Ethnic Reconciliation." *Evangelical Quarterly* 75.3 (2003) 195–213.
———. "Sent Like Jesus: Johannine Missiology (John 20:21–22)." *Asian Journal of Pentecostal Studies* 21.1 (2009) 21–45.
———. "Some New Testament Invitations to Ethnic Reconciliation." *Evangelical Quarterly* 75.3 (2003) 195–213.
———. *Spirit Hermeneutics: Reading Scripture in Light of Pentecost*. Grand Rapids: Eerdmans, 2016.
Ki, Tam. *From Darkness to Glorious Light: The Amazing True Story of a Myanmese Spirit Worshipper Turned Evangelist*. Translated by Lim Min. Singapore: Armour, 2011.
Kim, Sebastian, and Kirsteen Kim. *Christianity as a World Religion: An Introduction*. 2nd ed. London: Bloomsbury Academic, 2016.
———. "Editorial." *International Journal of Public Theology* 1.1 (2007) 1–4.
———. "Public Theology in the History of Christianity." In *A Companion to Public Theology*, edited by Sebastian Kim and Katie Day, 40–66. Leiden: Brill, 2017.
———. *Theology in the Public Sphere: Theology as a Catalyst for Public Debate*. London: SCM, 2011.
Kim Yong-Bock, ed. *Minjung Theology: People as the Subjects of History*. Singapore: CCA, 1981.
King, Sallie B. "Buddhism and Human Rights." In *Religion and Human Rights*, edited by John Witte and M. Christian Green, 103–18. Oxford: Oxford University Press, 2012.

Kingston, Jeff. *The Politics of Religion, Nationalism, and Identity in Asia*. Lanham, MD: Rowman & Littlefield, 2019.

Kooi, Cees Van der. "Three Models of Reconciliation: A Christian Approach." In *Religion, Conflict, and Peace*, edited by Jerald D. Gort et al., 104–16. Currents of Encounter 17. New York: Rodopi, 2002.

Koopman, Nico. "Public Theology as Prophetic Theology: More Than Utopianism and Criticism." *Journal of Theology for Southern Africa* 134 (2009) 117–30.

Köstenberger, Andreas J. *The Mission of Jesus and the Disciples According to the Fourth Gospel: With Implications for the Fourth Gospel's Purpose and the Mission of the Contemporary Church*. Grand Rapids: Eerdmans, 1998.

Kwa, Kiem-Kiok, and Samuel Ka-Chieng Law, eds, *Missions in Southeast Asia: Diversity and Unity in God's Design*. Carlisle, UK: Lanham Global Library, 2022.

Kwok, Pui-Lan. *Postcolonial Politics and Theology: Unraveling Empire for a Global World*. Louisville, KY: Westminster John Knox, 2021.

Koyama, Kosuke. *Water Buffalo Theology*. 25th anniversary ed. Maryknoll, NY: Orbis, 1999.

Küng, Hans. *Global Responsibility: In Search for a New World Order*. Translated by John Bowden. New York: Continuum, 1993.

Kymlika, W. "Multi-Nation Federalism in Asia." In *Federalism in Asia*, edited by Baogang He, Brian Gallingan and T. Inoguchi, 33–56. Cheltenham, UK: Edward Elgar, 2007.

Laoutides, Costas, and Anthony Ware. "Reexamining the Centrality of Ethnic Identity to the Kachin Conflict." In *Conflict in Myanmar: War, Politics, and Religion*, edited by Nick Cheesman and Nicholas Farrelly, 47–66. Singapore: ISEAS, 2016.

Lee, Jung Young. *The Trinity in Asian Perspective*. Nashville, TN: Abingdon, 1993.

———. "Yin-Yang Way of Thinking: A Possible Method for Ecumenical Theology." In *What Asian Christians Are Thinking*, edited by Douglas Elwood, 81–88. Manila: New Day, 1976.

Lehman, F. K. *Military Rule in Burma Since 1962*. Singapore: Maruzen Asia, 1981.

Lester, Robert C. *Theravada Buddhism in Southeast Asia*. Ann Arbor, MI: University of Michigan Press, 1973.

Leukel, Perry Schmidt, ed. *Buddhist-Christian Relations in Asia*. Munich: EOS, 2017.

Lehr, Peter. *Militant Buddhism: The Rise of Religious Violence in Sri Lanka, Myanmar and Thailand*. New York: Palgrave Macmillan, 2019.

Levison, Priscilla Pope, and John R. Levison. *Jesus in Global Contexts*. Louisville, KY: Westminster John Knox, 1992.

Ling, Samuel Ngun. *Christianity through Our Neighbors' Eyes: Rethinking the 200 Years Old American Baptist Missions in Myanmar*. Yangon, Myanmar: Judson Research Center, 2014.

———. *Communicating Christ in Myanmar: Issues, Interactions and Perspectives*. Yangon, Myanmar: Judson Research Center, 2005.

———, ed. *Ecumenical Resources for Dialogue: Between Christians and Neighbors of Other Faiths in Myanmar*. Yangon, Myanmar: Judson Research Center, 2004.

Ling, Salai Za Uk, and Salai Bawi Lian Mang. *Religious Persecution: A Campaign of Genocide against Chin Christians in Burma*. Ottawa: Chin Human Rights Organization, 2004.

Ling, Tan Sooi. "History of Christianity in Malaysia." In *Missions in Southeast Asia: Diversity and Unity in God's Design*, edited by Kiem-Kiok Kwa and Samuel Ka-Chieng Law, 47–60. Carlisle, UK: Lanham Global Library, 2022.

Ling, Trevor. *Buddhism, Imperialism, and War: Burma and Thailand in Modern Society.* London: George Allen & Unwin, 1979.

Lintner, Bertil. "Burma: Faith and Resistance in Kachin." https://therevealer.org/burma-faith-and-resistance-in-kachin/.

Liow, Joseph Chinyong. *Religion and Nationalism in Southeast Asia.* Cambridge: Cambridge University Press, 2016.

Lochman, Jan Milic. *Reconciliation and Liberation: Challenging a One-Dimensional View of Salvation.* Translated by Davis Lewis. Philadelphia: Fortress, 1980.

Longenecker, Bruce W. "The Story of Good Samaritan and the Innkeeper (Luke 10:30–35): A Study in Character Rehabilitation." *Biblical Interpretation* 17.4 (2009) 422–47.

Lorgunpai, Seree. "The Book of Ecclesiastes and Thai Buddhism." *Asia Journal of Theology* 8.1 (1994) 155–62.

Luther, Martin. "Sermon Psalm 5." In *Martin Luthers Werke: Kritische Gesamtausgabe* (Schriften), 151–57. Weimanr: Bohlau, 1883.

Mahadev, Neena. *Karma and Grace: Religious Difference in Millennial Sri Lanka.* New York: Columbia University Press, 2023.

Mang, Pum Za. "Burman, Burmanization, and Betrayal." *Studies in World Christianity* 8.2 (2012) 169–88.

Marsh, Charles. "Introduction—Lived Theology: Methods, Style, and Pedagogy." In *Lived Theology: New Perspectives on Method, Style, and Pedagogy,* edited by Charles Marsh et al., 1–22. Oxford: Oxford University Press, 2017.

Marsden, Lee. *Religion and Conflict Resolution.* Burlington, VT: Ashgate, 2012.

Marty, Martin E. *The Public Church: Mainline—Evangelical—Catholic.* New York: Crossroad, 1981.

———. Reinhold Niebuhr: Public Theology and the American Experience." *The Journal of Religion* 54.4 (1974) 332–59.

Marshall, I. Howard. *Commentary on Luke.* The New International Greek Testament Commentary. Grand Rapids: Eerdmans, 1978.

Marshall, Christopher. "Parables as Paradigms for a Public Theology." In *The Bible, Justice and Public Theology,* edited by David J. Neville, 23–44. Eugene, OR: Wipf & Stock, 2014.

Mason, Francis. *Memoir of Ko Tha Phyu.* Tavoy, Myanmar: Tavoy, 1943.

Mbiti, John. "When the Bull Is in a Strange Land, It Does Not Bellow." In *God and Globalization: Christ and the Domains of Globalization,* edited by Max L. Stackhouse and Diane B. Obenchain, 145–70. Harrisburg, PA: Trinity, 2002.

McGuire, Meredith B. *Lived Religion: Faith and Practice in Everyday Life.* Oxford: Oxford University Press, 2008.

Mendelson, E. M., and John Ferguson. *Sangha and State in Burma: A Study of Monastic Sectarianism and Leadership.* Ithaca, NY: Cornell University Press, 1975.

"Mission and History." *The Global Network for Public Theology.* https://gnpublictheology.net/about/#mision&history.

Miyahira, Nozomu. *Towards a Theology of the Concord of God: A Japanese Perspective on the Trinity.* Carlisle, UK: Paternoster, 2000.

Moe, David Thang. "The Church as the Image of the Trinity: Toward a Trinitarian Public Theology of Justice and Peace in Asia." *Asia Journal of Theology* 32.2 (2018) 22–49.

———. "A Cross-Cultural and Liberative Hermeneutics of Luke 10:25–37 in Asian and Asian-American Perspective: Reading One Text through the Two Lenses." *Expository Times* 130.10. (2019) 439–49.

———. "Nat-Worship and Paul Tillich: Constructing a Correlational Theology of Religion and Culture in Myanmar." *Toronto Journal of Theology* 31.1 (2015) 123–36.

———. *Pyithu-Dukkha Theology: A Paradigm for Doing Dialectical Theology of Divine Suffering and Human Suffering in the Asian-Burmese Context*. Lexington, KY: Emeth, 2017.

———. "Reaching Out and Receiving In: Reading Lukan Banquet (Luke 14:12–24) as a Trinitarian Theological Paradigm of Hospitality in a World of Hostility. *Journal of Pentecostal Theology* 28.1 (2019) 46–70.

———. "The Word to the World: Johannine Trinitarian Missiology (John 20:21–22)." *Journal of Pentecostal Theology* 26.1 (2017) 68–85.

Moltmann, Jürgen. *The Church in the Power of the Spirit: A Contribution to Messianic Ecclesiology*. Translated by Margaret Kohl. Minneapolis: Fortress, 1993.

———. *The Crucified God*. 40th anniversary ed. Minneapolis: Fortress, 2015.

———. *Experiences in Theology: Ways and Forms of Christian Theology*. Translated by Margaret Kohl. Minneapolis: Fortress, 2000.

———. *God for a Secular Society: The Public Relevance of Theology*. Minneapolis: Fortress, 1999.

———. "Political Theology and the Ethics of Peace." In *Theology, Politics, and Peace*, edited by Theodore Runyon, 31–42. Maryknoll, NY: Orbis, 1989.

———. *On Human Dignity: Political Theology and Ethics*. Translated by M. Douglas Meeks. Minneapolis: Fortress, 1984.

———. *The Spirit of Life: A Universal Affirmation*. Translated by Margaret Kohl. Minneapolis: Fortress, 1992.

———. *The Trinity and the Kingdom: The Doctrine of God*. Translated by Margaret Kohl. Minneapolis: Fortress, 1993.

Monogaran, Chelvadurai. *Ethnic Conflict and Reconciliation in Sri Lanka*. Honolulu: University of Hawaii Press, 1987.

Morgan, David L. *The SAGE Encyclopedia of Qualitative Research Methods*. Thousand Oaks, CA: SAGE: 2008.

Myint, Tun., and James C. Scott. "Myanmar's Transition to a New Inclusive Society." *Independent Journal of Burmese Scholarship*, Special Issue on the Rohingya: Politics of Inclusion and Exclusion in Myanmar 1 (2021) 3–11.

Nan, Lagai Zau. *Awmdawm Hte Anhte A Makam Laknak*. Yangon, Myanmar: Genesis Family Media, 2013.

Naw, Angelene. *The History of the Karen People of Burma*. King of Prussia, PA: Judson, 2023.

Neill, Stephen. *A History of Christian Missions*. New York: Penguin, 1964.

Newbigin, Lesslie. *The Gospel in a Pluralist Society*. Grand Rapids: Eerdmans, 1989.

Niebuhr, H. Richard. *Christ and Culture*, New York: Harper One, 1951.

Nyein, Swe, and Min Min. "Over 8,000 Soldiers and Police Officers Have Joined the Civil Disobedience." *Myanmar Now*, December 1, 2021. https://myanmar-now.org/en/news/over-8000-soldiers-and-police-officers-have-joined-the-civil-disobedience-movement-says, accessed January 10, 2022.

Okesson, Gregg A. *A Public Missiology: How Local Churches Witness to a Complex World*. Grand Rapids: Baker Academic, 2020.

Okey, Stephen. *A Theology of Conversation: An Introduction to David Tracy*. Collegeville, MN: Liturgical, 2018.

Palfrey, Barnabas, and Andreas Telser, eds. *Beyond the Analogical Imagination: The Theological and Cultural Vision of David Tracy*. Cambridge: Cambridge University Press, 2023.

Palihawadana, Mahinda. "The Theravada Analysis of Conflicts." In *Conflict, Violence in Modern Sri Lanka*, edited by Mahinda Deegalle, 67–77. London: Routledge, 2006.

Park, Andrew Sung. *The Wounded Heart of God: The Asian Concept of Han and the Christian Doctrine of Sin*. Nashville: Abingdon, 1993.

Perera, L. P. N. *Buddhism and Human Rights: A Buddhist Commentary on the Universal Declaration of Human Rights*. Colombo, Sri Lanka: Karunarane and Sons, 1991.

Phan, Peter C., ed. *Christianities in Asia*. Hoboken, NJ: Wiley-Blackwell, 2011.

———. "Crossing the Borders: A Spirituality for Mission in Our Time from Asian Perspective." *SEDOS Bulletin* 35 (2003) 8–19.

———. "Introducing Christianity in Asia." In *Uncovering the Pearl: The Hidden Story of Christianity in Asia*, edited by Amos Yong and Mark A. Lamport, xxxi–xl. Eugene, OR: Cascade, 2023.

———. *In Our Own Tongues: Perspectives from Asia on Interculturation and Mission*. Maryknoll, NY: Orbis, 2003.

Phan, Peter C., and Jonathan Y. Tan. "Interreligious Majority-Minority Dynamics." In *Understanding Interreligious Relations*, edited by David Cheetham et al., 218–40. Oxford: Oxford University Press, 2013.

Philip, T. M. *The Encounter between Theology and Ideology: An Exploration into the Communicative Theology of M. M. Thomas*. Madras: CLS, 1986.

Philpott, Daniel. *Just and Unjust Peace: An Ethic of Political Reconciliation*. Oxford: Oxford University Press, 2015.

Pieris, Aloysius. *An Asian Theology of Liberation*. Faith Meets Faith Series. Maryknoll, NY: Orbis, 1988.

———. "The Buddha and the Christ: Mediators of Liberation." In *The Myth of Christian Uniqueness: Toward a Pluralistic Theology of Religions*, edited by Paul F. Knitter and John Hick, 162–177. Faith Meets Faith Series. Maryknoll, NY: Orbis, 2004.

———. *Fire and Water: Basic Issues in Asian Buddhism and Christianity*. Faith Meets Faith Series. Maryknoll, NY: Orbis, 1996.

———. "Two Encounters in My Theological Journey." In *Frontiers in Asian Christian Theology*, edited by R. S. Sugirtharajah, 141–46. Maryknoll, NY: Orbis, 1994.

———. *The Genesis of Asian Theology of Liberation: An Autobiographical Excursus on the Art of Theologizing in Asia*. Gonawala-Kelaniya, Sri Lanka: Tulana Jubilee, 2013.

———. *God's Reign for God's Poor: A Return to the Jesus Formula*. Kelaniya, Sri Lanka: Tulana Jubilee, 1999.

———. *Love Meets Wisdom: A Christian Experience of Buddhism*. Faith Meets Faith Series. Maryknoll, NY: Orbis, 1988.

———. "Political Theology in Asia." In *The Blackwell Companion to Political Theology*, edited by Peter M. Scott and William T. Cavanaugh, 256–70. Hoboken, NJ: Wiley-Blackwell, 2004.

———. "Religion and Politics in Sri Lanka—The Role of the Sinhala Monk." *Dialogue* 3.3 (1976) 113–16.

Po, San C. *Burma and the Karens*. Bangkok: White Lotus, 2001.

Pohl, Christine D. *Making Room: Recovering Hospitality as a Christian Tradition*. Grand Rapids: Eerdmans, 1999.

Porter, Stanley. "Reconciliation as the Heart of Paul's Missionary Theology." In *Paul as Missionary: Identity, Activity, and Theology, and Practice*, edited by Trevor J. Burge and Brian S. Rosner, 169–79. London: T&T Clark, 2011.

Powery, Emerson B. *The Good Samaritan: Luke 10 for the Life of the Church*. Grand Rapids: Baker Academic, 2022.

Purser, W. C. B. *Christian Mission in Burma*. Westminster, UK: Society for the Propagation of the Gospel in Foreign Parts, 1913.

Queen, Christopher S. and Sallie B. King, eds. *Engaged Buddhism: Buddhist Liberation Movements in Asia*. Albany, NY: SUNY Press, 1996.

———. "Introduction: The Shapes and Sources of Engaged Buddhism." In *Engaged Buddhism: Buddhist Liberation Movements in Asia*, edited by Christopher S. Queen and Sallie B. King, 1–44. Albany, NY: SUNY Press, 1996.

Rajaskekar, Paul. "M. M. Thomas." In *The Cambridge Dictionary of Christian Theology*, edited by Ian A. McFarland, 505. Cambridge: Cambridge University Press, 2005.

Ramachandra, Vinoth. *Christian Integrity in a Multicultural World: Faiths in Conflict?* Downers Grove, IL: IVP Academic, 1999.

———. *Church and Mission in the New Asia: New Gods, New Identities*. Edited by Kimhong Hazra. Singapore: ARMOUR, 2009.

———. *The Recovery of Mission: Beyond the Pluralist Paradigm*. Carlisle: Paternoster, 1996.

———. *Subverting Global Myths: Theology and the Public Issues Shaping Our World*. Downers Grove, IL: IVP Academic, 2008.

Ream, Todd C, et al. *Public Intellectuals and the Common Good: Christian Thinking for Human Flourishing*. Downers Grove, IL: IVP Academic, 2021.

Robert, Dana L. *Christian Mission: How Christianity Became a World Religion*. Hoboken, NJ: Wiley-Blackwell, 2009.

Ross, Denise. "Hybridity among the Chin of Myanmar." In *Scripting Pentecost: A Study of Pentecostals, Worship and Liturgy*, edited by Mark L. Cartledge and A.J. Swoboda, 167–85. London: Routledge, 2016.

Ross, Kenneth R, et al. *Christianity in East and Southeast Asia*. Edinburgh Companions to Global Christianity 4. Edinburgh: Edinburgh University Press, 2020.

Russell, Letty M. *Just Hospitality: God's Welcome in a World of Difference*. Louisville, KY: Westminster John Knox, 2009.

Sakhong, Lian H. *In Defence of Identity: The Ethnic Nationalities' Struggle for Democracy, Human Rights, and Federalism in Burma*. Bangkok: Orchid, 2010.

———. *In Search of Chin Identity: A Study in Religion, Politics, and Ethnic Identity in Burma*. Copenhagen: NIAS Press, 2002.

Sanneh, Lamin O. *Disciples of All Nations: Pillars of World Christianity*. Oxford: Oxford University Press, 2007.

———. *Whose Religion Is Christianity? The Gospel beyond the West*. Grand Rapids: Eerdmans, 2003.

Schattauer, Thomas A. *Inside Out: Worship in an Age of Mission*. Minneapolis: Fortress, 1999.

Schmemann, Alexander. *Church, World, and Mission*. Crestwood, NY: St. Vladimir's Seminary Press, 1979.

Schober, Juliane. *Modern Buddhist Conjunctures in Myanmar: Cultural Narratives, Colonial Legacies, and Civil Society*. Honolulu: University of Hawaii Press, 2011.

Scharen, Christian B., ed. *Explorations in Ecclesiology and Ethnography*. Studies in Ecclesiology and Ethnography. Grand Rapids: Eerdmans, 2012.

———. *Public Worship and Public Work: Character and Commitment in Local Congregational Life*. Collegeville, MN: Liturgical, 2004.
Schreiter, Robert J. *Constructing Local Theologies*. Maryknoll, NY: Orbis, 1985.
———. *Ministry of Reconciliation: Spirituality and Strategies*. Maryknoll, NY: Orbis, 1988.
———. *Mission and Ministry in a Challenging Social Order*. Maryknoll, NY: Orbis, 1992.
———. "Theology in the Congregation: Discovering and Doing." In *Studying Congregations: A New Handbook*, edited by Nancy T. Ammerman et al., 23–39. Nashville: Abingdon, 1998
———. "Teaching Theology from an Intercultural Perspective." *Theological Education* 26 (1989) 13–34.
Schroeder, Roger P. *What Is the Mission of the Church? A Guide for Catholics*. Maryknoll, NY: Orbis, 2008.
Schuessler, Jennifer. "James C. Scott: Professor Who Learns from Peasants." *The New York Times*, December 4, 2012. https://www.nytimes.com/2012/12/05/books/james-c-scott-farmer-and-scholar-of-anarchism.html.
Schwartz, Regina. *The Curses of Cain: The Violent Legacy of Monotheism*. Chicago: University of Chicago Press, 1997.
Scott, James C. *The Art of Not Being Governed: An Anarchist History of Upland Southeast Asia*. New Haven, CT: Yale University Press, 2009.
———. *Domination and the Arts of Resistance: Hidden Transcripts*. New Haven, CT: Yale University Press, 1990.
———. *The Moral Economy of the Peasant: Rebellion and Subsistence in Southeast Asia*. New Haven, CT: Yale University Press, 1976.
———. *Weapons of the Weak: Everyday Forms of Peasant Resistance*. New Haven, CT: Yale University Press, 1985.
Segundo, Juan Luis. *The Liberation of Theology*. Translated by J. Drury. Maryknoll, NY: Orbis, 1976.
Shenk, Wilbert R. "Contextual Theology: The Last Frontier." In *The Changing Face of Christianity*, edited by Lamin Sanneh and Joel A. Carpenter, 191–229. Oxford: Oxford University Press, 2015.
Shepherd Andrew. *The Gift of the Other: Levinas, Derrida, and a Theology of Hospitality*. Princeton Theological Monograph Series. Eugene, OR: Pickwick, 2017.
Shils, Edward. "Primordial, Persona, Sacred and Civil Ties." In *British Journal of Sociology* 8.2 (1957) 130–45.
Silverstein, Josef. *The Political Legacy of Aung San*. Ithaca, NY: Cornell University Press, 1993.
Silverstein, L. B., and Auerbach, C. F. *Qualitative Data: An Introduction to Coding and Analysis*. Oxford: New York University Press, 2003.
Simpson, Adam, and Nicholas Farrelly, eds. *Routledge Handbook of Contemporary Myanmar*. London: Routledge, 2018.
Sin, Simone. "Introduction." In *Interactive Pluralism in Asia: Religious Life and Public Space*, edited by Simone Sin and Tong Wing-Sze, 9–16. Geneva: WCC. 2016.
Smith, Anthony. *Nationalism: Theory, Ideology, and History*. 2nd ed. Cambridge, Polity: 2010.
Smith, Donald E. *Religion and Politics in Burma*. Princeton: Princeton University Press, 1965.
———. "The Origins of Nation." *Ethnic and Racial Studies* 12.3 (1989) 349–56.
Song, C. S. *The Believing Heart: An Invitation for Story Theology*. Minneapolis: Fortress, 1999.

———. *Christian Mission in Reconstruction: An Asian Analysis*. Maryknoll, NY: Orbis, 1977.
———. *The Compassionate God: An Exercise in the Theology of Transposition*. Maryknoll, NY: Orbis, 1982.
———. *In the Beginning Were Stories, Not Texts: Story Theology*. Eugene, OR: Wipf & Stock, 2011.
———. *Jesus and the Reign of God*. Minneapolis: Fortress, 1993.
———. *The Tears of Lady Meng: A Parable of People's Political Theology*. Geneva: WCC, 1981.
———. *Tell Us Our Names: Story Theology from an Asian Perspective*. Maryknoll, NY: Orbis, 1984.
———. *Third-Eye Theology: Theology in Formation in Asian Settings*. Maryknoll, NY: Orbis, 1979.
Soper, J. Christopher., and Joel S. Fetzer. *Religion and Nationalism in Global Perspective*. Cambridge: Cambridge University Press, 2018.
Spencer, Nick. *The Political Samaritan: How Power Hijacked a Parable*. London: Bloomsbury Continuum, 2018.
Spiro, Melford E. *Burmese Supernaturalism*. Eaglewood Cliffs, NJ: Prentice Hall, 1967.
Stackhouse, Max L. "Pastor as Public Theologian." In *The Pastor as Public Theologian*, edited by Earl E. Shelp and Ronald H. Sunderland, 106–29. New York: Pilgrim, 1988.
———. *Public Theology and Political Economy: Christian Stewardship in a Modern Society*. Grand Rapids: Eerdmans, 1989.
Stanley, Brian. "Inculturation: Historical Backgrounds, Theological Foundations and Contemporary Questions." *Transformation* 24.1 (2007) 21–27.
Steinberg, David I. *Burma: The State of Myanmar*. Washington, DC: Georgetown University Press, 2001.
———. *Burma/Myanmar: What Everyone Needs to Know*. 2nd ed. Oxford: Oxford University Press, 2013.
Stern, Theodore. "Ariya and the Golden Book: A Millenarian Buddhist Sect among the Karen." *Journal of Asian Studies* 27.2 (1968) 297–328.
Sugirtharajah, R. S. *Postcolonial Criticism and Biblical Interpretation*. Reprint, Oxford: Oxford University Press, 2009.
Suh, Nam Dong. *Exploring Minjung Theology*. Seoul: Hangil. 1983.
———. "Toward a Theology of Han." In *Minjung Theology: People as the Subjects of History*, edited by Kim Yong-Bock, 51–65. Singapore, CCA, 1981.
Sunquist, Scott W., ed. *A Dictionary of Asian Christianity*. Grand Rapids: Eerdmans, 2001.
———. *The Unexpected Christian Century: The Reversal and Transformation of Global Christianity, 1900–2000*. Grand Rapids: Baker Academic, 2015.
Suu Kyi, Aung San. *Freedom from Fear*. 2nd ed. Penguin, 2010.
Stout, Jeffrey. *Ethics after Babel: The Languages of Morals and Their Discontents*. Princeton: Princeton University Press, 2001.
Swamy, Muthuraj. *The Problem with Interreligious Dialogue: Plurality, Conflict, and Elitism in Hindu-Muslim Relations*. London: T&T Clark, 2016.
Taylor, Charles, et al. *Reconstructing Democracy: How Citizens Are Building from the Ground Up*. Cambridge: Harvard University Press, 2020.
Takenaka, M. "A New Understanding of the World and the Need of Theological Renewal." In *Witnesses Together*, edited by U Kyaw Than, 33–42. Rangoon, Myanmar: EACC, 1959.
Tegenfeldt, Herman. *Through the Deeper Water*. Valley Forge, PA: Judson, 1968.

Thant, Myint-U. *The Hidden History of Burma: Race, Capitalism, and The Crisis of Democracy in the 21st Century*. New York: Norton, 2020.
Thomas, M. M. "Some Notes on a Christian Interpretation of Nationalism in Asia." *South East Asia Journal of Theology* 2.2 (1960) 16–26.
———. "My Pilgrimage in Mission." *International Bulletin of Missionary Research* 13.1 (1989) 28–31.
Thawnghmung, Ardeth Maung. *The "Other" Karen in Myanmar: Ethnic Minorities and the Struggle without Arms*. Lanham, MD: Lexington, 2011.
Thayer, Philip Warren, ed. *Nationalism and Progress in Free Asia*. Baltimore: The Johns Hopkins University Press, 1956.
Thomas, M. M. *The Acknowledged Christ of the Indian Renaissance*. Madras: CLS, 1969.
———. *The Christian Response to the Asian Revolution*. London: SCM, 1966.
———. "Indian Nationalism: A Christian Interpretation." *Religion and Society* 6 (1959) 4–26.
———. "The Meaning of Salvation Today: A Personal Statement." *International Review of Mission* 62.246 (1973) 158–69.
———. *Salvation and Humanization: Some Crucial Issues of the Theology of Mission in Contemporary India*. Madras: CLS, 1971.
———. *The Secular Ideologies of India and the Secular Meaning of Christ*. Madras: CLS, 1976.
———. *Some Theological Dialogues*. Madras: CLS, 1977.
———. "The Struggle for Human Dignity as a Preparation for the Gospel." *National Council of Churches Review* LXXXVI.9 (1966) 356–59.
———. *Towards a Theology of Contemporary Ecumenism*. Madras: CLS, 1978.
———. "The World in Which We Preach Chris." In *Witness in Six Continents—Records of the Commission on World Mission and Evangelism*, edited by Ronald K. Orchard, 11–19. London: Edinburgh House, 1964.
Thomas, M. M., and Lesslie Newbigin, "Baptism, the Church, and Koinonia." *Religion and Society*, 1.1 (1972) 69–90.
Thomas, M. M., and Paul D. Devanandan, eds. *Christian Participation in Nation-Building: The Summing Up of a Corporate Study on Rapid Social Change*. Bangalore: NCCI, 1960.
Tombs, David. "Liberating Christology: Images of Christ in the Work of Aloysius Pieris." In *Images of Christ Ancient and Modern*, edited by Stanley E. Porter et al., 173–88. Sheffield, UK: Sheffield Academic, 1997.
Tracy, David. *The Analogical Imagination: Christian Theology and the Culture of Pluralism*. New York: Crossroad, 1981.
———. "Defending the Public Character of Theology." *Christian Century* 98 (1981) 350–56.
———. *Dialogue with the Other: The Inter-Religious Dialogue*. Grand Rapids: Eerdmans, 1990.
———. *Fragments: The Existential Situation of Our Time. Selected Essays I*. Chicago: University of Chicago Press, 2020.
———. "Three Kinds of Publicness in Public Theology." *International Journal of Public Theology* 8.3 (2007) 330–34.
Turner, Alicia. *Saving Buddhism: The Impermanence of Buddhism in a Colonial Burma*. Honolulu: University of Hawaii Press, 2014.
Trager, Helen. *Burma through Alien Eyes*. New York: Praeger, 1966.

Vanhoozer, Kevin J. *The Drama of Doctrine: A Canonical Linguistic Approach to Christian Theology.* Louisville, KY: Westminster John Knox, 2005.

———. *Faith Speaking Understanding: Performing the Drama of Doctrine.* Downers Grove, IL: IVP Academic, 2014.

———. *First Theology: God, Scripture and Hermeneutics.* Downers Grove, IL: IVP Academic, 2002.

———. "One Rule to Rule Them All: Theological Method in an Era of World Christianity." In *Globalizing Theology: Belief and Practice in an Era of World Christianity*, edited by Craig Ott and Harold A. Netland, 85–126. Grand Rapids: Baker Academic, 2006.

———. "What Is Everyday Theology? How and Why Christians Should Read Culture." In *Everyday Theology: How to Read Cultural Texts and Interpreting Trends*, edited by Kevin J. Vanhoozer, 15–60. Grand Rapids: Baker Academic, 2007.

Vanhoozer, Kevin J., and Owen Strachan, eds. *Pastor as Public Theologian: Reclaiming a Lost Vision.* Grand Rapids: Baker Academic, 2015.

Volf, Miroslav. *After Our Likeness: The Church as the Image of the Trinity.* Sacra Doctrina. Grand Rapids: Eerdmans, 1998.

———. "Being as God is Trinity and Generosity." In *God's Life in Trinity*, edited by Miroslav Volf and Michael Welker, 2–13. Minneapolis: Fortress, 2006.

———. *Exclusion and Embrace: A Theological Exploration of Identity, Otherness, and Reconciliation.* Rev ed. Nashville: Abingdon, 2019.

———. *Flourishing: Why We Need Religion in a Globalized World.* New Haven, CT: Yale University Press, 2015.

———. *A Public Faith: How the Followers of Christ Should Serve the Common Good.* Grand Rapids: Brazos, 2011.

———. "On Being a Christian Public Intellectual." In *Public Intellectuals and the Common Good: Christian Thinking for Human Flourishing*, edited by Todd C. Ream et al., 3–20. Downers Grove, IL: IVP Academic, 2021.

———. "Theology, Meaning & Power: A Conversation with George Lindbeck on Theology & the Nature of Christian Difference." In *The Nature of Confession: Evangelicals & Postliberals in Conversation*, edited by Timothy R. Philips and Dennis L. Okholm, 45–66. Downers Grove, IL: IVP Academic, 1996.

———. "The Trinity Is Our Social Program: The Doctrine of God in the Trinity and the Shape of Social Engagement." *Modern Theology* 14.3 (1998) 1–20.

Volf, Miroslav, and Matthew Croasmun. *For the Life of the World: Theology That Makes a Difference.* Grand Rapids: Brazos, 2019.

Volf, Miroslav, and Ryan McAnnally-Linz. *The Home of God: A Brief Story of Everything.* Grand Rapids: Brazos, 2022.

Wa, Maung Shwe. *Burma Baptist Chronicle*, Book I. Yangon, Myanmar: Board of Publications, Burma Baptist Convention, 1963.

Walpola, Rahula. *What the Buddha Taught.* Rev ed. New York: Grove, 1974.

Walls, Andrew F. *The Cross-Cultural Process in Christian History.* Maryknoll, NY: Orbis, 2002.

———. *The Missionary Movement in Christian History: Studies in the Transmission of Faith.* Maryknoll, NY: Orbis, 1996.

Ward, Pete. "Introduction." In *Perspectives on Ecclesiology and Ethnography*, edited by Pete Ward, 1–12. Studies in Ecclesiology and Ethnography. Grand Rapids: Eerdmans, 2012.

———, ed. *Perspectives on Ecclesiology and Ethnography.* Studies in Ecclesiology and Ethnography I. Grand Rapids: Eerdmans, 2012.

Weber, Max. *The Protestant Ethics and the Spirit of Capitalism*. Translated by T. Persons. New York: Scribner's Sons, 1958.

———. *The Religion of India: The Sociology of Hinduism and Buddhism*. New York: Free, 1958.

Wee, Sui-Lee. "Thousands Flee Myanmar for India amid Fears of a Growing Refugee Crisis." *The New York Times*, October 19, 2021. https://www.nytimes.com/2021/10/19/world/asia/myanmar-refugees-india.html.

Weiner, Eugene. "Coexistence Work: A New Profession." In *The Handbook of Interethnic Coexistence*, edited by Eugene Weiner, 13–26. New York: Continuum, 1998.

Well, Tamas. "Making Sense of Reactions to Communal Violence in Myanmar." In *Conflict in Myanmar: War, Politics, and Myanmar*, edited by Nick Cheesman and Nicholas Farrelly, 245–60. Singapore, ISEAS, 2016.

West, Charles C. "M. M. Thomas." In *Biographical Dictionary of Christian Mission*, edited by Gerald H. Anderson, 666–67. New York: Macmillan, 1998.

Wheeler, Ray. "The Legacy of Shoki Coe." *International Bulletin of Missionary Research* 26.2 (2002) 77–80.

Wildavsky, Aaron. *Moses as Political Leader*. Salem, NJ: Salem, 2005.

Wiesel, Elie. *Night*. New York: Bantam, 1960.

Wilfred, Felix. *Asian Public Theology: Critical Concerns in Challenging Times*. Delhi: ISPCK, 2010.

———. "Asian Christianity and Public Life." In *Oxford Handbook of Christianity in Asia*, edited by Felix Wilfred, 558–74. Oxford: Oxford University Press, 2014.

———. *Margins: Site of Asian Theologies*. Delhi: ISPCK, 2008.

———. "On the Future of Asian Theology: Public Theologizing." In *Theology to Go Public*, edited by Felix Wilfred, 28–55. Delhi: ISPCK, 2013.

———. "Public Theology in Service of Liberation." *Vidyajyoti Journal of Theological Reflections* 83.7 (2019) 485–504.

———, ed. *Theology to Go Public*. Delhi: ISPCK, 2013.

———. "Towards an Asian Public Theology." *Vidyajyoti Journal of Theological Reflections* 74 (2010) 103–16.

———. "Theologies of South Asia." In *The Modern Theologians: An Introduction to Christian Theology Since 1918*, edited by David F. Ford and Rachel Muers, 502–17. 3rd ed. Hoboken, NJ: Wiley-Blackwell, 2005.

Winter, Bruce W. *Seek the Welfare of the City: Christians as Benefactors and Citizens*. Grand Rapids: Eerdmans, 1994.

Witte, John, Jr., and M. Christian Green, eds. *Religion and Human Rights: An Introduction*. Oxford: Oxford University Press, 2012.

Wolters, Hielke T. *Theology of Prophetic Participation: M. M. Thomas's Concept of Salvation and the Collective Struggle for Fuller Humanity in India*. Delhi: ISPCK, 1996.

Wolterstorff, Nicholas. *The Mighty and the Almighty: An Essay in Political Theology*. Cambridge: Cambridge University Press, 2012.

———. "Is There Justice in the Trinity?" In *God's Life in Trinity*, edited by Miroslav Volf and Michael Welker, 177–87. Minneapolis: Fortress, 2006.

Wormald, Benjamin. "Buddhists." *Pew Research Center*, April 2, 2015. https://www.pewforum.org/2015/04/02/buddhists/.

Wright, Christopher J. H. *The Old Testament Ethics for the People of God*. Downers Grove, IL: IVP Academic, 2013.

Wright, N.T. *Evil and the Justice of God*. Downers Grove, IL: IVP Academic, 2013.

———. *God in Public: How the Bible Speaks Truth to Power Today*. London: SPCK, 2016.

———. *Paul and the Faithfulness of God*. Minneapolis: Fortress, 2013.
———. "Paul's Gospel and Caesar's Empire." *Reflections* 2 (1999) 42–65.
———. *Into the Heart of Romans: A Deep Dive into Paul's Greatest Letter*. Grand Rapids: Zondervan Academic, 2023.
———. *Simply Good News: Why the Gospel Is News and What It Make Good*. New York: Harper One, 2015.
Wright, N. T., and Michael F. Bird. *Jesus and the Powers: Christian Political Witness in an Age of Totalitarian Terror and Dysfunctional Democracies*. Grand Rapids: Zondervan Academic, 2024.
———. *The New Testament in Its World: An Introduction to the History, Literature, and Theology of the First Christians*. Grand Rapids: Zondervan Academic, 2019.
Yeo, K. K. "Biblical Christologies of the Global Church: Beyond Chalcedon? Toward a Fully Christian and Fully Cultural Theology." In *Jesus without Borders: Christology in the Majority World*, edited by Gene Green et al., 162–79. Grand Rapids: Eerdmans, 2014.
Yeow, Choo Lak, ed. *Doing Theology with Asian Resources*, 1–94. Theology and Politics 1. Singapore: ATESEA, 1993.
Yi, Daw Khin. *Dobama Movement in Burma (1930–938)*. Ithaca, NY: Cornell University Press, 1988.
Yong, Amos. *Hospitality and the Other: Pentecost, Christian Practices, and the Neighbor*. Faith Meets Faith Series. Maryknoll, NY: Orbis, 2008.
———. *In the Days of Caesar: Pentecostalism and Political Theology*. Sacra Doctrina, Grand Rapids: Eerdmans, 2010.
———. "The Spirit, the Common Good, and the Public Sphere." In *Public Intellectuals and the Common Good: Christian Thinking for Human Flourishing*, edited by Todd C. Ream et al., 21–41. Downers Grove, IL: IVP Academic, 2021.
———. *The Spirit Poured Out on All Flesh: Pentecostalism and the Possibility of Global Theology*. Grand Rapids: Baker Academic, 2005.
Yoo Dong-Sik, *The Mineral Vein of Korean Theology*. Seoul: Jun Mang Sa, 1984.
Yun, Koo D. "Pentecostalism from Below: Minjung Liberation and Asian Pentecostal Theology." In *The Spirit in the World: Emerging Pentecostal Theologies in Global Contexts*, edited by Veli-Matti Karkkainen, 89–114. Grand Rapids: Eerdmans, 2009.
Yung, Hwa. *Mangoes or Bananas? The Quest for an Authentic Asian Christian Theology*. 2nd ed. Oxford: Regnum, 2014.
Zan, U., and Erville E. Sowards. "Baptist Work among the Karens." In *Burma Baptist Chronicle, Book II*, edited by Genevieve Sowards and Erville Sowards, 304–26. Yangon, Myanmar: Burma Baptist Convention, 1963.
Zurlo, Gina A. "A Demographic Profile of Christianity in East and Southeast Asia." In *Christianity in East and Southeast Asia*, edited by Kenneth R. Ross et al., 3–14. Edinburg Companions to Global Christianity 4. Edinburgh: Edinburgh University Press, 2020.
———. *Global Christianity: A Guide to the World's Largest Religion from Afghanistan to Zimbabwe*. Grand Rapids: Zondervan Academic, 2022.

Index of Subjects and Names

Abe, Masao, 147
Academy, 11, 19–20, 22, 24, 26–27, 31–34, 37, 49, 56, 114, 138
Academic-grassroots voices, 113
Academic public theology, xiii, 2, 33–34
Ahn Byung-Mu, 140
Alternative imagination, 151
Amyo, 16
Anatta, 145, 147–49
Anderson, Benedict, 15,
Asia Journal of Theology, 88
Asian cultures, 10
Asian theology, 2–3, 5–7, 9–11, 38, 43–45, 52, 57, 84–86, 89, 99, 101, 105, 150
Atonement, 66
Atta, 147

Bailey, Kenneth, 52, 140
Barth, Karl, 28, 86, 114, 139
Batha, 16
Beyond the academy, xiii, xiv, 3, 5, 24, 31, 34, 56
Bottom-up approach, 8, 29, 151
Bridging the gaps, xiii, 4
Brueggemann, Walter, 21–22, 30, 130
Bryman, Alan, 53, 55
Buddhist majority nations, 41
Buddhist nationalism, 2, 4, 5, 16, 72, 73, 111

Chan, Simon, 3, 7, 37, 57, 118
Chin, 17, 53, 67, 68, 73, 74
Chin spirit-worshiper, 67
Christian-Buddhist dialogue, 2, 6, 11
Christian Conference of Asia, 86, 116
The church's direct engagement with politics, 152
The church's ontological witness, 119
The church as the image of the trinity, 119
Civil Disobedience Movement, 139, 142, 145
Clash of imaginations, 18
Coe, Shoki, 85, 88–89, 95, 100
Common good, 103, 111, 115, 120
Common witness, 10
Communion, 29, 61–62, 121–23, 154
Compassion, 15, 37, 47
Confession, 97, 114, 148
Contextualization, 10, 89, 96, 98,
Contextual theologies, 89
Conversion, 11, 23, 28, 43, 69, 153, 104
Cosmic Christ/Christology, 92, 108, 110, 112, 116
Christo praxis, 112

Dana, 138
Dictatorship, 129, 151
Dobama Azi-ayone, 15–16
Domination, 16–18, 31, 43–44, 72, 76–77, 133, 136, 141, 145

INDEX OF SUBJECTS AND NAMES

Double minorities, 40–41
Dukkha, 131

East Asia Christian Conference, 86
Ecclesial flourishing among grassroots Christians, xiii
Ecclesiology, 50, 94, 116, 153
Eco-healing, 128–29
Ethnic conflict, 2, 13, 14, 55, 145
Ethnic identity, 18, 48, 50, 76, 148–52, 155
Ethnic minority groups, 41, 87
Ethnic reconciliation, xiv, 13, 19, 139–40, 142–43, 145, 147, 149
Ethnography, 50–51
Embrace, 145–49
Engaged Buddhism, 132
Erudite literation, 89
Exclusion, 146–48, 152
Exodus paradigm, 84
External crisis of public theology, xiii
Everyday theology, 114–15, 148

The Federation of Asian Bishops' Conferences, 10, 100
Fasting prayer, 65, 154
First America (Myanmar), 131
First theology, 28–29
Freedom from fear, 131

Genesis of Asian Theology of Liberation, 9
Global Network for Public Theology, 1, 99
The Good Samaritan, xiv, 137, 142, 145,
Grassroots Christians, xiii–xiv, 2,4, 6–7, 9, 20, 22, 35–36, 42–45, 47–48, 51–52, 54, 56–59, 62–65, 67, 69–73, 75, 78–82, 94, 99, 112–13, 116–17, 125, 132–33, 138–39, 150–51
Grassroots Expression of Soteriology, 66
Grassroots religion, 35, 39
Green, Joel, 143
Guder, Darrell, 124
Gunewardene, R.S.S, 135
Gutiérrez, Gustavo, 20

Hanh, Thich Nhat, 132
Hastings, Thomas J, xviii, 37, 119,
Hauerwas, Stanley, 21

Healing, xiv, 27, 42, 44, 48, 65, 68, 70–71, 80–81, 105, 112, 116, 124–26, 128–29, 137–38, 141, 144–45, 151–52
Hector, Kevin, 36–37
Hidden resistance, 133
Hidden transcripts, 30, 133–34
Holistic mission, 48
Hospitality, 139–41, 144–45, 149
Humanization, 92, 94–95
Huntington, Samuel, 14
Hutchinson, John and Anthony D. Smith, 18

Imagined communities, 15
Interacademic dialogue, 6
Intercultural witness, 139, 149
Internal life of the church, 117, 151
International Journal of Public Theology, 1
Interreligious dialogue, 6, 10–11, 13, 28, 32–33, 90, 93–94, 104, 106, 110, 112, 117
International Journal of Asian Christianity, 100
Intrareligious dialogue, 6, 11, 33, 37
Intrareligious witness, 30
Interreligious solidarity, 152

Jenkins, Philip, 40
The Journal of Religion, 85
Judson Research Center, 109

Kachin, 17–18, 41, 53, 67–68, 71, 73–74, 76–79, 81
Karen, 17, 41, 53, 73, 79, 81, 87
Kamdar, Mira, 131
Karma, 132
Kawanami, Hiroko, 144
Keener, Craig S, 8, 125
Kenosis, 47–49
Ki, Tam, 67,69
Kim, Sebastian, 100, 102
Kingdom, 24–26, 75, 102, 130, 139, 143, 150
Koyama, Kosuke, 52

Lama, Dalai, 142

176

INDEX OF SUBJECTS AND NAMES

Liberation, xv, 2, 4, 5–10, 13, 19–20, 151–52, 33, 42, 76–77, 84–85, 89, 92, 96–97, 99, 101, 103–13, 116–17, 132, 136, 138–39, 143, 145, 151–52
Liberation theology, 6, 9, 101, 103, 136
Liberation of theology, 89
Liturgical theology, 28
Lived Asian public theology of religions, 1, 4, 11, 13, 25–26, 32, 112, 116, 148
Lived Christianity, 39
Lived experiences, 4, 11, 13, 26, 35–36, 44–45, 50, 59, 94, 99, 113
Lived faith, 25, 30, 33–34, 44, 52, 57–58, 75, 78, 87, 151
Lived religion, 35–36, 56
Lived story theology, 46–47
Lived theology, 3, 26
Lochman, Jan Milic, 139
Luther, Martin, 49

Majority World liberation theologies, 84
Marty, Martin E, 1, 19, 85
Meditation, 136
Methodology, xiii–xv, xviii, 3, 9, 32–33, 35, 38, 50–51, 56, 58, 98, 150
Minjung theologians, 140
Minjung theology, 6–7, 103, 140,
Minority Christians, 5, 13–18, 25, 39–44, 67, 72–74, 76–79, 84, 87, 105, 110–11, 145–46, 148–52
Miracles, 125–26,
Moe, David Thang, ix-x, 28–29, 128, 141
Moltmann, Jürgen, 6, 22, 24, 37, 46, 117, 120, 142–43
Multiple witnesses, 48, 123, 151
Myanmar, 4, 5, 15, 57, 78, 110

The Nazareth public manifesto, 84
Nat-worship, 127–28
Native religion across Southeast Asia, 118
Neighborly love, 143
Neighbors, 10–11, 23, 29, 79, 140–41, 144–45, 148
Newbigin, Lesslie, 49–50, 95
A New Perspective on Grassroots Christianity, 35
Niebuhr, Reinhold, 1

Okesson, Gregg, 48
Origin of Asian public theology, 85

Paradigm shifts, xiii, xiv, 1, 3, 31, 44
Paradox of Christianity in Southeast Asia, 40
The pastor as public theologian, 48–49
Pastoral witness, 49, 125, 149
Peasant Christians, xviii
Phan, Peter, 10, 41
Pohl, Christine, 144
Pieris, Aloysius, 2, 6, 9, 101, 105
Pioneer Asian public theologians, 88
Political engagement, 74, 136
Political liberation, 89
Political powers, 4, 42, 108, 112, 130–31, 133, 136, 151–52
Post-colonial period/context/Asia, 11, 88, 92–93, 95
Post-colonial nationalism, 16
Poverty, 13, 107
Pre-Christian indigenous cultural practices of ritual sacrifices, 67
Preaching, 75, 78–82, 94, 99, 102, 104, 108, 114, 120, 148, 151
Primal religion, 128–29, 149
Private witness, 25
Privatization of faith, 116
Prophetic imagination, 132–33
Prophetic witness, 28, 93, 116, 123, 129–31, 136–37, 149
Public life, 51, 54, 58, 64, 72, 78–84, 87, 91, 94, 100–101, 103–4, 111, 114, 116, 123–24, 128, 151
Public mission, 114, 116, 120, 124–25, 129
Public theology, 1, 2, 3, 4, 5, 7, 8, 11, 12, 23
Public theology for four communities, 19
Public theology with confession, 20
Public theology with conversation, 23
Public theology with courage, 24
Public theology with critical reflection, 22
Public theologian of the bridge, 4
Public witness, 20–21, 25, 30–31, 44–45, 148, 36, 80–83, 96, 98, 112, 119, 124–26, 128, 133, 136–37, 139, 148–49, 151–52
Publicization of faith, 117
Pulpit and politics, 64

INDEX OF SUBJECTS AND NAMES

Pyithu-dukkha theology, 131

Rahula, Walpolo, 141
Ramachandra, Vinoth, 18
Reconciliation, 4–5, 13, 19, 22, 51–52
Relational identity, 145, 149, 152
Reconciliation and liberation, 139, 152
Religion and resistance, 132
Religio-ethnic boundaries, 141
Religious diversity, 6, 105–6
Religious nationalism, 14, 43
Ritual rites, 66–68
Resistance, 99, 106–7, 110, 132–34, 136–37, 139, 152
Rohingya Muslims, 142

Sakhong, Lian Hmung, 17
Salvation, 5, 9, 20, 22, 42, 50, 54, 58, 64, 66–72, 74, 77, 79–80, 82, 92–94, 97–99, 104–5, 110, 112–13, 116–19, 125–26, 128, 138–39, 151
Sangha, 15
Schreiter, Robert J, 145
Second-generation Asian theologian, 89
Sin, 66–67, 99, 108, 112–13, 151
Social injustices, 4, 7, 106,
Scott, James C, 31, 133–34
Solidarity, 106, 110, 136, 140–42, 145–46, 154, 152
Song, C.S, 44–47, 89, 98, 100, 115, 143
Southeast Asia, xviii, 15, 25, 31, 40–41, 88, 92, 128, 135
Southeast Asian villages, 42
Speaking truth to powers, 129–30, 132–33, 136, 149
Spirit-worshipers, 78–79
Spiritual powers, 42, 124–25
Spirituality, 66, 151
Stackhouse, Max, 48
Steinberg, David I, 17, 44
Story theology, 46–47
Suffering, 4, 7, 37, 43, 45, 61, 63, 107, 109, 131–32, 136, 140, 142–43
Sugirtharajah, R.S, 111, 136
Suh, Nam-Dong, 140
Suu Kyi, Aung Sa, 131
Synthesis, 113

Synthetic methodology, xv, 9

Thant Myint-U, 131
Thathana, 16
Theology of liberation, 89
Third-Eye Theology, 115
Thomas, M.M, 7, 85–95, 99, 104
Threefold reality of Asian context, 13
Tracy, David, 19, 22–23
Tribal leaders, 18
Trinitarian, 114
Trinitarian doxology, 120
Trinity, 117–24
Triple dialogue, 9–11, 13, 32
The twin principles, 12
Twofold liberation, 89
The unhappy gaps, 1, 5, 31
Top-down approach, 8,
Twofold reality of Asia, 6, 13, 84

Vanhoozer, Kevin, 25, 114
Village churches, xiii, xiv, xvii, 5
Volf, Miroslav, 23–24, 34

Walls, Andrew, 52,
Weber, Max, 12
Western dualistic worldview of sacred-secular dichotomy, 128
Western political theology, 24–25
Wiesel, Elie, 46
Wilfred, Felix, 2, 27, 85, 94, 100–102
Withness, 119–20, 124
Witnesses together, 87
Wolterstorff, Nicholas, 118
World Christianity, 9–12, 39–40, 50–51, 86
World Council of Churches, 10
World religions, 93, 127,
Worship, 20–22, 59–62, 89, 118–20, 127–29
Wright, N.T, 43, 117, 126, 130, 134

Yong, Amos, 20, 29, 38, 123
Yun, Koo Dong, 7
Yung, Hwa, 3, 37, 88, 100

Zurlo, Gina, 39–40

www.ingramcontent.com/pod-product-compliance
Lightning Source LLC
Chambersburg PA
CBHW051741230426
43670CB00012B/2111